Time Off With Baby:
The Case for Paid Care Leave

Edward Zigler, Susan Muenchow, and Christopher J. Ruhm

With a chapter coauthored by Sami Kitmitto

Foreword by Matthew E. Melmed and Kelsey Quigley

ZERO TO THREE
National Center for Infants,
Toddlers, and Families

Washington, DC

Published by

ZERO
TO
THREE®
National Center for Infants,
Toddlers, and Families

ZERO TO THREE
1255 23rd St., NW, Ste. 350
Washington, DC 20037
(202) 638-1144
Toll-free orders (800) 899-4301
Fax: (202) 638-0851
Web: www.zerotothree.org

The mission of the ZERO TO THREE Press is to publish authoritative research, practical resources, and new ideas for those who work with and care about infants, toddlers, and their families. Books are selected for publication by an independent Editorial Board.

The views contained in this book are those of the authors and do not necessarily reflect those of ZERO TO THREE: National Center for Infants, Toddlers and Families, Inc.

These materials are intended for education and training to help promote a high standard of care by professionals. Use of these materials is voluntary and their use does not confer any professional credentials or qualification to take any registration, certification, board or licensure examination, and neither confers nor infers competency to perform any related professional functions.

The user of these materials is solely responsible for compliance with all local, state or federal rules, regulations or licensing requirements. Despite efforts to ensure that these materials are consistent with acceptable practices, they are not intended to be used as a compliance guide and are not intended to supplant or to be used as a substitute for or in contravention of any applicable local, state or federal rules, regulations or licensing requirements. ZERO TO THREE expressly disclaims any liability arising from use of these materials in contravention of such rules, regulations or licensing requirements.

The views expressed in these materials represent the opinions of the respective authors. Publication of these materials does not constitute an endorsement by ZERO TO THREE of any view expressed herein, and ZERO TO THREE expressly disclaims any liability arising from any inaccuracy or misstatement.

Cover and text design: Design Consultants, Inc.

Cover photo: © iStockphoto.com/jonya

Library of Congress Cataloging-in-Publication Data

Zigler, Edward, 1930-

Time off with baby : the case for paid care leave / Edward Zigler, Susan Muenchow, and Christopher J. Ruhm ; with one chapter coauthored by Sami Kitmitto.

p. ; cm.

Includes bibliographical references.

ISBN 978-1-934019-97-9 -- ISBN 0-934019-97-6 (print) 1. Parental leave--United States. 2. Parental leave. I. Muenchow, Susan. II. Ruhm, Christopher J. III. Title.

[DNLM: 1. Parental Leave--United States. 2. Infant Care--United States. 3. Parent-Child Relations--United States. HD 6065.5.U6]

HD6065.5.U6Z54 2012

331.25'763--dc23

2012010214

For permission for academic photocopying (for course packets, study materials, etc.) by copy centers, educators, or university bookstores or libraries, of this and other ZERO TO THREE materials, please contact Copyright Clearance Center, 222 Rosewood Drive, Danvers, MA 01923; phone, (978) 750-8400; fax, (978) 750-4744; or visit its Web site at www.copyright.com.

10 9 8 7 6 5 4 3 2 1

ISBN 978-1-934019-97-9

Printed in the United States of America

Suggested citation:

Zigler, E., Muenchow, S., & Ruhm, C. J. (2012). *Time off with baby: The case for paid care leave.* With one chapter coauthored by S. Kitmitto. Washington, DC: ZERO TO THREE.

To Congresswoman Lynn Woolsey, a diligent champion of paid family leave

Marin, Sonoma
retired 2013

Table of Contents

Foreword vii

   References xi

Acknowledgments xiii

Introduction   An American Conundrum: Balancing Work and Baby 1

   References 7

Chapter 1   Time Off With Baby: Who Gets It, and Who Doesn't 9

   Timing of Employment Postbirth 10

   Public Policies on Leave Following Childbirth 15

   History of the FMLA 16

   Impact of the FMLA 22

   State Policies Affecting Time Off With New Babies 25

   Private Sector Leave Policies 26

   Summary 28

   References 29

Chapter 2   The Medical and Child Development Case for Time Off 33

   Maternal, Family, and Child Health Evidence 34

   Child Development Evidence 41

   Summary 50

   References 51

Chapter 3   Infant Care Leave and Quality Infant Care 57

   Use of Nonparental Care for Infants 58

   Impact of Early Nonparental Care on Child Development 59

   Impact of Early Nonparental Care on Children's Health and Safety 67

   What Is the Quality of the Care Available? 70

What Does Quality Care for Infants Cost? 72
Summary: What Is the Role of Paid Leave in a Child Care Policy? .73
References 77

Chapter 4   The Economics of Paid Leave for Infant Care 83
Potential Economic Benefits of Paid Parental Leave 83
Private Labor Markets and Paid Parental Leave 89
Public Policy Options for Promoting Rights to Paid Parental Leave 94
Additional Considerations 95
Summary 97
References 98

Chapter 5   Parental Leave Policies in Europe and Canada 101
A Brief History of Parental Leave Policies in Western Europe 102
Current Parental Leave Policies in Western Europe and Canada .104
Leave Policies in Canada and Australia 110
Consequences of Parental Leave Entitlements 112
Conclusion 117
References 117

Chapter 6   Paid Family Leave: Lessons From California 123
Introduction 123
Statutes Affecting Pregnancy and Infant Care Leave in California 126
A Closer Look at California's PFL 129
Provisions of PFL 130
Assessing the Impact of California's PFL 132
Summary 146
References 147

Chapter 7   Recommendations for a Paid Care Leave Policy 151
Duration of Leave Package 155
Wage Replacement Rate 159
Eligibility—Worker Characteristics 161
Eligibility—Prior Work History 161
Business Size Requirement 163
Finance Mechanism 164
Administration 166
Scope of Leave Legislation—Stand-Alone Parental Leave or Comprehensive
    Family and Medical Leave 168
Conclusion 170
References 171

About the Authors and Contributor 173

Foreword

Over the past hundred years, society has undergone dramatic changes. Yet the developmental needs of babies have been unchanged for generations.

One of the most profound social transitions during recent years has been women's entrance into the workforce. Once limited to home and children, women's purview has expanded to include a variety of professional and personal pursuits. In the United States today, 59% of mothers with children less than 1 year old are in the labor force (National Association of Child Care Resource & Referral Agencies [NACCRRA], 2011). And yet society has not adapted to accommodate these new responsibilities. About half of working mothers in America lack access to job-protected leave to care for a newborn or adopted child, and almost none have the option to take paid leave. In today's economy, these circumstances make it unfeasible for parents to take the leave that is critical to the health and development of both their child and their family.

While the American workforce and women's roles within it have evolved, young children's needs have remained the same. Babies depend on positive, consistent care by someone who will take the time to observe them, understand them, and create for them a safe, supportive, and nurturing environment. As Urie Bronfenbrenner (1991), father of ecological systems theory, so concisely summed it up, "Development, it turns out, occurs through the process of progressively more complex exchange between a child and somebody else—especially somebody who's crazy about that child." Because infants and toddlers experience the world through and with their primary caregivers, early relationships become the portals through which each individual first encounters the world. Becoming a child's guide is a daunting, time-consuming, and physically exhausting role, and it isn't relegated to nights and weekends. As any parent can attest, babies operate according to no schedule but their own. Their needs are immediate and unyielding.

The title of this book, *Time Off With Baby,* therefore aptly expresses the issue at stake: The birth or adoption of a baby requires "time off" from the flow of daily life—not only to adjust to the new physical demands of breastfeeding and sleepless nights—but to decipher the nuanced patterns and communications of a newborn. In their first days and months together, parent and child choreograph the intricate dance of development. As their relationship grows, each becomes highly attuned to the cues of the other as they hone the subtle synchrony that will satisfy every need and soothe every discomfort. Just think: Mothers are notoriously able to distinguish among their baby's cries of hunger, frustration, fear, and fatigue. And seemingly inconsolable babies become peaceful in their father's arms. Theirs is a rhythm unknown to anyone else. In developmental terms, this process is comprised of three stages: bonding, attunement, and attachment formation. The parent and child's navigation of these three tasks lays the foundation upon which all future relationships will be built.

When the tasks go unattended—when the dance breaks down—babies learn that they cannot rely on their parents or other caregivers to meet their needs, and they become dysregulated. Where positive, consistent relationships breed security and confidence, inconsistent or unresponsive caregiving produces fear and distrust. Children who grow up in these relationships learn that their needs might not be met, that they cannot rely on others, and that the world is unsafe, inhospitable, and lonely. This opens the door to a variety of troubling developmental outcomes: Children raised in unreceptive or unstimulating environments perceive that their coos and cries will not elicit a response, and so they stop trying. In these children, clinicians and researchers find low affect, diminished conceptions of self-worth, and maladaptive attention-getting methods. Later in life, these challenges can trigger the formation of other unstable and unhealthy relationships. Furthermore, these children often exhibit impaired cognition because, in the absence of a secure base from which to venture and return, they lack the confidence and curiosity to explore their environment. This often leads to poor performance in school and decreased productivity as a member of the workforce.

These and other psychological discoveries accumulated over the past several decades have made it clear that young children need more than a safe place to stay while their parents work. To develop appropriately, they need a stimulating environment. For babies, every minute— every interaction—is a lesson in how the world works, how individuals relate to one another, and how they are valued. Ed Tronick's "Still Face" study, in which a mother is instructed to make her face completely still and affectless and not respond to her baby, shows the striking effects of just a few minutes of deprivation on an otherwise healthy child. The baby moves through a series of attention-getting tactics, first straining and shrieking and then waving her arms, pointing, and even issuing a fake cough. As she exhausts her repertoire without response, however, she becomes still and resigned. This healthy baby's reaction to just minutes of deprivation gives us an eerie preview of what long-term deprivation can do. An environment that is physically safe but does not include continuous interaction with a consistent caregiver simply will not suffice.

This, however, is the choice that many parents face. With the majority of American workers unable to afford substantial leave time and the high cost of quality early care and education, too many parents are forced to settle for inadequate care. (The annual cost of full-time, center-based child care for an infant ranges from $4,650 in Mississippi to $18,200 in the District of Columbia [NACCRRA, 2011]. By comparison, the average annual cost of public higher education is $7,600 [NACCRRA].) A recent survey showed that 55% of new mothers return to work within 6 months of giving birth, and 64% return within a year (NACCRRA). Babies' needs during this crucial period of development are well known. And yet no suitable option exists for the vast majority of American families, who can neither afford to take unpaid leave nor pay upwards of 69% of their income for full-time child care.[1]

Perhaps most troubling of all is that current policy and practice disproportionately jeopardize the development of babies living in low-income and poor households. The parents of these children are less likely than more-affluent parents to have access even to the unpaid leave provided by the Family and Medical Leave Act (FMLA),[2] and if they do have FMLA benefits, they cannot afford to use them. Many of these parents work multiple shifts and long hours, and still child care costs can be prohibitive (Berkeley Center on Health, Economic, and Family Security and Workplace Flexibility, 2010). All of this means that these families are faced with the impossible calculus of balancing a family budget in which solvency is pitted against children's needs for quality care. As a result, these babies are more likely to land in unsuitable care arrangements, and their parents, in general, can ill afford to take sufficient time off before returning to work. These facts are particularly concerning because a growing body of research on resilience—the ability to develop successfully despite adversity—demonstrates that positive, consistent relationships mitigate the impacts of adversity and can be the difference between positive and negative outcomes. In other words, children living in poor and low-income households have so much more to gain from the formation of secure attachments—and they stand to lose so much from their absence.

The case for family leave, however, is not only clear from the developmental and familial perspectives. There are equally compelling economic arguments to be made, many of which are laid out in this book. Workers whose benefits support their families tend to be more loyal to their employers and productive in their work. Women who have access to job-protected leave following birth or adoption are more likely to return to the same position, thus reducing costly employee turnover, new-hire processes, and job training. As the authors point out, even unpaid leave, like that provided by FMLA, increases work participation and productivity by retaining workers who might otherwise leave the labor force. While some in the business

---

[1] *Full-time child care costs for an infant are equivalent to between 7% and 16% of a married family's income and between 25% and 69% of a single mother's income (NACCRRA, 2011).*

[2] *FMLA covers only about half of the workforce. Low-income and part-time workers are less likely to have access (Berkeley Center on Health, Economic, and Family Security and Workplace Flexibility, 2010).*

sector continue to oppose state-mandated leave, research shows that it poses distinct economic gains to employers and to the workforce in general.

Indeed, there is reason to believe that the benefits of paid family leave extend to society more broadly and reach far into the future. Nobel Prize-winning economist James Heckman (n.d.) determined that investment in the earliest years yields higher returns than can be achieved by investments in any other period of the lifespan. Studies by Heckman and others have found that for every dollar invested in early childhood programs, between $4 and $17 are saved through crime reduction, increased schooling, workforce productivity, and reductions in teen pregnancy and welfare dependency (Heckman, 2006; Heckman, Grunewald, & Reynolds, 2006). Stock market followers can attest to the soundness of such an investment. And these findings are not mere estimates; multiple studies bear out the same results.[3] Although this research has not specifically examined paid family leave, Heckman's model (see chapter 4) indicated that the earliest investments have the greatest potential. If $1 invested in quality early care returns $4 to $17, what return might be expected on $1 invested in providing parents the time to foster a positive, secure caregiving relationship in the first weeks and months of life?

As the authors have so comprehensively argued in this book, *time off with baby* is critical to children's health and development, to family well-being, to economic sustainability, and to current and future society. And yet today, the United States is the only developed country without some form of paid family leave. Mothers and fathers are expected to juggle jobs and parenting, contribute to the economy, pay the bills, and rear responsible future citizens—all with minimal support. All Americans lose under this regime, but none lose more than the vulnerable babies who depend on strong, healthy relationships to overcome adversity. Without paid family leave, being born in America today is like being born in the Wild West, a land where families must fend for themselves. To quote Bronfenbrenner again,

> In today's world parents find themselves at the mercy of a society which imposes pressures and priorities that allow neither time nor place for meaningful activities and relations between children and adults, which downgrade the role of parents and the functions of parenthood, and which prevent the parent from doing things he wants to do as a guide, friend, and companion to his children. (1970)

Adults have shaped this world, and in doing so have incurred an obligation to carve into it a safe space for babies and families. The alternative is unacceptable: By leaving this question up to circumstance, America ensures that the families who cannot afford leave will not take it. This

---

[3] *The Abecedarian Project also provides evidence for the importance of early intervention. Research was originally conducted by Craig Ramey, with follow-up analyses at ages 15 and 21 by Frances A. Campbell, University of North Carolina (Burchinal, Campbell, Bryant, Wasik, & Ramey, 1997; Campbell & Ramey, 1995; Campbell, Pungello, Miller-Johnson, Burchinal, & Ramey, 2001).*

precarious approach is dangerous for young children and induces high costs to society in the long run, yet policies continue to favor reaction over prevention. In examining both policy and practice, we must ask ourselves as a country whether we would really rather pay for remedial education or juvenile justice than promote health, self-sufficiency, and success in young families. It is time to cast off this short-sightedness and heed the important arguments made in this book. In doing so, we attune our national priorities to the needs of children and parents and, in enacting paid family leave, we respond.

Matthew E. Melmed, Executive Director, ZERO TO THREE, with Kelsey Quigley, Federal Policy Analyst, ZERO TO THREE

References

Berkeley Center on Health, Economic, and Family Security and Workplace Flexibility. (2010). *Family security insurance: A new foundation for economic security.* Berkeley, CA: Berkeley Law and Georgetown Law.

Bronfenbrenner, U. (1970). *Two worlds of childhood: U.S. and U.S.S.R.* Retrieved January 25, 2012, from *Iridescent Learning:* http://iridescentlearning.org/vision/problem/

Bronfenbrenner, U. (1991). As quoted in *Childhood: A viewer's guide.* R. H. Wozniak, WNET, Educational Broadcasting Corporation, Public Broadcasting Service (U.S.), National Science Foundation, The Childhood Project, Inc., Channel Four Television Corporation (U.K.), Antelope Films, Ltd., PBS.

Burchinal, M. R., Campbell, F. A., Bryant, D. M., Wasik, B. H., & Ramey, C. T. (1997). Early intervention and mediating processes in cognitive performance of children of low-income African American families. *Child Development, 68*(5), 935–954.

Campbell, F. A., Pungello, E. P., Miller-Johnson, S., Burchinal, M., & Ramey, C. T. (2001). The development of cognitive and academic abilities: Growth curves from an early childhood educational experiment. *Developmental Psychology, 37*(2), 231–242.

Campbell, F. A., & Ramey, C. T. (1995). Cognitive and school outcomes for high-risk African American students at middle adolescence: Positive effects of early intervention. *American Educational Research Journal, 32*(4), 743–772.

Heckman, J. (n.d.). *The case for investing in disadvantaged young children.* Retrieved from www.heckmanequation.org/content/resource/case-investing-disadvantaged-young-children

Heckman, J. (2006). *Investing in disadvantaged young children is an economically efficient policy.* Committee for Economic Development/The Pew Charitable Trusts/PNC Financial Services Group Forum on Building the Economic Case for Investments in Preschool.

Heckman, J., Grunewald, R., & Reynolds, A. (2006). The dollars and cents of investing early: Cost–benefit analysis in early care and education. *Zero to Three, 26*(6), 10–17.

National Association of Child Care Resource & Referral Agencies. (2011). *Child care in America: 2011 state fact sheets.* Retrieved from www.naccrra.org/sites/default/files/default_site_pages/2011/childcareinamericafacts_2011_final.pdf

U.S. Department of Labor. (2000). Balancing the needs of family and employers: Family and medical leave survey. Retrieved from www.dol.gov/whd/fmla/cover-statement.pdf

Acknowledgments

We would like to express our appreciation to the Smith Richardson Foundation for their financial support to make this book possible, and to Mark Steinmeyer, Senior Program Officer at the Foundation, for his guidance throughout the project. We thank Amy Merickel, Charles Muenchow, and Deborah Parrish for their editing of chapters; Suzanne Claussen, Phil Esra, and Tassie Jenkins for their additional editorial assistance; and Peter Hoffmann for his copyediting of the entire manuscript. We also gratefully acknowledge the support of the American Institutes for Research for supporting the final stages of the work necessary to complete the book.

In this book we draw on the expertise of many researchers and policy experts. These include but are far from limited to Eileen Appelbaum; T. Berry Brazelton; the late Urie Bronfenbrenner; Ronald Elving; Netsy Firestein; Ellen Galinsky; Deanna Gomby; Janet Gornick; Wen-Jui Han; James Heckman; Jody Heymann; Tallese Johnson; Sheila Kamerman; J. Ronald Lally; Lynda Laughlin; Lilian Miwa Maher; Marcia Meyers; Ruth Milkman; Sharon Masling; Deborah Phillips; Peggy Pizzo; Ross A. Thompson; Jack Shonkoff; Jane Waldfogel; and Elizabeth Washbrook.

An American Conundrum: Balancing Work and Baby

A month before each is due to give birth, a part-time sales clerk, a small-business office manager, and an engineer working for a start-up technology firm share the typical concerns about the delivery process and setting up a nursery. But they also have some other circumstances in common: None of the three has a paid maternity leave, a job protected by the Family and Medical Leave Act (FMLA), or the promise of continued employment if she takes more than a few weeks off after the birth.

Bringing a new life into the world is a serious as well as joyful undertaking everywhere. Giving birth in the United States is safer and easier than in most countries. But in one respect, expectant parents in this nation encounter a challenge atypical among developed nations. By international standards, new mothers in the United States return to work much more quickly than those in other advanced nations. Four times as many first-time mothers in the United States as in the United Kingdom return to work by the time their child is 2 months old (Washbrook, Ruhm, Waldfogel, & Han, 2011).[1] Of all new mothers in the United States, nearly three in five are back at work—the majority full-time—9 months after giving birth, compared to only one in five of their Canadian counterparts (Han, Ruhm, Waldfogel, & Washbrook, 2008).

The customarily rapid return to work following childbirth in the United States raises the following questions:

- How much time is needed to recover from pregnancy and childbirth, and how long should at least one parent stay home to ensure that a new baby gets off to a healthy start?

---

[1] *According to an analysis of Early Childhood Longitudinal Study Birth Cohort (ECLS-B) data, 28% of first-time American mothers return to work by the time their babies are 2 months old, as compared to only 7% of their British counterparts.*

- How many months of focused attention does it take to become a responsive caregiver, establishing patterns that will influence a baby's long-term cognitive, social, and emotional development?

- How much leave can parents take off from work to care for an infant without jeopardizing not only the family's short-term income but also its long-term employment and earning prospects?

Decades of social science research demonstrate that parents and their infants need time to establish a reciprocal pattern of interaction. The interactive patterns established in the first half-year of life foreshadow the quality of the infant's later social and emotional development. Recent studies also show that when a parent is able to stay home with an infant during the early months, child health improves, with a greater likelihood of breastfeeding and up-to-date immunizations that protect against disease and a decrease in child mortality rates, especially in the postneonatal period. During the past 2 decades, there have been great advances in understanding how the human brain develops and, in particular, how profound changes in the brain's circuitry and neurochemistry occur during prenatal and early postnatal development. Now researchers know that early interactions between parent and child help shape the development of the brain. The brain research underscores the wisdom of promoting adequate time for parents to get to know and nurture their newborn or adopted infants.

At the same time that the understanding of infancy as a sensitive period has increased, there have been profound changes in the social and economic circumstances affecting families that may limit their options to devote time to caring for an infant at home. Women's patterns of employment increasingly resemble those of men, and parents at all income levels report greater difficulty balancing workplace and family responsibilities. In 1968, only one in five women with a child less than 1 year old was in the labor force; today, more than half of these mothers work outside the home. Most mothers work for the same reason men do: to help support their families. Moreover, as a result of welfare reform legislation enacted in 1996, many states make returning to work as early as 3 months after the birth of a child a condition for the continued receipt of cash assistance. Growing numbers of children therefore spend considerable time in child care settings of highly variable quality, with some entering out-of-home care 2 weeks after birth or even earlier. Over the last 20 years, there has been intense debate about the effects of early nonparental care on child development, and infant day care is the most controversial form of child care. Many experts advise not placing infants in child care, and at one time the official position of the Child Welfare League of America was that no child less than 1 year old should be placed in out-of-home child care. In our view, this is unrealistic, and the debate should focus less on *whether* families should use out-of-home care and more on how to improve the *quality* of care. Nonetheless, a balanced perspective suggests using caution and ensuring that parents have other options and hence a choice of whether—and how soon—to use out-of-home arrangements.

Reconciling the need for adequate time for parent–child interaction with the economic interests of families and their employers is a challenge. One approach is to adopt paid parental leave policies like those adopted by as many as 173 nations, including all of the United States' major competitors, as well a handful of U.S. states and many private firms (Heymann, Earle, & Hayes, 2007). There is evidence that such leave policies not only help promote parent–child attachment and improve child health but also improve the economic conditions of families by increasing the long-term employment and earning prospects of working parents, while benefiting employers by reducing staff turnover. If paid parental leave is viewed as a form of investment in early intervention, the policy may also lead to long-term economic benefits such as improvements in children's educational and life performance. According to Nobel laureate and University of Chicago economist James Heckman, early intervention programs are a form of capital investment, and the earlier the intervention, the greater the return on this investment (Heckman, 2000).

Implementing a paid parental leave policy in the United States for the period surrounding childbirth would, of course, have costs as well as benefits. Business opponents of the existing (unpaid) FMLA in the United States tend to focus their complaints on intermittent absences related to employees' illnesses, not on the provisions that allow a parent to stay home to care for a newborn or newly adopted baby. However, organizations representing small business strongly oppose extending the job protection provisions to enterprises with fewer than 50 employees. In 2004, California implemented a leave program that provides partial wage replacement, though not job protection, to employees regardless of business size. Although business organizations predicted that the paid family leave would have dire consequences for small business, the policy does not appear to have adversely affected employers or to pose a burden for small business. In chapter 6, we examine the provisions of the California leave package in some depth, its impact on families with new babies, and its lessons for a national leave policy.

From the standpoint of promoting equality in the workplace, there is some concern that a paid leave policy, unless carefully constructed to motivate men to take part, could have the unintended consequence of promoting employment discrimination against women of childbearing age and of curtailing progress toward narrowing the gender wage gap. We therefore look carefully at the most recent research on the experience in Europe, where negative consequences of leave policies on earnings of women appear to be limited to cases where new mothers have rights to extended leave (of a year or more), and especially to cases where they take multiple leaves. At the same time, some nations are adopting policies intended to increase the share of parental leave taken by fathers. This direction fits the growing body of social science literature indicating that the greater the involvement of the father with the child, the better the child's development.

In the chapters that follow, with a multidisciplinary team representing the fields of developmental psychology, economics, and early care and education policy, we carefully weigh the implications of existing research on child health and development along with what is known about the economic impact of parental leave policies as they have evolved in other nations and in the United States.

We begin by defining the various types of leave—maternity leave, paternity leave, parental leave, family leave, and newborn care leave—that could be applied to the infant care leave concept. In the United States today, who does—and doesn't—have access to time off to care for a new baby, and why? Who benefits from the unpaid job protection in the FMLA? To what extent are private firms providing paid maternity, paternity, and/or parental leave for the care of infants or newly adopted children?

Turning to the social science and medical case for paid parental leave for infant care, we tackle the following practical issues:

- How long does it take to recover from childbirth and to get a baby off to a healthy start? How important is breastfeeding, and how strong is the evidence that infant care leave might improve child health outcomes, especially in reducing postneonatal mortality?

- What are the important tasks to be accomplished in a family during the 1st year following the birth of a baby? How many months do pediatricians and psychologists recommend that at least one parent stay home to attune and attach to a new baby? What about the role of fathers in these early months—does the term "parent" really include "dad"?

- What is the evidence on the effects of early use of infant day care, and could paid parental leave during the first months of life serve as a cornerstone of a national child care policy?

Next, we look at the economics of parental leave policies, based on the growing body of research on the implementation and use of such leaves both in the United States and abroad. Here we address the following:

- What does economic theory predict about the effects of paid family leave on the labor force participation, employment, wages, and human capital accumulation of women? What are the predicted effects on employers? How might overall productivity be affected?

- What are the potential long-term economic benefits of investing in paid leave? To the extent that paid parental leave represents an early intervention, might it be a highly cost-effective investment in human capital?

- To what extent has the FMLA achieved its goals? Were business concerns about the enactment of the act borne out, and what are the lessons learned? How much has the FMLA cost employers, and what challenges have resulted from its implementation?

- How is the paid leave law enacted in California in 2002 and implemented in 2004 working out? Has it succeeded in broadening leave usage beyond the better educated, most highly skilled employees?

- What do Europe and Canada offer in the way of paid leave, and how do those policies affect families, child outcomes, and employers? Does taking leave jeopardize a parent's—and especially a woman's—long-term employment and earning prospects? What impact have policies in place for some time in Europe had on gender equality?

Finally, we look at the various policy options and financing mechanisms for paid parental leave in the United States. Specifically, we consider:

- What are the pros and cons of vehicles for financing and implementing paid parental leaves for infant care: payroll deduction, unemployment insurance, attachment to temporary disability insurance, general revenue tax, and other proposals?

- What is the optimal amount of paid leave to offer from a child development and economic perspective? What are the trade-offs involved in offering more generous durations of paid leave, and what would be the most efficient combination of paid and unpaid, job-protected leave balancing the needs of families and employers?

- Although most leave policies require prior work history, many new mothers do not qualify because they work part-time or have not worked long enough for the same employer to qualify. How many hours of work with the same employer should be required for job-protected leave, and how should prior earnings affect calculation of paid leave benefits?

- Which types of employers offer paid leave, and what kinds of employees take it? Are employers more likely to offer paid leave to their better paid workers who, because they are more skilled or better educated, are more difficult to replace? How could a policy promote equity so that leave provisions also cover the lower paid workers?

- What fraction of family and medical leave is currently used for care of newborn or newly adopted infants? What are the pros and cons of combining paid maternity and parental leave with other forms of family and medical leave? Should paid leave be extended to family members caring for an ill child or elderly parent?

- Should paid leave be based on income level? We look at the experience in Europe, where some countries apply a means test to some forms of parental leave, and the pros and cons of targeting paid leave to low-income workers.

- Is there a feasible way to make paid leave available to employees in small businesses and to those who are self-employed? If so, what accommodations should be made?

- What vehicles are available to make parental leave with a new baby more accessible to fathers, and have any national policies proven effective in encouraging fathers to take it?

- In short, from the perspective of both child development and the economy, would paid parental leave during some period of the 1st year of life be desirable and feasible in the United States, and if so, how might it work?

Nearly 20 years after the passage of the FMLA, it is time to take stock of U.S. policy on parental leave, particularly as it affects infant care and child development. After carefully reviewing the evidence, our view is that the current system of unpaid leave is inadequate, leaving far too many parents without any real option but to return to work far too soon after childbirth. We offer recommendations for a partially paid leave policy combined with expanded job protection. The recommended duration of partial wage replacement would be similar to what is called paid maternity and paternity leave in some nations but could be taken by either parent. Although less generous than parental leave policies in Europe and Canada, our recommended policies would build on U.S. and state law and go a long way toward promoting significant improvements in child health and development. All families are different, and there is no one-size-fits-all approach to balancing employment with the care of a new baby. Our goal is to suggest a policy that will give families reasonable choices.

References

Han, W. J., Ruhm, C. J., Waldfogel, J., & Washbrook, E. (2008). The timing of mothers' employment after childbirth. *Monthly Labor Review, 131*(6), 15–27.

Heckman, J. (2000). Public policies to foster human capital. *Research in Economics, 54*(1), 3–56.

Heymann, J., Earle, A., & Hayes, J. (2007). *The work, family, and equity index: How does the United States measure up?* Project on Global Working Families, Institute for Health and Social Policy. Montreal, Quebec, Canada: McGill University. Retrieved December 9, 2011, from www.mcgill.ca./files/ihsp/WFEIFinal2007Feb.pdf

Washbrook, E., Ruhm, C. J., Waldfogel, J., & Han, W.-J. (2011). Public policies, women's employment after childbearing, and child well-being. *The B.E. Journal of Economic Analysis & Policy, 11*(1), Article 43. Retrieved December 9, 2011, from www.bepress.com/bejeap/vol11/iss1/art43

CHAPTER

Time Off With Baby: Who Gets It, and Who Doesn't

N ew mothers in the United States return to the workforce rapidly—and far more quickly than their counterparts in other advanced industrialized nations. Within the United States, there are wide disparities in the timing of employment after childbirth based on education, where one works, and even where one resides. These disparities in turn reflect variations in the provisions of public and private sector leave policies: who is covered, for how long, and whether the leave is paid or unpaid. Following a period of expanding access to job-protected family leave in the United States and the adoption of paid family leave in a handful of states as well as in many private businesses, there is evidence that access to employer-supported paid leave may actually be declining.

In this chapter, we review the dramatic changes that have occurred in the United States over the last 40 years in the timing of return to employment following the birth or adoption of an infant. We then explain why differences in leave policies are the major factor accounting for the earlier return to employment postbirth in the United States than in other advanced industrialized nations. The chapter's major focus is on the history and impact of the Family and Medical Leave Act (FMLA) of 1993 on parental leave-taking for newborn care. Although this hard-won legislation has certainly expanded access to such leave, large sectors of employees are left out and, in the absence of paid leave, cannot afford to use it even if they are eligible. Finally, we consider the extent to which private sector leave policies support families following childbirth or adoption.

What emerges is a complicated portrait: Compared to their mothers and grandmothers, women in the United States today are delaying birth, working longer into their pregnancies, and returning to work sooner after giving birth, and they are much more likely to continue working while bearing and rearing children. Well-educated mothers and fathers employed full-time in the private sector by relatively large employers generally have access to federally job-protected unpaid leave and often to employer-provided paid leave as well. This not only gives them time to attune to their new babies but also strengthens their ties to the workforce. However, less educated mothers and fathers who have a more tenuous position in the workplace, and also even highly trained professionals who are employed by small businesses or only part-time, typically do not have access to job-protected, much less paid, leave. As a result, large numbers of Americans in all income groups are under pressure to return to work far sooner than they would prefer, or sooner than their own well-being or their child's well-being would dictate.

Timing of Employment Postbirth

■ **Maternal employment during the 1st year of a baby's life has become the norm in the United States.**

Participation in the workforce by mothers with infants has risen sharply. In 1968, only one in five mothers with a child less than 1 year old was in the labor force. This pattern began to change in the 1970s, and, in every year since 1986, more than half of mothers of infants have been in the workforce (Han, Ruhm, Waldfogel, & Washbrook, 2008). Although this increase has slowed and appeared to stabilize since 2000, current data indicate that a majority of mothers of infants are back at work by the end of the 1st year postbirth. Forty-one percent of American mothers, including both first-time mothers and those with more than one child, have returned to work within 3 months of giving birth, and 28% by 2 months, as compared to only 7% in the United Kingdom (Washbrook, Ruhm, Waldfogel, & Han, 2011). Nearly three in five mothers in the United States are working 9 months after giving birth, compared to fewer than one in five of their Canadian counterparts (Han et al., 2008).

■ **First-time mothers are typically at work within 3 months after their baby's birth.**

The most striking increase has been in the percentage of first-time mothers in the workforce who have babies 3 months old or younger. In 1961–1965, among women who worked during their pregnancies, only 17% of first-time mothers were in the labor force 3 months after their child's birth. By 2005–2007, according to a U.S. Census Bureau study, among first-time mothers who worked late into their pregnancies, 59% were in the workforce 3 months postdelivery, with about 30% back at work within 2 months, and about 15% within 1 month (Laughlin, 2011).[1]

---

[1] *Authors' interpretation of Figure 4: Percentage of Women Working During Pregnancy and Percentage Working After Their First Birth, by Month Before or After Birth: Selected Years, 1961–1965 to 2005–2007 (Laughlin, 2011, p.13).*

It is not surprising that prebirth employment is the strongest predictor of postbirth employment, and the mothers most apt to be in the workplace soon after the arrival of a new baby are those who were employed just prior to giving birth (Han et al., 2008). Thus, it is significant that women generally work much longer into their pregnancies than was the case just a few decades ago. In 1961–1965, only about one third of employed mothers pregnant with their first child continued to work during the last month before their child's birth. By 2006–2008, 82% of employed women pregnant with a first baby worked during the last month before giving birth (Laughlin, 2011), and many of them also returned early to work.

■ In the United States, mothers with a high school education but no college degree return to work most quickly.

To provide some parameters on the timing of postbirth employment, most new mothers in the United States are able to spend the 1st month at home with their new babies. Of all mothers with infants, including women who worked and those who were not employed during their pregnancies, only 7% are at work within 1 month after giving birth (Han et al., 2008). As indicated above, even among first-time mothers who worked late into their pregnancies, only about 15% were back at work within a month postdelivery and about 30% within 2 months (Johnson, 2008). Nonetheless, more than 1.3 million first-time mothers return to work before their babies reach 3 months old (Laughlin, 2011). The mothers most likely to work during the 1st or 2nd month after giving birth are those with a high school education or some college but no post-secondary degree. Among first-time mothers who worked during their pregnancies, nearly half of those with no more than a high school education returned to work within 2 months postdelivery, as compared to just over one third of those with a bachelor's degree (Johnson; Laughlin). Mothers with less than a high school education are the most likely to quit their jobs following the birth of a baby, and mothers with a bachelor's degree or higher typically return within 3 to 5 months. Hence, it is the mothers with a high school education or some college but no degree who return to work most rapidly. And, as we discuss in chapter 3, it is this same group of relatively less educated, lower-paid new mothers who are unlikely to be able to afford good-quality child care or to qualify for publicly subsidized child care.

The disproportionately higher early employment rate among the mothers with fewer resources also makes it unlikely that the decision to work soon after birth is purely a matter of choice. As we discuss in chapter 2, a survey of new mothers—including professionals, laborers, and those in clerical positions—indicated that a majority of them would prefer to take 6 months off after childbirth, twice as long as the time they actually took (Farber, Alejandro-Wright, & Muenchow, 1988). Women returned sooner than they preferred because they needed the money and feared losing their jobs.

■ **Better educated, higher paid mothers typically take at least 3 months off but are generally back at work 9 months after giving birth.**

An interesting pattern emerges in the timing of employment among new mothers with greater resources: Women who are married, have a bachelor's degree or higher, and are 30 years old or older tend to wait at least 3 months after giving birth before resuming work. However, these same women are more apt than their less educated counterparts to be at work 9 months postbirth. Based on an analysis of the Early Childhood Longitudinal Study, Birth Cohort study, Han et al. (2008) found that 68% of mothers in this nation with a bachelor's degree or higher were working by the 9th month postbirth, compared to 60% of those with a high school diploma and 47% of mothers with less than a complete high school education.

Of course, this pattern makes sense. Better educated women have invested more in preparation for careers and generally receive higher earnings than do their less educated peers. After a period of time at home with their infants, these are the mothers who have the greatest incentive—and most likely the greatest opportunity—to work. The better educated mothers are also more likely to have access to job-protected maternity leave, a period of employer-sponsored paid leave, or their own savings to compensate for the lack of a paid leave benefit.

However, the fact that the rate of employment by the 9th month postbirth in the United States is noticeably higher than among other industrialized nations suggests that personal preference and career opportunities may not be the only factors that are at play. Canada recently expanded its part-paid maternity leave benefits to cover a full year after childbirth. Under the previous policy of 6 months paid leave, 53% of mothers were at work by 9 months postbirth, a percentage comparable to that in the United States. After changing the paid leave policy to cover a full year, the share of mothers working by 9 months in Canada fell to only 20% (Han et al., 2008).

■ **Several other demographic changes have contributed to the rise in maternal participation in the workforce but do not account for the striking cross-national differences in the timing of employment postbirth.**

It is important to note that several other demographic changes have accompanied, and most likely contributed to, the dramatic increase in the participation of mothers with infants in the workforce in the United States. During the same period that the duration of work during pregnancy and the percentage of mothers in the workforce with infants increased, women obtained access to safe, effective contraception and began to delay childbearing. Women in the United States are typically older now when they have their first baby (on average, 24.9 years in 2000, as compared to 21.4 years in 1970). By 2000, nearly one in four first-time mothers, as compared to only 4% in 1970, was at least 30 years old (Johnson, 2008). Being older, of course, means that these mothers are more likely to have established work histories, which in turn may make it easier to return to work relatively soon after giving birth; their work histories provide them with established reputations and relationships with colleagues, and they may, therefore, be cut more slack during the initial transition back to work.

New mothers also typically have considerably more education than their counterparts did just a few decades ago. By 2000, 25% of new mothers had at least a couple of years of postsecondary education, as compared to only 9% in 1970, and women occupied nearly half of the seats in U.S. medical and law schools (Collins, 2009) and slightly more than half of managerial and professional jobs (Belkin, 2010). More educated women tend to have more rewarding, better paid jobs, which may in turn influence their decisions about how long to work during their pregnancies and how soon to return to work following the birth or adoption of a child.

However, neither the increase in years of education for women nor the delay in childbearing accounts for the striking cross-national differences in the timing of return to employment. For example, of all advanced industrialized nations, the United Kingdom has the highest percentage of women with university degrees (National Science Foundation, 2002), and yet women in the United Kingdom stay home far longer with a new baby than do similarly educated women in the United States. Furthermore, the trend toward delayed childbearing is evident not only in the United Kingdom but also in many other nations in Western Europe as well as in Canada (Royal College of Obstetricians and Gynaecologists, 2009). Typically, however, these new mothers stay home far longer than mothers in the United States following the birth of a baby.

Even the overall rate of female employment does not explain why women in the United States return to work so much sooner than do their counterparts in Western Europe and Canada. Of the 37 most advanced industrialized nations, 11 have higher female employment rates than does the United States (Organization for Economic Cooperation and Development [OECD], 2009). For example, both the United Kingdom and Canada have slightly higher overall female employment rates than the United States, but those countries have dramatically fewer mothers working in the 1st year after giving birth. Among the Scandinavian countries with the highest percentage of women in the workforce, new mothers generally spend a much larger portion of the 1st year at home with their babies than do mothers in the United States (Han et al., 2008).

■ Most fathers in the United States now take some time off after the birth or adoption of a baby, but usually 1 week or less.

By 2001, the vast majority of fathers (89%) took some time off after the birth of their child, though two thirds took 1 week or less, and the time off was largely confined to the birth month (Nepomnyaschy & Waldfogel, 2007). Better educated fathers in higher prestige occupations tended to take somewhat longer leaves. Also, fathers were more likely to spend a longer time at home following the birth of their first child, as compared to their subsequent children. It is interesting that the small fraction of fathers who took more time off to be with their newborn infants were found to be more involved with their children at 9 months of age. It is unclear whether the longer period of time off taken to spend with the baby led to the greater parental involvement, or the reverse. But, as we discuss in chapter 2, the same processes of attunement and attachment apply to fathers as to mothers with their infants, and establishing a reciprocal relationship with a new baby requires time on the part of both parents.

Even in nations where few new mothers are at work within the 1st year after giving birth, and where fathers have generous access to paid leave, fathers generally take much less time off than mothers—usually little more than 2 weeks (OECD, 2008). Part of the reason fathers tend not to be the primary parent taking time off after childbirth is biological—they can't breastfeed. But there are also cultural and economic pressures at play. Three fourths of women and two thirds of men responding to a poll in 2000 said they thought fathers should take more than 2 weeks of paternity leave (Dunnewind, 2003). However, fathers fear that taking longer leaves for infant care may affect their chances of promotion and damage their careers; men may pay a penalty for displaying too much interest in hearth and home and doing what is still widely perceived as "women's work" (Ludden, 2010).

Concerned about the gender gap in parental leave usage, some nations have begun to implement incentives to encourage fathers and mothers to share a more extended period of time off to bond and attune with their infants. Where countries offer full wage replacement for paternity leave of 2 weeks or less, men generally claim the full leave. Also, in the wake of legislative reforms designed to promote gender equity in leave usage, claims by fathers for more extended parental leave are expanding. For example, Canada has recently implemented "use it or lose it" provisions whereby after a brief period of maternity leave, the remaining parental leave must be split between the father and mother. As a result, about 55% of fathers took some leave in 2006, compared to 38% in 2001 (OECD, 2008). Since similar leave reform was introduced in Germany, the take-up rate of parental leave by fathers increased from 3.5% of eligible fathers in 2006 to 14.3% in the first quarter of 2008 (OECD, 2008).

Public Policies on Leave Following Childbirth

One explanation for why new parents in Western Europe and Canada stay home longer after giving birth or adopting a baby is that they can—without losing their jobs or significant income. Public policies in these nations provide not only job protection but also wage replacement for both mothers and fathers following the birth or adoption of an infant. Of 173 nations, including all of the United States' major competitors and many far less affluent nations, the United States is joined by only three others—Liberia, Papua New Guinea, and Swaziland—in guaranteeing no paid leave for mothers in any segment of the workforce (Heymann, Earle, & Hayes, 2007). Australia, once an outlier along with the United States among advanced nations in offering no paid maternity leave, established a paid family leave starting in 2011 (Daly, 2009). Thus, the United States is now the only advanced industrialized nation that does not provide some wage replacement to care for a new baby.

> ■ There are several types of leave policy relevant to recovery from childbirth and caring for a new or adopted baby.

To understand the wide variation across nations and within the United States to access to time off from employment to care for a new baby, it is important to define the relevant types of leave. In this book, we primarily focus on the period covering the 1st year after the birth of a baby. At one point in the evolution of leave policy in this nation, the first author of this book, Edward Zigler, led the Yale Bush Center Advisory Committee on Infant Care Leave. Convened in 1983, the group included such figures as pediatricians T. Berry Brazelton of Harvard Medical School and Sally Provence of the Yale Child Study Center; Wilbur Cohen, former Secretary of Health, Education, and Welfare under President Johnson; Sheila Kamerman, Columbia University professor of social work and noted expert on international leave benefits; Wendy Williams, Georgetown law professor and civil rights expert; and Jo Ann Gasper, a representative from President Reagan's Department of Health and Human Services. For reasons that will be explained later, the United States ultimately chose to include infant care leave in a broader package of family and medical leave. However, the following types of leave could all be applied to the infant care leave concept:

- *Maternity Leave (or Pregnancy Leave)*: This is a job-protected leave for employed women at the time they are due to give birth and following childbirth (or adoption).

- *Paternity Leave*: This is a job-protected leave from employment for fathers at the time of childbirth, usually much briefer than maternity leave.

■ *Parental Leave*: This is a gender-neutral, job-protected leave from employment that usually follows maternity leave and allows either men or women to take advantage of the leave policy. In some countries, maternity and paternity leaves are not specific entitlements but are included in provisions for parental leave. Recently, some nations have reserved a portion of parental leave for fathers on a "use it or lose it" basis to provide an incentive for fathers to use the leave.

■ *Family Leave*: This is a leave policy that addresses several different family-related reasons for taking time off from work, including childbirth, care of an infant, and bonding with an adopted child, but also extending to care of a sick child, spouse, or parent (Rudd, 2004).

Yet another term, *newborn family leave*, clearly applies to the kind of leave policy discussed in this book (Gomby & Dow, 2009). However, in medical terms, newborn is usually defined as the neonatal period lasting through the first 28 days of life (*Mosby's Medical Dictionary*, 2009). To avoid any confusion, because our book focuses on leave policies extending considerably beyond that neonatal period, we generally use the term *parental leave* for infant care.

■ Most advanced industrialized nations offer a package of paid maternity, paternity, and parental leave benefits.

The International Labor Organization convention on maternity leave stipulates a period of at least 14 weeks of paid maternity leave (OECD, 2008). The average length of maternity leave that is job-protected and at least partially paid is 18 weeks in the 37 advanced industrialized nations that constitute the OECD (2008). Two thirds of these nations, such as France and the United Kingdom, also offer a brief period of paid paternity leave and a subsequent period of job-protected parental leave that can be taken by either parent (OECD, 2008). Canada, as noted earlier, recently extended paid maternity and parental leave benefits to cover a full year postbirth (Han et al., 2008). The United Kingdom planned to expand the period of fully paid maternity leave from 39 weeks to a full year by April 2010, though the conservative government has since postponed that expansion indefinitely (Local Government Employers, 2010). Twenty-two nations offer both paid maternity leave and an extended period of job-protected parental leave, with a total leave package ranging from 6 months to more than 2 years, at an average of 14 months.[2] For a more complete portrait of international leave policies and the rationale behind them, see chapter 5.

History of the FMLA

Until the passage of the FMLA in 1993, the United States, in stark contrast to its European competitors, did not offer any type of job-protected leave (much less paid leave) to care for a

---

[2] *Authors' calculations from Table PF7.1 in OECD Family Database (OECD, 2008).*

newborn or adopted infant. For most of the 20th century, American women were expected to quit their jobs once they were visibly pregnant (Elving, 1995). One of the authors of this book recalls the sudden midyear disappearance in the 1950s of her highly regarded fifth-grade teacher; only many months later were students informed that Mrs. "Z" had left to have a baby. But by the 1980s, more than half of the nation's women were working outside the home, many of them out of financial necessity, and most of them were or still expected to become mothers. A basic American concept of fairness was at stake: Pregnancy and childbirth were a natural part of the life cycle for most women, but they were being considered cause for embarrassment or grounds for forced exit from employment.

▇ The FMLA was the culmination of a decade-long battle.

Legislative action to provide job-protected maternity and paternity leave began at the state level. Between 1972 and 1992, at least 12 states and the District of Columbia passed laws mandating job-protected maternity leave, and 10 enacted parental leave statutes (Waldfogel, 1999). Advised by Edward Zigler and following up on the Yale Bush Center Advisory Committee on Infant Care Leave convened in 1983, John B. Larson, then president pro tem of the Connecticut State Senate and now serving in Congress, introduced the broader concept of family and medical leave (*Larson Paid Parental Leave Act Puts Families First*, 2009). The initial Connecticut leave statute, which went into effect 3 years before the FMLA, offered 16 weeks of job-protected leave for new parents and caregivers, a more generous leave duration than ended up being in the FMLA.

From 1984 to 1993, there were multiple efforts to enact similar legislation at the national level. The first version of what ultimately became the FMLA was a 1984 bill by House members Howard Berman (D-CA) and Patricia Schroeder (D-CO) that provided 18 weeks of job-protected leave for the birth, adoption, or serious illness of a child. As eloquently chronicled by Ronald Elving, then political editor for the *Congressional Quarterly*, in his book *Conflict and Compromise: How Congress Makes the Law* (1995), it took six sessions of Congress, and starting over after two vetoes by President George H. W. Bush, before the legislation finally was signed into law by President Bill Clinton. Hillary Rodham Clinton, who had chaired the board of the Children's Defense Fund, had long-standing ties with supporters of family leave legislation, and the FMLA was the first legislation signed by the new president.

On one side of the decade-long battle was a coalition of civil rights lawyers, the Women's Legal Defense Fund, the National Organization for Women, labor officials, the U.S. Catholic Conference, the Association of Junior Leagues, pediatricians, social scientists, and the American Association of Retired Persons. On the other side were business lobbyists, such as the U.S. Chamber of Commerce, the National Association of Manufacturers, the National Association of Wholesaler-Distributors, and the National Federation of Independent Business. These groups saw the proposed legislation as another wave in a rising tide of government mandates threatening American business. It is important to remember that during roughly the same time period, the momentum was building for passage of the Americans with Disabilities Act, which would impose a federal mandate for employers to spend billions on ramps and facilities for people with disabilities.

■ Business groups mounted strong opposition to proposed leave legislation.

One business argument against the proposed family leave legislation was its purported cost to employers: The first U.S. Chamber of Commerce estimate was $16.2 billion, largely based on the presumption that every worker taking leave would be replaced full-time, for the entire length of the leave, by a temporary employee (Elving, 1995). After businesses with fewer than 50 employees were exempted from the bill, the Chamber revised this estimate to $2.6 billion. It is interesting that a similar provision is in the 2010 health care reform legislation, which exempts businesses with fewer than 50 employees from penalties for not providing health insurance.

Despite the small business exemption from the proposed family leave legislation, most business groups continued to oppose it. "The organized business lobby in Washington is out of step with the real world and that includes conscientious, no-nonsense, bottom-line business people at the grassroots," said Congresswoman Marge Roukema (R-NJ), an early advocate of the leave policy (Roukema, 1990, p. 4). Roukema had supported the small business exemption as a necessary compromise to secure passage of the bill. Disappointed that her efforts did not lead to more business support, she added, "The lobbyists have overreacted in a way that no one can explain to me."

The central business complaint was that the proposed legislation imposed a governmental mandate, and that even if it might be in the interest of employers to offer family and medical leave benefits, they should not be forced to do so. "Any mandated benefit is likely to replace other, sometimes more preferable, employee benefits," testified Earl Hess, president of Lancaster Laboratories, on behalf of the U.S. Chamber of Commerce (*Testimony on Behalf of U.S. Chamber of Commerce*, 1993). Summing up the case for the business opposition, then Congressman Jim Bunning (R-KY) said, "This is not a baby bonding bill, it is a one-size-fits-all business bondage bill" (Bunning, 1990, p. 9). The bill "is just another nail in that coffin in which we will bury competitiveness and productivity," added then Congressman Tom DeLay (R-TX), pleading with his fellow members to reject "this federal, nationalistic mandate" (DeLay, 1990. p. 17). By imposing a federal mandate, the FMLA "robs employers and employees of personal freedom and flexibility in designing their benefits packages" said Senator Orrin Hatch (R-UT; 1993, p. S1006) just before the FMLA passed the Senate and was signed into law. Hatch, who often sided with advocates of child care legislation at the time, said he recognized the need for family and medical leave legislation but called for tax incentives as an alternative approach.

Actually, business opposition to family and medical legislation was not unanimous. Senator Christopher Dodd (D-CT), the father of family leave in the Senate, was pleased to announce that the National Retail Federation, estimated to represent 20% of the workforce and many small employers, supported the legislation on the grounds that it would be good not only for families but also for their businesses (Dodd, 1993). A study by the Small Business Administration concluded that the net cost to employers of placing employees on leave was always lower than the cost of terminating and permanently replacing an employee (Dodd, 1993).

Finally, as pointed out by economist David Weil (2008), many larger employers already voluntarily offered leave policies. Although most organizations representing these employers continued to side publicly with lobbyists opposed to the family and medical leave legislation, their opposition may have been tempered by seeing some benefit to legislation that would codify existing policies. That is, the employers who already voluntarily offered job-protected leaves may have privately welcomed legislation that would level the playing field, requiring their competitors to do the same.

◼ Family leave legislation won bipartisan support.

Although Dodd, often referred to as the children's senator, was at the time unmarried with no children, he acted like a door-to-door salesman on behalf of family and medical leave, tenaciously reaching across the aisle for support of the various incarnations of the proposed legislation (Elving, 1995). Among his Republican supporters were Senators Kit Bond of Missouri, Dan Coats of Indiana, and Ted Stevens of Alaska. John McCain of Arizona ultimately voted for the legislation, as did Frank Murkowski of Alaska and Alfonse D'Amato of New York. Key House champions included not only many Democrats, such as Berman and Schroeder, George Miller of California, and William Clay of Missouri, but also several Republicans, such as Roukema and Henry Hyde of Illinois. Hyde was instrumental in the first floor victory in the House on the legislation, basing his position on the pro-life argument that pregnant working women needed job security as an incentive not to terminate their pregnancies to avoid losing their jobs (Elving). Thus, as the final version of the FMLA neared passage in the Senate, Dodd could rightly claim, "This is not a partisan bill. It has never been a partisan bill" (Dodd, 1993).

◼ The FMLA represents a hard-won, uniquely American achievement.

The leave legislation that finally emerged from the legislative process is a one-of-a-kind American approach (Rudd, 2004) which might be summed up as "broadest possible purpose with the narrowest public investment." Although the battle began and was driven essentially by a focus on maternity leave, it ended with a much broader definition of the conditions eligible for leave. Moreover, although proponents such as the Yale Bush Center Advisory Committee on Infant Care Leave had advocated for at least partial wage replacement (75% of salary) for 3 months following the birth or adoption of a child, the final legislation was limited to job protection along with maintenance of benefits, such as health insurance (Zigler & Frank, 1988).

■ The FMLA covers a broad range of conditions.

In what amounts to a distinctly American innovation, the FMLA combines access to what are usually several different types of leave in Europe—maternity, paternity, and parental—in one package. Further broadening the definition of conditions eligible for leave, the FMLA includes family "medical" leave. The FMLA guarantees 12 workweeks of job-protected, unpaid leave during any 12-month period for childbirth, adoption, or foster care placement, but also for the employee's own serious medical condition or care of a sick child, spouse, or parent. Broadening was important to unions and to the American Association of Retired Persons, whose support Dodd needed to push against business opposition. Members of Congress were enthralled by T. Berry Brazelton's videotapes of new mothers bonding with their new babies, but they were at least as moved by testimony by a mother who was fired for staying home to care for her sick child. And, if it was important to grant employees job protection for caring for a sick child, was it not also only right to grant the same privilege for care of a sick spouse?

Not only does the FMLA broadly define the conditions eligible for job-protected leave, but the legislation is also intentionally gender-neutral. Whereas the European maternity leaves initially focused exclusively on mothers in order to increase birth rates and help working women fulfill family roles, the FMLA from the outset made all forms of leave available to both men and women (Rudd, 2004). Another major reason why the FMLA expanded to include family medical leave was the concern voiced very early by feminists, union officials, and other activists that a focus on pregnancy and childbirth alone would invariably lead to leave that only women would take, with all of the unintended consequences of employment discrimination against women of child-bearing age and gender-segregated occupations (Elving, 1995). Indeed, several members of the Yale Bush Center Advisory Committee on Infant Care Leave led the way in advocating a gender-neutral policy. Wendy Williams had long believed that any legislation providing special treatment for women would ultimately backfire. Sheila Kamerman, testifying before the House Select Committee on Children and Families in 1984, called for "parental" as distinct from "maternity" leave. The first author of this book, testifying before the same committee, weighed in on the side of equal treatment, introducing the concept of "infant care leave" and endorsing the concept of parental leave so that at least one parent "could be home with a newborn" (Elving, 1995).

■ The FMLA offers relatively modest benefits.

Despite its broad scope, however, the FMLA offers modest benefits compared to those offered in other industrialized nations. The FMLA offers only 12 weeks of unpaid, job-protected leave, less than the 14 weeks stipulated by the International Labor Organization as the minimum for maternity leave, and far less than the 6 months recommended by the Yale Bush Center Advisory Committee on Infant Care Leave (Zigler & Frank, 1988). Many supporters, as well as some critics, of the FMLA legislation expressed concern that the 12 weeks were not sufficient to promote attunement and attachment. Furthermore, as discussed earlier, European leave policies are not limited to maternity leave. Taken together, European maternity, paternity, and parental leave policies provide an average of 14 months of job-protected leave, and most countries provide at least partial wage replacement for the maternity and paternity leave portions.

Politics, of course, is the art of the possible, and legislators often have to settle, at least for the day, for what they can win. Thus, although the FMLA does not include wage replacement, the provision of job protection itself was no small victory. The FMLA also requires a covered employer to maintain group health insurance coverage, including family coverage, for an employee on FMLA-covered leave on the same terms as if the employee continued to work. For example, if the group health plan involves copayments by the employer and the employee, an employee on unpaid FMLA leave must make arrangements to pay his or her normal portion of the insurance premiums to maintain insurance coverage, as must the employer. In a nation without publicly supported health insurance, the importance of this benefit should not be underestimated.

■ The FMLA offers job-protected leave to three in five American workers.

One of the main limitations of the FMLA coverage is that only three in five American workers are estimated to be eligible to take the job-protected leave (Cantor et al., 2001). The FMLA restricts eligibility in several ways: Only employees who have at least 12 months of tenure with their employer qualify, which leaves out a lot of people who have recently initiated or changed jobs. Also, employees must have worked at least 1,250 hours for the same employer during the 12 months preceding the leave period; even workers who work full-time hours by combining multiple part-time jobs would not qualify under the FMLA (Fass, 2009). Both of these restrictions tend to make younger workers who have the least work experience, as well as low-wage workers, less apt to qualify. Low-wage workers are less likely to be eligible because they typically have less stable employment histories and are more apt to work intermittently, seasonally, or part-time.

Even young highly trained professionals may not qualify. Consider a 34-year-old woman we interviewed who started a residency in veterinary medicine at a major northeastern school about the same time she learned she was pregnant. Despite several prior years of continuous, full-time work with a previous employer, this new mother, whose baby spent time in the neonatal intensive care unit, did not qualify for FMLA-job-protected leave. Especially for women who have deferred childbearing while they obtained post-graduate training, launching a career and launching a family are likely to occur in the same years.

Another key restriction, as discussed earlier, is that the FMLA exempts small business employers with fewer than 50 employees working within a 75-mile radius of all worksites. Illustrative of this group ineligible for FMLA-protected leave are the small-business office manager and the engineer working for the start-up technology firm mentioned in the introduction to this book. As a result of this exemption based on company size and the other restrictions based on job tenure and work history, only 19% of all new mothers and 31% of those employed for 1 year prior to childbirth are estimated to be eligible for benefits under the FMLA (Ruhm, 1997). Many new mothers, in particular, are not eligible because they are more apt than men to work less than full-time or for employers with fewer than 50 employees.

Impact of the FMLA

■ The FMLA has expanded access to job-protected leave.

Despite its relatively modest benefits and less-than-universal coverage, the FMLA has succeeded in expanding access to job-protected leave, particularly maternity and paternity leave. Prior to the enactment of the FMLA, only one in five businesses offered job-protected leave; by 2000, one in three establishments, including one in five not covered by the FMLA, offered similar benefits (Cantor et al., 2001). According to an analysis of data from the National Survey of America's Families, most working parents now report that they have access to at least some period of job-protected maternity or paternity leave during the birth month (Phillips, 2004). The FMLA appears to have had a spillover effect, leading firms to offer job-protected leave even to part-time workers not eligible for FMLA-protected benefits and encouraging employers with fewer than 50 employees to provide leave (Phillips).

Under the FMLA, 60 million Americans have taken time off from work to care for a new baby or newly adopted child; an ill child, spouse, or parent; or their own serious medical condition. Of those taking leave under the FMLA, nearly half took their longest leave to attend to their own serious health condition, and more than one quarter took time off to care for a seriously ill family member. Nearly one in five took leave under the FMLA to take care of a newborn or newly adopted child (Cantor et al., 2001; Melmed, 2008). The FMLA has led to mothers covered by the law taking from 2 to 6 weeks more unpaid leave. Three quarters of the workers claiming FMLA-covered leave earn less than $75,000 per year (Cantor et al., 2001; Ness, 2008).

■ The FMLA has tended to benefit better educated, higher paid employees—and their employers.

Although expansion of parental leave rights is associated with increased leave-taking by mothers in the months following birth, the magnitude of the change is much greater for college-educated or married mothers than for their less educated or single counterparts (Han, Ruhm, & Waldfogel, 2009). In the absence of paid parental leave, legal entitlement to leave benefits under the FMLA may not amount to real-world access. As one labor lobbyist remarked during early hearings on the legislation, "The idea of an unpaid leave tends to leave working people with an eyebrow cocked" (Elving, 1995). Even some opponents of the FMLA referred to it disparagingly as the "yuppie bill" on the grounds that it would benefit only higher paid employees who could afford to take unpaid leave (Hatch, 1993).

Nearly 20 years after the enactment of the legislation, these warnings about the impact of unpaid leave seem prescient. According to Congresswoman Lynn Woolsey (personal communication, November 9, 2011), who entered Congress the year the FMLA was enacted, "The law has worked up to a point, but only for those who have the means to take leave without pay." A pattern of unequal usage has developed, where FMLA-covered leave-taking is more frequent among better educated, higher paid employees. National survey data reveal that three fourths of FMLA-eligible workers who needed but did not take a leave indicated that they could not afford the associated loss of wages, and 88% said they would have taken leave had some wage replacement been available (Cantor et al., 2001; Fass, 2009).

At the same time, the law seems to have strengthened the ties of the best educated, most highly trained mothers to the workforce, with three in four new mothers with bachelor's degrees or higher back at work 5 months after giving birth and 80% returning to their prebirth employer (Johnson, 2008; Laughlin, 2011). Thus, the FMLA, although enabling these parents to take time off in the short term, actually promotes higher work participation in the medium term (Han et al., 2008). In this respect, as we discuss in more detail in chapter 4, the FMLA may benefit employers as much as employees by promoting the retention of the most highly trained workers who are the most difficult and expensive to replace.

■ The impact of FMLA on leave use by fathers is less clear.

The impact of the FMLA on leave use by fathers is more difficult to assess but appears less robust than the law's impact on maternal leave-taking. To minimize loss of income, many men use paid vacation or sick leave to cover the short time they take off after the birth or adoption of an infant; very few use unpaid paternity leave per se as protected by the FMLA. However, using a more expansive definition of leave, Han et al. (2009) found that, since the passage of the FMLA, a small but growing number of fathers have taken some type of brief leave, such as vacation or personal days, to be with their new babies. As a result, a parental leave law is estimated to increase the percentage of the birth month that employed fathers spend on leave from 7% to 11%, representing approximately 2 extra days off work, seemingly a small increase but large in relative terms (Han et al., 2009).

■ The FMLA has cost employers far less than estimated.

Perhaps not surprisingly given the law's lack of wage replacement, the costs to employers associated with the FMLA have been found to be minimal. Two years after the enactment of the FMLA, between 89% and 98% of covered worksites reported little if any cost associated with the general administration of the act, continuing health insurance benefits, or hiring and training replacements for employees on leave (Commission on Family and Medical Leave, 1996). Five years later, a survey of employers commissioned by the U.S. Department of Labor found that two thirds of covered establishments considered the FMLA easy to administer, and an even larger majority reported that the FMLA had had no adverse effects on their business (Cantor et al., 2001). Large employers with more than 250 employees did report a somewhat greater administrative burden than did smaller establishments, but some employers actually reported a positive effect of the law on business productivity, profitability, and growth (Cantor et al., 2001).

The dire predictions that the FMLA would bankrupt American business have not come true because business lobbyists were mistaken in a key assumption: The U.S. Chamber of Commerce estimated that employers would hire temporary employees to cover for employees on leave. On the contrary, as it turns out, virtually all employers cover work when an employee takes leave by assigning the work temporarily to another existing employee. For example, in the course of writing this book, the second author assumed part of the workload of a colleague on maternity leave with a premature baby. Thus, to the extent that there is a cost associated with the FMLA benefits, it is shared by employees, who do so for a variety of reasons—because the people we work with tend to become our friends, because assuming the workload temporarily for an employee on leave has become a standard workplace expectation, and because anyone providing coverage for an employee on leave knows that he or she may one day need similar assistance.

State Policies Affecting Time Off With New Babies

■ Several states offer more generous maternity, paternity, or family leave policies, or a combination of these.

A number of states—both prior to and since the enactment of the FMLA—have enacted similar legislation that may apply to more workers, offer less restrictive requirements for unpaid leave, or even provide some access to paid leave. By 2009, 14 states and the District of Columbia had parental leave laws more generous than the federal law (Washbrook et al., 2011). Of these, five states—California, Hawaii, New Jersey, New York, and Rhode Island—have temporary disability insurance (TDI) laws that provide a short (typically 6 weeks) period of partial wage replacement. Most of these TDI programs were enacted in the 1940s but did not apply to pregnant women until the 1970s with the passage of the Pregnancy Discrimination Act (Fass, 2009). In addition, nine states and the District of Columbia offer job-protected leave to employees who work part-time, seven states and the District require firms with fewer than 50 employees to offer job-protected leave, and four states and the District offer more than 12 weeks of job-protected leave (Washbrook et al.). Of particular significance to new parents who changed jobs in the year before they gave birth, five states require less than 12 months history with an employer to qualify for job-protected leave; for example, Oregon requires 6 months tenure, and two states set no minimum requirement.

Finally, three states—California, New Jersey, and Washington—have enacted statutes that provide paid family leave. In 2002, California became the first state to pass such legislation. The Paid Family Leave Insurance Program builds on the state's TDI program and offers 6 weeks of partial wage replacement (up to 55% of weekly earnings, with a maximum of $959 per week in 2009) for workers to care for a seriously ill child, spouse, or domestic partner, or to bond with a newborn or newly adopted child or recently placed foster child. The paid family leave is financed entirely by employee contributions. Because California is a TDI state, new parents can receive partial wage replacement for 4 weeks prior to a child's birth and 6–8 weeks after birth. Following the expiration of the TDI benefits, a parent can claim an additional 6 weeks of bonding leave through Paid Family Leave Insurance. However, these additional weeks of leave are job-protected only if the parent also is covered under the FMLA (Fass, 2009).

Similarly, in 2008, New Jersey enacted paid family leave legislation building on its TDI program. The law offers wage replacement up to two thirds of weekly pay, up to a maximum of $546 in 2009 (Fass, 2009). Like California's paid leave legislation, the New Jersey statute does not include job protection, with that provision still dependent on the employee's eligibility for coverage under the FMLA (Warner, 2009). Like California's law, the New Jersey paid leave is also financed exclusively by employee contributions.

The state of Washington enacted a Family Leave Insurance program in 2007 intended to provide 5 weeks of partial wage replacement for parents to spend time with a newborn or newly adopted child (Fass, 2009). However, the administration of the program was not spelled out, no permanent funding source was identified, and, at the onset of the financial crisis of 2008, the governor suspended work on implementing the program until 2012 (Economic Opportunity Institute, 2009).

For a more detailed analysis of the impact of the paid family leave legislation in California and a more complete description of the laws enacted in New Jersey and Washington and those under consideration in many other states, see chapter 6.

Private Sector Leave Policies

■ **Access to paid leave for newborn care varies greatly based on where one works.**

Except in the few states described above that mandate partial wage replacement under TDI or through other legislation, access to paid leave around the time of childbirth depends on where one works. According to the 2008 National Study of Employers (Galinsky, Bond, Sakai, Kim, & Giuntoli, 2008, p. 7), the employers most likely to offer generous wage replacement benefits

■ are larger;

■ are nonprofit;

■ have a greater percentage of union members;

■ have a greater percentage of racial and ethnic minorities; and

■ have less difficulty finding and hiring employees whom they consider "honest, reliable and hardworking self-starters."

Half of the employers with more than 50 employees, according to the above study, provide at least some replacement pay for employees on maternity leave. However, the percentage of employers providing full pay during the period of maternity-related disability has actually declined, from 27% in 1998 to 16% in 2008. This parallels the cutback in employers' contributions to health care premiums. In addition, within the above group of employers, three quarters of those with 1,000 or more employees offer some type of wage replacement for maternity leave. By contrast, fewer than half of employers with 50 to 99 employees provide any wage replacement, and access to paid leave among those with fewer than 50 employees is thought to be far less frequent yet (Galinsky et al., 2008).

On the basis of an analysis of U.S. Department of Labor data by the Institute for Women's Policy Research (2007), it appears that access to extended time off through disability plans in the private sector varies along occupational lines, with service and part-time workers and those earning less than $15 per hour the least apt to qualify. Almost none of the lowest earning workers have access to paid family leave, whereas the employees who do have paid leave are usually managers or professionals and among the highest paid workers.

Some companies that put a high premium on retaining talented employees do offer generous wage replacement. Perhaps most notable are the major accounting firms—not only for the generosity of their benefit policies but also for the rationale that led to them. The Big Four accounting firms—Ernst & Young, Deloitte, KPMG, and PricewaterhouseCoopers—generally offer 12 weeks of paid maternity leave and 6 weeks of paid paternity leave, and that is on top of the 12 weeks of unpaid leave provided to families under the FMLA (Greenhouse, 2011). These firms calculated that the cost of hiring and training a new employee can be 1.5 times a departing worker's salary. Thus, according to an example cited by Greenhouse, reducing turnover by 200 employees earning an average of $100,000 per year could mean $30 million in savings. Sharon Allen, Deloitte's chairwoman, said her firm's flexibility and leave policies saved more than $45 million a year in reduced turnover (Greenhouse).

■ Many families use vacation leave, sick leave, or disability leave to help finance time off with a new baby.

One of the challenges in assessing the extent of access to paid maternity or paternity leave in the United States is that many mothers and fathers use other forms of paid leave to help piece together time off to care for a new or adopted child. For example, the U.S. Census Bureau lumps together paid maternity, sick, vacation, and other paid leave in one definition of paid leave (Johnson, 2008; Laughlin, 2011). Of the more than 3 million first-time mothers who worked during pregnancy from 2001 through 2003, nearly one third of the new mothers had at least a few days of paid time off, but many used multiple forms of leave, including both paid and unpaid sick leave, vacation leave, or disability leave to cover their time off from work. Bundling these different types of leave not only makes it difficult to assess the extent of paid leave specifically provided to help parents with newborn care, but more important, it poses potential problems for these parents when they return to work. After all, it is not as if a parent can promise not to get ill later just because she or he had the privilege of taking time off to care for a new baby. Moreover, Americans already get less time off for vacation than do employees in other industrialized nations (Wade, 2010), and it is questionable whether requiring them to use their vacation time for family and medical leave will enhance their own or the nation's productivity.

Finally, it is clear that employees with little education have much less access to paid sick leave, vacation leave, and disability leave. Employees with a bachelor's degree or higher, according to the U.S. Census Bureau, are nearly 4 times more likely to receive some type of paid leave—even of a few days in duration—than are their counterparts with less than a high school education (Laughlin). Fewer than one third of women who are high school graduates receive any type of paid leave following childbirth as compared to two thirds of women with a bachelor's degree or more (Laughlin).

▪ Access to job protection and to private sector policies providing paid leave may be eroding.

Compared with a decade ago, according to *Wall Street Journal* columnist Sue Shellenbarger (2008), there is some evidence that employers may actually be reducing postchildbirth pay and offering shorter paid leaves for short-term disability, for both men and women. New parents are also being hit by a cost-cutting move not aimed at them per se but rather at reducing pay for workers on short-term disability, as an incentive for workers to return to work as soon as they are able.

In the midst of an economic downturn, workers worried about losing their jobs may also be less likely to use benefits even if they have them, according to Debra Ness of the National Partnership for Women and Families (Goodman, 2009). There is also evidence that job protection for those on maternity leave is less secure. "It is entirely legal to lay off a pregnant woman or woman on maternity leave," notes *New York Times* business reporter Lesley Alderman (2009), "as long as the employer can make the case that she is being let go for a reason unrelated to her pregnancy." Although employers may not be singling out employees on maternity leave, it is convenient to lay off a person who is on leave and hence not working on any projects that might get disrupted.

In 2008, 30 years after the passage of the Pregnancy Discrimination Act, the number of pregnancy-based discrimination charges filed with the Equal Employment Opportunity Commission was up nearly 50% from a decade earlier, to a total of 6,285 (Alderman, 2009). In part, these statistics probably reflect an increase in employees' awareness of their legal rights and greater enforcement of those rights. However, a 6-fold increase in monetary awards related to Equal Employment Opportunity Commission charges also suggests a greater percentage of well-founded complaints (Grossman, 2008).

Summary

In summary, women represent half of the workforce and occupy half of the professional and managerial positions in the United States; they also continue to have babies. Mothers in the United States return to work much earlier after giving birth than do their counterparts in other advanced industrial nations, with first-time mothers typically resuming work within 3 months after giving birth, and a significant minority (15%) within 1 month or less. Fathers take more time off to be with their newborn babies than in the past, but rarely more than a week.

The FMLA was a hard-won legislative achievement, opposed vehemently by many business organizations who wanted to create a firewall against more government mandates. Nearly 2 decades later, it is clear that the FMLA has significantly increased access to job-protected maternity and paternity leave, even among employers not required to comply. Business lobbyist predictions that the FMLA would impose high costs and heavy administrative burdens on employers were vastly overblown, and the legislation has actually helped strengthen the ties of better paid, more highly educated employees to the workforce.

However, although the 12 weeks of unpaid leave have certainly been a help to many new parents, the duration is not sufficient to fully address many of the maternal and child health issues we raise in chapter 2. Strict prior work requirements leave many workers unprotected, and, without wage replacement, many low-income workers cannot afford to take the leave provided by the FMLA. Some employers have concluded that voluntarily providing paid leave for infant care and other purposes ultimately saves money for their business, and a few states are now offering paid family leave. Thus, although the FMLA has had an impact, real access to time off to care for a newborn or adopted baby still depends largely on where one works, with the lesser educated, lower income parents the least likely to qualify.

References

Alderman, L. (2009, March 28). When the stork carries a pink slip. *The New York Times*, p. B6.

Belkin, L. (2010, October 24). Calling Mr. Mom? Why women won't have it all until men do, too. *The New York Times Magazine*, pp. 13–14. Retrieved July 24, 2011, from www.nytimes.com/2010/10/24/magazine/24fob-wwln-t.html?_r=1

Bunning, Rep. J. [KY]. (1990, May 10). Statement. In *Congressional Record* 136, 9. 101st Cong.

Cantor, D., Waldfogel, J., Kerwin, J., McKinley Wright, M., Levin, K., Rauch, J., et al. (2001). *Balancing the needs of families and employers: Family and medical leave surveys, 2000 update.* Rockville, MD: Westat.

Collins, G. (2009). *When everything changed: The amazing journey of American women from 1960 to the present.* New York: Little, Brown.

Commission on Family and Medical Leave. (1996). *A workable balance: Report to Congress on family and medical leave policies.* Washington, DC: U.S. Department of Labor, Women's Bureau.

Daly, L. (2009, August 3). The case for paid family leave: Why the United States should follow Australia's lead. *Newsweek.* Retrieved September 23, 2010, from www.newsweek.com/2009/08/03/the-case-for-paid-family-leave.print.html

DeLay, Rep. T. [TX]. (1990, May 10). Statement. In *Congressional Record* 136, H17. 101st Cong..

Dodd, Sen. C. [CT]. (1993, February 2). Statement. In *Congressional Record- Senate*, 139, S985. 103rd Cong.

Dunnewind, S. (2003, November 19). Attitudes about paternity leave are changing. *The Seattle Times*. Retrieved February 11, 2011, from www.azcentral.com/families/articles/1120fam_paternityleave.html?&wired

Economic Opportunity Institute. (2009). *Keeping your job while you care for your family.* Retrieved July 25, 2011, from www.eoionline.org/work_and_family/family_leave_insurance.htm

Elving, R. D. (1995). *Conflict and compromise: How Congress makes the law.* New York: Touchstone Books.

Family and Medical Leave Act of 1993, Pub. L. No. 103-3, 107 Stat. 6, 29 U.S.C. § 2601 et seq. (1993).

Farber, E., Alejandro-Wright, M., & Muenchow, S. (1988). Managing work and family: Hopes and realities. In E. Zigler & M. Frank (Eds.), *The parental leave crisis: Toward a national policy* (pp. 161–176). New Haven, CT: Yale University Press.

Fass, S. (2009). *Paid leave in the states: A critical support for low-wage workers and their families.* Retrieved April 15, 2009, from The National Center for Children in Poverty Web site: www.nccp.org/publications/pub_864.html

Galinsky, E., Bond, J. T., Sakai, K., Kim, S. S., & Giuntoli, N. (2008). *2008 national study of employers.* New York: Families and Work Institute.

Gomby, D., & Dow, J. P. (2009). *Newborn family leave: Effects on children, parents, and business.* The David and Lucile Packard Foundation. Available from http://www.paidfamilyleave.org

Goodman, E. (2009). *Just grateful to have a job.* Retrieved January 20, 2011, from www.boston.com/jobs/news/articles/2009/09/11/just_grateful_to_have_a_job/

Greenhouse, S. (2011, January 8). The retention bonus? Time. In accounting, firms find flexible hours pay dividends. *The New York Times*, p. B1.

Grossman, J. (2008, April 1). *A marked increase in pregnancy discrimination claims and other key developments illustrate the continuing struggle of pregnant workers: Part one in a two-part series of columns.* Retrieved September 9, 2010, from http://writ.lp.findlaw.com/grossman/20080401.html

Han, W. J., Ruhm, C., & Waldfogel, J. (2009). Parental leave policies and parents' employment and leave-taking. *Journal of Policy Analysis and Management, 28*(1), 29–54.

Han, W. J., Ruhm, C., Waldfogel, J., & Washbrook, E. (2008). The timing of mothers' employment after childbirth. *Monthly Labor Review, 131*(6), 15–27.

Hatch, Sen. O. [UT]. (1993, February 2). Statement. In *Congressional Record* 139, S1006. 103rd Cong.

Heymann, J., Earle, A., & Hayes, J. (2007). *The work, family, and equity index: How does the United States measure up?* Project on Global Working Families, Institute for Health and Social Policy. Montreal, Quebec, Canada: McGill University. Retrieved July 26, 2011, from www.mcgill.ca./files/ihsp/WFEIFinal2007Feb.pdf

Institute for Women's Policy Research. (2007, August). *Maternity leave in the United States: Paid parental leave is still not standard, even among the best U.S. employers* (IWPR Fact Sheet A131). Retrieved July 26, 2011, from www.iwpr.org/publications/pubs/maternity-leave-in-the-united-states-paid-parental-leave-is-still-not-standard-even-among-the-best-u.s.-employers

Johnson, T. D. (2008). *Maternity leave and employment patterns of first-time mothers: 1961-2003* (Current Population Reports, P70–113). Washington, DC: U.S. Census Bureau.

Larson: Paid parental Act leave puts working parents first. (2009). Retrieved January 20, 2011, from House Democrats Web site: www.dems.gov/press/larson-paid-parental-leave-act-puts-working-families-first

Laughlin, L. (2011). Maternity leave and employment patterns of first-time mothers: 1961-2008. (Current Population Reports, P70-128). Washington, DC: U.S. Census Bureau.

Local Government Employers. (2010). *Legal timetable: Guide to implementation of recent or forthcoming employment legislation.* Retrieved January 20, 2010, from www.lge.gov.uk/lge/core/page.do?pageID=119649

Ludden, J. (2010, June 10). *More workers alleging bias against caregivers.* Retrieved February 21, 2011, from www.npr.org/templates/story/story.php?storyId=127531355

Melmed, M. (2008). *Statement of Matthew Melmed, Executive Director, ZERO TO THREE, Submitted to the Committee on Health, Education, Labor and Pensions, Subcommittee on Children and Families, United States Senate: Hearing on Writing the Next Chapter of the Family and Medical Leave Act – Building on a Fifteen Year History of Support for Workers.* Retrieved August 30, 2010, from http://main.zerotothree.org/site/DocServer/FMLATestimony.pdf?docID=4921

Mosby's medical dictionary (8th ed.). (2009). Maryland Heights, MO: Elsevier Health Services.

National Science Foundation. (2002). Higher education in science and engineering: Increasing global capacity. *Science and Engineering Indicators 2002. Division of Science Resources Statistics, Chapter 2.* Retrieved July 25, 2011, from www.nsf.gov/statistics/seind02/c2/c2s4.htm

Nepomnyaschy, L., & Waldfogel, J. (2007). Paternity leave and fathers' involvement with their young children: Evidence from the American ECLS-B. *Community, Work & Family, 10,* 427–453.

Ness, D. (2008). *Written testimony of Debra Ness for the Committee on Health, Education, Labor and Pensions, Subcommittee on Children and Families: Hearing on Writing the Next Chapter of the Family and Medical Leave Act – Building on a Fifteen Year History of Support for Workers.* Retrieved January 20, 2011, from www.nationalpartnership.org/site/DocServer/DebraNess_WrittenTestimony_2-13-08.pdf?docID=2941

Organization for Economic Cooperation and Development. (2008). *OECD family database.* Retrieved from www.oecd.org/els/social/family/database

Organization for Economic Cooperation and Development. (2009). *OECD factbook 2009: Economic, environmental, and social statistics.* Paris: Author.

Phillips, K. R. (2004). *Getting time off: Access to leave among working parents* (Policy Brief B-57). Washington, DC: The Urban Institute. Retrieved July 27, 2011, from www.urban.org/url.cfm?ID=310977

Roukema, Rep. M. [NJ]. (1990, May 10). Statement. In *Congressional Record* 136, 4. 101st Cong.

Royal College of Obstetricians and Gynaecologists. (2009). *RCOG statement on later maternal age.* Retrieved January 19, 2011, from www.rcog.org.uk/what-we-do/campaigning-and-opinions/statement/rcog-statement-later-maternal-age

Rudd, E. (2004). *Family leave: A policy concept made in America.* Retrieved January 20, 2011, from the Sloan Work and Family Research Network, Boston College. Web site: http://wfnetwork.bc.edu/encyclopedia_entry.php?id=233

Ruhm, C. (1997). Policy watch: The Family and Medical Leave Act. *Journal of Economic Perspectives, 11*, 175–186.

Shellenbarger, S. (2008, June 11). Downsizing maternity leave: Employers cut pay, time off. *The Wall Street Journal*, p. D1.

Testimony on behalf of U.S. Chamber of Commerce, 103d Cong., Minority Views on H.R. 1, Rep. No. 103-10 (1993) (testimony of Earl Hess).

Wade, L. (2010). Paid vacation days in the U.S. versus other OECD countries. *Sociological images.* Retrieved February 1, 2011, from http://thesocietypages.org/socimages/2010/01/31/paid-holidaysvacation-days-in-the-u-s-versus-other-oecd-countries

Waldfogel, J. (1999, October). Family leave coverage in the 1990s. *Monthly Labor Review*, 13–21.

Warner, J. (2009, March 19). Families to care about. *The New York Times.* Retrieved March 19, 2009, from http://warner.blogs.nytimes.com/2009/03/19/families-to-care-about/

Washbrook, E., Ruhm, C. J., Waldfogel, J., & Han, W. -J. (2011). Public policies, women's employment after childbearing, and child well-being. *The B.E. Journal of Economic Analysis & Policy, 11*(1), Article 43. Retrieved July 30, 2011, from www.bepress.com/bejeap/vol11/iss1/art43

Weil, D. (2008). Mighty monolith or fractured federation? Business opposition and the enactment of workplace legislation. In A. Bernhardt, H. Boushey, L. Dresser, & C. Tilley (Eds.), *The gloves off economy: Workplace standards at the bottom of the labor market* (pp. 287–314). Ithaca, NY: Cornell University Press.

Yale Bush Center Advisory Committee on Infant Care Leave. (1988). Recommendations. In E. Zigler & M. Frank (Eds.), *The parental leave crisis: Toward a national policy* (pp. 343–345). New Haven, CT: Yale University Press.

Zigler, E., & Frank, M. (Eds.). (1988). *The parental leave crisis: Toward a national policy.* New Haven, CT: Yale University Press.

CHAPTER

2

The Medical and Child Development Case for Time Off

There is abundant evidence that parents need some time off from employment after the birth or adoption of a baby. As a result, obstetricians recommend that mothers take at least several weeks off from work to recover from pregnancy and childbirth. Pediatricians counsel taking time to get the baby off to a healthy start. Psychologists stress the importance of mothers—and increasingly fathers—spending a period of time focusing primarily on their infants, developing patterns of reciprocal interaction that will influence the quality of all of the child's future development.

Research over the last 2 decades has strengthened both the medical and child development case—and provided a clear biological basis—for infant care leave. Studies show a link between breastfeeding and reductions in neonatal mortality, underlining the wisdom of allowing employed mothers to stay home long enough to facilitate the practice. Recent research provides a neurological explanation for the lasting impact of an infant's early experiences on his long-term behavior—namely that these early experiences actually influence the "wiring" and developing structure of the baby's brain.

Child developmental research, once focused almost exclusively on the mother's interaction with a new baby, has also expanded to explore the role of fathers in the infant's early development. A growing body of studies confirms the special contribution of fathers in encouraging infant play and cognitive development, and these studies show that fathers who take some time off after the birth or adoption of a baby are more apt to be involved in their child's life from then on.

In this chapter, we summarize the findings and implications for parental leave policy for the care of new or adopted infants from several streams of research. We begin with findings from maternal and child health, family adjustment to the birth or adoption of a baby, and early identification of and amelioration of disabilities. We then turn to research on bonding, attunement, and attachment; neurological findings on brain development; and studies of the impact of the timing of parental return to employment on children's long-term cognitive and social and emotional development. Interspersed amid the review of applicable research are a few illustrations of postpartum experiences drawn from the authors' own observations and work lives. What emerges is a case for parental leave policies that allow time for both mothers and fathers to participate in the early nurture of babies. The birth or adoption of a child is a profoundly moving experience for both parents. Human infants are very dependent creatures, and parents are programmed to provide the nurture that babies need.

Maternal, Family, and Child Health Evidence

> ■ We start with the most basic question: Why do physicians routinely recommend 6 to 8 weeks for mothers to recuperate from pregnancy and labor?

Childbirth has become so safe in the United States that most parents may take for granted that an expectant mother will enter the hospital in labor and emerge 2 days later not only with a healthy bundle of joy but also with no serious complications herself. Over the last century, there have been tremendous advances in reducing maternal mortality following childbirth in the United States. In 1900, 1 in 100 mothers died within 42 days of giving birth; in 2004, the rate was 13 in 100,000 (Centers for Disease Control and Prevention, n.d.-b), although recently, maternal mortality has begun to rise slightly. The increase is attributed to several factors: the rising incidence of obesity, the growing number of cesarean deliveries, the rising age of mothers, and the continuing problem of pockets of the population who do not receive proper prenatal care. Mothers' postnatal stays in the hospital have also decreased sharply from the standard 8 to 14 days in the 1950s to 2 to 3 days in 2002 (Brown, Small, Faber, Drastev, & Davis, 2002). For a variety of social and financial reasons, postnatal discharge might take place even more quickly had the United States not enacted the Newborns' and Mothers' Health Protection Act of 1996, which requires insurance companies to cover at least 48 hours of hospitalization following a vaginal delivery or 96 hours following a cesarean. Physical recovery from childbirth is typically viewed as a process that takes care of itself, requiring little assistance from health care providers, as demonstrated by the single postpartum visit typically recommended several weeks after delivery (Gjerdingen, Froberg, Chaloner, & McGovern, 1993).

Notwithstanding the image of *The Good Earth* (Buck, 1931) heroine who gives birth and resumes work in the rice paddies the same day, however, the fact that childbirth is a natural and commonplace event does not necessarily mean that it is easy. Consider the dramatic physical changes that occur in a woman's body during pregnancy, childbirth, and postdelivery. During pregnancy, the weight of the uterus (not counting the contents!) increases at least 15-fold (BabyCenter, n.d.-b). Although postpartum changes differ for every woman, it generally takes 6 weeks for the uterus to shrink to its prepregnancy size (Cunningham et al., 2010; Curtis & Schuler, 2002). Childbirth stretches and distends the muscles and ligaments that normally hold up the reproductive and digestive organs, and it typically takes weeks, not to mention pelvic floor exercises, to restore muscle tone. No wonder it may be a few weeks before new mothers begin to feel more like themselves. At a minimum, giving birth is physically exhausting.

Many new mothers also contend with several minor to moderate physical discomforts for weeks, if not months, after giving birth—breast soreness, discomfort from stitches, pelvic bone pain, and skin problems, to mention a few of the more annoying and humiliating, though admittedly not life-threatening, possibilities (Gjerdingen et al., 1993). One month following delivery, for example, breast soreness and nipple irritation have been found to affect 45% of new mothers who were breastfeeding and 28% even of those who were not (Gjerdingen et al.). Painful conditions associated with breastfeeding include engorgement; plugged milk ducts; cracked, blistered, and bleeding nipples; and infection of the breast (mastitis).

Inadequate milk supply is another common and worrisome problem. Having some medical knowledge about breastfeeding and reading about it prior to the arrival of the baby does not necessarily prevent these problems, as a colleague's daughter, a pediatrician, recently discovered in the first weeks after the birth of her son. Difficulties with breastfeeding can usually be overcome, but doing so requires time and patience, perhaps consultation with a lactation consultant, and sometimes medical treatment. Breast infections most commonly occur in mothers who are stressed and exhausted or who have not been able to resolve some of the other common breastfeeding problems mentioned above (*Overcoming Breastfeeding Problems*, 2009). Thus, breastfeeding, although highly recommended by the American Academy of Pediatrics to promote children's health (benefits of breastfeeding for children are discussed later), often presents challenges for new mothers and does not always proceed easily.

About one in four vaginal deliveries in the United States is accompanied by an episiotomy, a surgical incision between the vaginal opening and the anus (perineum) during childbirth. Another third of women experience a spontaneous tear or "rip." Whether the cut to this sensitive area occurs spontaneously or is done deliberately to prevent a larger tear, full recovery typically requires 4 to 6 weeks (Frankman, Wang, Bunker, & Lowder, 2009; Kettle & Tohill, 2008).

Cesarean sections, which have increased 50% since 1996 and now represent nearly one in three of all deliveries in the United States, constitute major abdominal surgery (Martin et al.,

2009). Cesarean deliveries pose a greater danger of infection, hemorrhage, or surgical complications, and a mother is advised not to pick up anything heavier than the baby for 6 to 8 weeks (Brigham and Women's Hospital, 2010). A man or woman experiencing other forms of abdominal surgery would be advised to go home for 6 to 8 weeks, focus on good nutrition, and get lots of rest. However, mothers who have just experienced cesarean deliveries go home to take on a demanding new job—caring for and feeding a baby—often accompanied by major disruptions in sleep.

Although the birth of a baby is typically a joyous event, postpartum blues also affect most mothers in the first few days or up to 2 weeks after delivery. As a result of rapid hormonal changes, as many as 80% of all new mothers experience sadness, crying for no apparent reason, loneliness, and anxiety (Brigham and Women's Hospital, 2010). Reflecting on the first time, after giving birth, that she found herself alone with her new baby at home, a colleague said, "I just sat there and cried—and called a neighbor to ask for help."

The so-called "baby blues" usually pass within a few days, but a more serious form of clinical depression affects 10%–20% of women within days of delivery and up to a year later (Brigham and Women's Hospital, 2010; Miller, 2002; U.S. Department of Health and Human Services, 2009). Symptoms include feelings of anxiety and inability to cope, despair, panic, either lack of feeling or extreme concern for the baby, fear of harming the baby or oneself, poor concentration or memory, and feelings of unworthiness. These symptoms are usually temporary, but they require treatment and professional help.

In summary, recovery from childbirth is not always simple, typically takes 6 to 8 weeks, and sometimes requires substantially more time. Even by 6 months postpartum, some women do not feel completely recovered from childbirth. In a study of 96 mothers of healthy, full-term infants 6 months after delivery, one in four women did not feel physically recovered from childbirth and reported problems with lack of sleep, difficulty losing weight, and emotional volatility (Tulman & Fawcett, 1991). The wide range in recovery time from childbirth, noted University of Minnesota professor and family practice physician Dwenda Gjerdingen and her colleagues (1993), should be taken into account by women as they plan their postpartum activities, by physicians who advise women about postpartum health care, and by employers and legislators who have the power to influence the duration of maternity leave.

■ How does the timing of return to employment affect the new mother's health?

Research on the impact of early maternal employment has traditionally focused on its effects on children, with much less exploration of how the timing of return to employment might affect the health of the mothers themselves. To the extent that researchers have explored the impact of return to employment on the physical health of new mothers, most have not identified a higher rate of doctor visits among those returning early to work. However, a study of first-time mothers in Minnesota found that employed postpartum mothers had higher rates of respiratory infections, breast symptoms, and gynecological problems compared to postpartum mothers who were not employed (Gjerdingen et al., 1993). Another study found that short maternity leaves of 6 weeks, as compared to 12 weeks, increased the probability of depression, though only among mothers who also had marital concerns and who considered their work unrewarding (Hyde, Klein, Essex, & Clark, 1995).

More recent research has suggested that time off from employment, to the extent that it facilitates breastfeeding, has maternal health benefits, such as diminishing the risk of ovarian and premenopausal breast cancer, pregnancy-induced obesity, osteoporosis, and hip fractures (Calnen, 2007). For example, based on an analysis of data from the Nurses' Health Study, a long-term study of 100,000 women in 14 states, women with a family history of breast cancer were 59% less likely to develop breast cancer themselves if they breastfed their children (Stuebe, Willett, Xue, & Michels, 2009). The reduction in risk was similar whether women breastfed for a lifetime total of 3 months or for more than 3 years. Although the duration of the breastfeeding did not seem to make a difference, to the extent that access to time off from employment facilitates the initiation of breastfeeding, this study provides indirect evidence that leave policies may contribute to the health of mothers at risk of breast cancer.

Perhaps the most definitive post-Family and Medical Leave Act (FMLA) findings relating to the impact of the timing of return to employment on both the physical and mental health of new mothers come from a study by economists Pinka Chatterji and Sara Markowitz (2008). On the basis of an analysis of interviews with 3,366 mothers who were employed before giving birth and who participated in the Early Childhood Longitudinal Study, Birth Cohort, the authors found that somewhat longer maternity leaves (e.g., 4 months), both paid and unpaid, were associated with maternal benefits that included declines in depressive symptoms, a reduction in the likelihood of severe depression, and improvement in overall health.

Chatterji and Markowitz (2008) focused on depression as a maternal health outcome because clinical depression and self-reported depressive symptoms among mothers put children, particularly in the early years, at risk of adverse emotional and cognitive development. Maternal depression was measured using a widely used psychiatric scale that captures mood, sleeping problems, and motor functioning level. On the basis of results from this scale, doubling total maternal leave from 9 to 18 weeks was estimated to reduce maternal depressive symptoms by a small but significant amount (Chatterji & Markowitz). Self-reports from the mothers responding to the Early Childhood Longitudinal Study, Birth Cohort indicated that more weeks of leave, both paid and unpaid, were also associated with a greater likelihood of their being in excellent physical health and a lower probability of their being in poor health.

Although the magnitude of the effects on maternal physical health was small, the authors considered them still significant, especially because health outcomes could not be measured until about 9 months after childbirth, and many mothers who had been experiencing health problems early on would be expected to have started to recover.

■ How does the arrival of the baby—and the timing of the parents' return to employment—affect the health and well-being of the whole family?

In many ways, it is difficult to separate the impact of the birth or adoption of a new baby on the mother's health from the impact on the entire family system. Having a new baby is one of life's most exciting and joyful events, but it is also one of its more stressful. In a study of more than 2,500 adults, Dohrenwend, Krasnoff, Askenasy, and Dohrenwend (1978) found that the birth of a first child was the sixth most stressful event out of a list of 102 events.

Fatigue is likely to contribute to both parents' feelings of stress (Hopper & Zigler, 1988). For the first few weeks after birth, most babies sleep no more than 2 to 4 hours at a time, day or night. Low birth weight babies typically have even shorter periods of sleep. Between 3 to 6 months of age, many babies begin to sleep through the night, but that is defined as 5 to 6 hours a night, not the 8 hours many adults consider their due (BabyCenter, n.d.-a; Hopper & Zigler). The baby's sleep patterns may continue to conflict with parental work schedules for some time, as one of our colleagues who has a 4-month-old daughter recently discovered: "She wakes up at midnight, 3:30 a.m., and 6:30 a.m. It is then difficult to have to wake her at 8 a.m. to take her to child care. Sometimes I can barely get out of bed in time to go to work."

The transition to parenthood, however much welcomed, also puts stress on a marriage. The couple, now that they are parents, have less time to maintain and build marital intimacy (Cowan et al., 1985; Hopper & Zigler, 1988). Many doctors recommend waiting 4 to 6 weeks before resuming sex, to allow the cervix to close, bleeding to stop, and tears to heal. At 4 weeks postpartum, more than half of the postpartum mothers in two studies expressed concerns about emotional tension, fatigue, sexual function, and relationships with their husbands (Gjerdingen et al., 1993; Gruis, 1977; Harrison & Hicks, 1983). Fathers may have mixed feelings about the birth and feel that they will not be able to measure up to the mother's expectations. Or a father may simply worry that the new baby will replace him in the mother's affection.

The arrival of a new infant also introduces a period of adjustment for other children in the family. The birth of a sibling transforms the lives of firstborn children, and all of the children in the family must begin to adjust to their new roles as brother or sister to what they may regard as the little interloper (Hopper & Zigler, 1988). We recall an instance in which an existing child in the household feared that he would have to move out when the new baby arrived. As a pediatrician once remarked to a mother concerned about her toddler's less-than-enthusiastic reception of a baby sister, "How would you feel if someone younger and cuter suddenly moved into your household?"

The transition to parenthood can be even more challenging for individuals or couples who adopt (Hopper & Zigler, 1988). Adoptive parents may have been waiting for years for the opportunity to adopt a child, only to have just a few days to prepare for the child's arrival. When families adopt an infant, they encounter many of the same physical challenges experienced by biological families (such as sleep disruption) but often with less support. And the period of emotional and social adjustment, as we discuss in more detail later, is likely to be at least as demanding.

In summary, the birth or adoption of an infant is a sensitive period in a family's life, and it takes time for both parents to adjust physically and emotionally. According to Farkas, Duffett, and Johnson (2000), four out of five parents believe that new mothers are pressured to return to work too quickly. Moreover, recent research indicated that the length of paternity leave also contributes to maternal health outcomes. According to the study discussed by Chatterji and Markowitz (2008), having a husband who took a paternity leave, even of typically less than 2 weeks, appeared to reduce the likelihood of maternal depression. When both parents share at least the initial joys and adjustments of welcoming a small but demanding new family member into the household, new mothers feel better about the partnership.

■ How does the timing of a mother's return to employment in the 1st year of life and access to parental leave affect a child's health?

A substantial body of research has indicated that the timing of parental return to employment as influenced by access to paid leave can affect child health. Cross-national studies link paid leave to reductions in infant mortality. For example, one of us (Ruhm, 2000) looked at the impact of paid parental leave—defined broadly to include both the initial period available only to mothers and broader forms of family leave that could be available to either parent—on child health in 16 European countries between 1969 and 1994. In the first 30 days after the birth of a baby, parental access to paid leave did not have much of an effect on infant mortality, most likely because neonatal deaths relate more to the type of medical care a mother and baby receive or whether the infant is born with a congenital defect of some kind. But for the rest of the 1st year of life, there was a clear link between access to leave and reduction in postneonatal mortality. Specifically, a 10-week extension in paid leave is predicted to reduce the death rate for infants between 28 days and 1 year of life by 3.7% to 4.5% (Ruhm). Building on this study and extending it to include the United States and Japan up to the year 2000, Tanaka (2005) found the same link between extensions in paid leave and reduction in postneonatal mortality. It is interesting that only paid leave had a beneficial impact on child health; unpaid leave had no significant effect. The absence of effect may be explained in part, as we discussed in chapter 1, by the fact that parents are less likely to take leave when it is unpaid. Or it is possible that even when parents do take unpaid leave, the positive health benefits of the time off are offset by the stress of dealing with lost income. That said, a recent study by Rossin (2011) found that the FMLA led to small increases in birth weight and reductions in premature births and infant mortality for U.S. children born to college-educated and married mothers, who are most likely to be able to afford to take the unpaid leaves provided by the law.

Another body of research suggests why access to paid leave contributes to a reduction in postneonatal mortality: A mother's ability to take time off during the 1st year helps facilitate breastfeeding, which in turn helps the young child develop immunities against bacterial meningitis, diarrhea, respiratory infections, ear infections, and even childhood leukemia. A 2010 study in *Pediatrics* projected that if 90% of women in the United States breastfed their babies for the first 6 months of life, the lives of nearly 900 babies would be saved each year, along with $13 billion in reduced expenditures for treating the above diseases and other conditions such as asthma, juvenile diabetes, and childhood obesity (Bartick & Reinhold, 2010).

Since 1997, recognizing the health benefits of breastfeeding, the American Academy of Pediatrics has recommended "human milk" as the exclusive food for the first 6 months of life, to be followed by a mixed diet of solid food and human milk until at least the end of the 1st year. In 2001, the World Health Organization made the same recommendation. Providing breast milk exclusively even for 4 months and partially thereafter, according to a study of more than 4,000 subjects conducted in the Netherlands (Duitjts, Jaddoe, Hofman, & Moll, 2010), is associated with a significant reduction in respiratory and gastrointestinal illness in infants. However, partial breastfeeding, even for 6 months, was not associated with significantly lower rates of infection. On the basis of their findings, the study authors recommended health policy strategies to promote exclusive breastfeeding for at least 4 months, but preferably 6 months, in industrialized nations.

Despite the overwhelming medical evidence for the benefits of breastfeeding, however, exclusive breastfeeding for the recommended time period is still the exception in the United States. In 2006, while three fourths of new mothers in the United States started breastfeeding, only one third continued to breastfeed their babies exclusively for 3 months, and only 14% for 6 months (Centers for Disease Control and Prevention, n.d.-a). One reason so many women stop breastfeeding early is that they go back to work. The logistics of finding a way to continue the practice after returning to work can be daunting. A British study found that the longer a mother delayed her return to work, the more likely she was to breastfeed for at least 4 months (Hawkins, Griffiths, Dezateux, Law, & the Millennium Cohort Study Child Health Group, 2006).

Employers are responding by offering "pumping" stations, but this approach does not address some of the key issues. A bottle of human milk offered by a caregiver may give a baby as much protection against infection as would the mother's breastfeeding, but it would not afford the same sense of comfort and security. For example, a new mother in one of our offices who recently returned from a 3-month leave tried pumping her own milk, but she could not get her baby to take a bottle. To follow the doctor's orders, this new mother had to leave work twice a day—every 4 hours—to drive 25 minutes across town to the child care center to feed her baby, not a practice she could sustain very long.

Access to parental leave may also facilitate either the mother's or father's taking a child to the doctor for well-baby care and to obtain recommended immunizations, as well as the early identification of disabilities and interventions to minimize them. Adequate time with parents is especially crucial for infants traditionally considered at high risk for a variety of developmental difficulties, such as those born preterm or with illnesses, birth defects, or low birth weight. Of the 4.3 million babies born in the United States in 2007, more than 350,000 (8.3%) weighed less than 5.5 pounds, and more than 64,000 (1.5%) weighed less than 4.4 pounds (Hamilton, Martin, & Ventura, 2009). Largely as a result of the greater numbers of multiple-birth babies who are apt to be born early and weigh less, the incidence of very low birth weight is increasing in the United States. Low birth weight babies cry more and are more demanding. Engaging in special activities to soothe and comfort as well as appropriately stimulate these fragile and initially difficult babies is especially important for minimizing developmental delays and any long-term cognitive deficits or behavioral problems (Hopper & Zigler, 1988). But learning these techniques takes time and energy on the part of the families; even the opportunity to obtain assistance from professionals trained to work with low birth weight infants assumes that a parent has the time to seek and receive the instruction.

Child Development Evidence

■ **How much time do parents think they need to get to know their babies?**

Although the maternal and child health evidence for parental time off from employment after the birth or adoption of a child is compelling, parents themselves seem more concerned about just having enough time to enjoy and nurture and get to know their new babies. As one of our colleagues recently said on her first day back to work after 3 months at home with her new baby, "It's sad. I don't want to be away from her. I am dropping her off at a university-based child care center, and it's a good place, but I know what she needs best."

Some years ago, before the passage of the FMLA, researchers (including one of us) at the Yale Bush Center in Child Development and Social Policy interviewed a random sample of 181 new mothers who had delivered babies in the prior year span in Connecticut. What we found was that mothers who had to return to the workplace before they felt ready to do so not only felt stressed and guilty but, most important, cheated out of an important experience (Farber, Alejandro-Wright, & Muenchow, 1988). Although the median length of leave taken by these mothers was 3 months, when the women were asked how long a leave they would have preferred, the median response was 6 months. There were many practical reasons for this preference, such as adjusting to the baby's schedule and waiting until the baby slept through the night. But one of the major reasons was to have sufficient time to get to know the baby. Thus, although the women said they felt physically ready to return to work within 3 months after delivery, they were not emotionally ready to return for 6 months, though some said they would be willing to return to work earlier if they could work part-time and gradually increase their work hours.

About the same time that the above study was conducted, the senior author of this book, in a speech at a conference in Salt Lake City, UT, mentioned the possibility of paid parental leave as a cornerstone of a comprehensive child care policy. Following the speech, a young woman came up to the podium and asked, "Dr. Zigler, do you think that there is any real chance that the United States will get a paid national leave policy so that a mother can stay home with a new baby?" While she was talking, the woman started to cry, explained that she was a reporter for a newspaper and had recently had a baby, and this was her first day back at work. "And I am so sad," she said.

As the late developmental psychologist Urie Bronfenbrenner often stated, "in order to develop normally, a child needs the enduring, irrational involvement of one or more adults in care of and joint activity with that child…. In short, somebody has to be crazy about that kid" (Bronfenbrenner, 1988, p. 145). Multiple theories account for the type of irrational commitment—the willingness to walk through fire, if need be—that parents develop toward their children. Probably it is a survival mechanism that is rooted in evolutionary development. Human beings have the longest period of dependency, and children have to rely on their parents for a long time. Parents—and we would add, based on our own experiences, grandparents—simply like to look at their children's faces; they derive pleasure from their baby's smile; they chuckle just thinking about their toddler's latest antics; they can be moved to tears of pride by their son's or daughter's first attempt to sing for company, even if the child sounds a bit off-key.

One recent and very practical explanation comes from behavioral economist Dan Ariely (2010). People tend to place the highest value on the products in which they most personally invest, and parents' value of their own children is one excellent manifestation of this phenomenon. Parents tend to think that their own children are the cutest, brightest, most marvelous creatures, and they assume that others will assess them the same way. In fact, largely because parents invest so much time and energy in their own children, they tend to "overvalue" them—or care more about them and see them in a more positive light than other people do.

Clearly, the Salt Lake City mother mentioned earlier was smitten by her new baby, and returning to her full-time job as a reporter was not going to diminish her love for the child. But her concern was that she who, along with the baby's father, was the person most interested in the child's development, was going to miss out on a key opportunity for joint activity that could promote the baby's growth and build a solid foundation for all that would follow.

■ What are the early psychological and biological processes influencing the parent–child relationship?

Pediatricians, psychologists, and neuroscientists offer both biological and experiential explanations for the profound commitment between parent and child. It is almost as if parents and babies are programmed to care for each other. Developmental psychologist Ross Thompson, a noted authority on early relationships and social and emotional development, and his colleagues explained that at least three distinct though related processes are at work:

- *Bonding* "typically refers to the establishment of an emotional connection of the mother to the infant, often shortly after birth, that is closely tied to the hormonal processes associated with birth.... Bonding is not essential to the development of attachment (as studies of adopted infants show)" but usually contributes to it (Thompson et al., 2006, p. 353).

- *Attunement* is learning to read and respond to each other's verbal and nonverbal cues, a process that starts in the infant's first weeks and helps to lead to attachment (Thompson et al., 2006).

- *Attachment* is the affective tie that develops between infants and their primary caregivers later in infancy. Attachment evolves but starts to be readily apparent in the first half year of life (Thompson et al., 2006).

To the above list we—and Thompson—would now add *brain development*, which in turn is affected by all of the above processes. How bonding, attunement, and attachment transpire can have long-term effects on the child because these processes affect the neural connections in the brain, according to Thompson, who served on a panel of experts that gave rise to the joint National Research Council and Institute of Medicine report *From Neurons to Neighborhoods* (National Research Council & Institute of Medicine, 2000), which is discussed later. The wiring of the brain that takes place in the early years provides a foundation for the development of all of the more advanced capacities in the years that follow.

■ How central a role do hormones play in promoting bonding?

The manner in which nature interacts with nurture is perhaps most apparent in the period immediately following birth. During the delivery process, mothers release large amounts of oxytocin, a hormone that promotes bonding patterns, priming mothers to nurse, groom, have contact with, and protect the infant (Thompson et al., 2006). Oxytocin helps the new mother identify (and prefer) her own baby's scent. Opioids, naturally produced morphine-like chemicals, also create feelings of elation and a predisposition toward bonding. Typically within the first 72 hours following childbirth, mothers begin to lactate, prompting further release of hormones, and nursing and holding the baby continue to contribute toward elevated levels of oxytocin.

As Thompson et al. (2006) pointed out, hormones may play a less exclusive role in promoting a bond between human mothers and their infants than they do among smaller brained mammals; human experience and knowledge regarding the needs of babies undoubtedly also help prompt maternal (and we might add paternal) "instincts" to care for a new baby. Researchers have shown that fathers who are given the opportunity to hold their newborn babies are just as involved with and nurturing toward their babies as are mothers (Hopper & Zigler, 1988; Parke & O'Leary, 1976; Parke & Tinsley, 1982). Visit the newborn nursery in a hospital and observe the father stroking his baby daughter's cheek; see the grandparents peering in the window of the nursery eager for a glance at their first new grandchild. So it is clear that the experience of bonding need not be limited to the mother–baby dyad. Nonetheless, it is striking how maternal biology reinforces maternal behavior.

■ Attunement plays a larger role than bonding in the development of attachment.

Decades of research on parent–infant interaction by the noted pediatrician T. Berry Brazelton and many others has demonstrated that parents and their infants need time to establish a pattern of interaction that will enable them to recognize and respond to each other's signals, a process known as attunement (Zigler, Finn-Stevenson, & Hall, 2002). Although bonding helps initiate ties between babies and their parents, successful attunement between parent and child appears to play an even larger role in the development of attachment. Even during the infant's earliest weeks, research has shown that the interactions between infants and parents are reciprocal and bidirectional, meaning that infants influence the nature of these interactions rather than being passive objects of parental behavior. These early interactions have been compared to a carefully choreographed dance in which both partners synchronize their steps (Hopper & Zigler, 1988), each modifying his or her behavior in response to that of the other. When parents respond to a baby's signals or expressions of need, they teach the baby that care is forthcoming and predictable, helping the infant to accomplish what Erik Erikson called the most fundamental task of all—the formation of basic trust (Erikson, 1950, 1963).

The interactive patterns established during the first half-year of life influence the child's feeling of effectiveness and, according to the late Stanley Greenspan (1990), foreshadow the quality of the infant's later social and emotional development. Responsive care by an adult who recognizes a baby's distinct cry, who knows when the child is hungry or in pain, and who gives the child the opportunity to explore his surroundings safely is important even for the optimum cognitive development of the child (Nelson et al., 2007). Thus, when parents say, "We can take care of our baby best. We are best attuned to his needs," they are expressing not just a subjective sentiment but a verifiable claim that is based on the accumulated experiences they have shared with the child.

Attunement is not limited to the relationship between parent and baby, of course; babies and their other frequent caregivers can also develop these patterns of reciprocal interaction. When the process of attunement between parent and infant proceeds properly, however (and it typically does), parents are best positioned to have the kind of continuous exposure that allows them to know their babies best. Thus, the strength of the attunement process between babies and their parents (and, for that matter, other caregivers) depends on having sufficient time together to get to know each other.

The precise time needed to establish a pattern of reciprocal parent–infant interaction may vary, but there is some consensus that it takes at least several months. Brazelton and Als (1979) outlined four stages in the development of early mother–infant interaction, with the fourth stage typically not even beginning until the 4th month after birth. Greenspan and Lewis (1999) described six stages in the emotional development of infants and toddlers, with the second stage—"falling in love" with the caregiver—beginning about the 4th month. Although much of the research has focused on the interaction between mother and child, fathers, too, need time to attune to their infants; the style of interaction may differ from the pattern between mother and infant, but the process is no less important to the child's long-term development.

A program in Vermont that was designed to help parents adjust to the care of their low birth weight infants and, indirectly, to enhance the babies' development provides a striking illustration of the attunement process and its importance (Rauh, Achenbach, Nurcombe, Howell, & Teti, 1988). Beginning during the final week of the baby's hospitalization, a neonatal intensive care nurse provided sessions teaching mothers—and fathers, when available—how to recognize the baby's states of distress or disorganization as opposed to composure and stability; how to bring the baby to the quiet, alert state in which the baby would be most responsive to social interaction; how to be sensitive and responsive in daily caretaking routines; and how to prepare for the transition to caring for the baby at home. In four subsequent home visits over the next 3 months, the nurse focused on building the mother's repertoire of interactive play experiences with the child and ways to enhance the fit between mother and child by taking into account the baby's individual rhythms and capacities. By the time the low birth weight babies participating in the program were 1 year old, their scores on a cognitive test were virtually the same as those of the normal birth weight babies in a control group (Rauh et al.). The intervention program helped the mothers' initial adjustment to their low birth weight infants and appeared to reduce the babies' risk of impaired cognitive development.

Although the intervention program focused on low birth weight infants, its lessons apply more broadly. To promote cognitive, physical, and social-emotional development, there are a number of important tasks to be accomplished during the relatively discrete period of the first 3 months of life, and really during the 1st year. Many of the same activities designed to minimize adverse effects of low birth weight during the first few months of life would also help babies with normal birth weight. But these activities require time to learn and practice, and, in some cases, outside support and instruction. Someone growing into the role of a responsive parent, therefore, is likely to benefit from a period of time off from employment.

Not only is the success of the attunement process important to the child's cognitive development, but it also affects the attachment process, which in turn affects a variety of the child's other behaviors. In studies of 10 caregiver characteristics that might contribute to children's secure attachment to their caregivers, researchers identified three as being the most important (Dunst & Kassow, 2008). The top three characteristics were *caregiver–child synchrony*, characterized by interactions that are rewarding to both caregiver and child; *caregiver–child mutuality*, characterized by positive interactions in which both the caregiver and the child are attending to the same thing simultaneously; and *response quality*, characterized by the caregiver's ability to perceive infant signals accurately and respond promptly and appropriately. Taken together, the three characteristics add up to a textbook definition of attunement.

According to J. Ronald Lally, codirector of the WestEd Center for Child and Family Studies, somewhere around the 4th month of life, a baby "needs to be wooed into a loving relationship" (Lally, 2009, p. 51). Parents and other caregivers must learn what is special about a baby's way of dealing with sensations, taking in and acting on information, and organizing her movements to calm or soothe herself, and they must act accordingly. Parents can try many different "wooing" tactics, such as facial expressions, types of touch, and sounds, to respond to what the baby shows she likes or dislikes. Perhaps not surprisingly, therefore, a baby is more likely to develop a secure attachment to a parent who has learned to respond to the child's unique expression of needs for contact, comfort, and stimulation. Might the same not be said of most close friendships, not to mention intimate relationships?

■ How long does it take for parents and a new baby to develop an attachment?

Compared to bonding or even the process of attunement, the development of an attachment relationship requires considerably more time. First, according to Thompson et al. (2006), the baby has to have the cognitive capacity to recognize the caregiver's distinctive voice, face, or smell, and to recognize consistently that these features belong to the attachment figure, a capacity that emerges sometime around the 3rd month of life. At that point, the baby begins to respond uniquely to familiar caregivers. Second, before attachment can take place, the baby must begin to associate the parent's (or other caregiver's) presence with the relief of stress and the experience of heightened pleasure and joy (Thompson et al.). During the second half of the 1st year, for example, just the sound of the mother's particular footsteps as she approaches the crib can comfort a baby in distress. At this stage of developing an attachment, babies are likely to protest separation from their mothers, as well as express pure joy upon reunion with them.

As Mary Ainsworth (Ainsworth, Blehar, Waters, & Wall, 1978) illustrated with her landmark laboratory test called the strange situation assessment, an infant's preferentially seeking contact with a parent or other caregiver, or turning to that figure as a secure base, is an important marker of attachment. Once babies learn to crawl or walk, they follow their mothers or other attachment figures wherever they go, as any parent who has tried to get a moment of privacy in the bathroom while in the presence of a year-old baby has certainly experienced.

In summary, the human infant is a social animal—programmed to recognize faces over nonfaces, to learn to identify the mother's voice, and to form an attachment to persons who provide sensitive care. These early stages of attunement and attachment provide the foundation for all future development.

■ How do the processes of attunement and attachment affect brain development?

Recent neurological research provides a biological explanation for the lasting impact of the infant's early experiences. That is, how the processes of attunement and attachment transpire helps shape the actual architecture of the brain. In their compelling book *From Neurons to Neighborhoods*, Shonkoff and Phillips (National Research Council & Institute of Medicine, 2000, p. 384) pointed out that "what happens during the first months and years of life matters a lot" not because this period of development provides "an indelible blueprint for adult outcomes," but because it sets "either a sturdy or fragile stage on which subsequent development is constructed." Thanks to advances in neuroscientific research over the last 20 years, scientists now know that virtually every aspect of early human development, from the brain's evolving circuitry to the young child's capacity for empathy, is affected by the environments and accumulated experiences beginning in the prenatal period and extending throughout the early childhood years (National Research Council & Institute of Medicine). As just one example, there is evidence that early experiences affect the development of the right hemisphere of the brain, the part of the brain that develops most quickly during the first 2 years of life and the one that affects a person's ability to regulate impulses and to learn how to relate to others (Schore, 2001, 2005; Spence, Shapiro, & Zaidel, 1996).

Ross Thompson's research probed more deeply into the relationship between behavioral and biological prerequisites for forming attachments, and the integration of biological and behavioral insights into what he called "the most compelling question of all: How does early experience influence later behavior?" (Thompson et al., 2006, p. 379). According to Thompson, developmental neuroscience "confirms that the early years establish the foundation on which later development is built, much as a house is structurally firm or weak based on the foundation on which it is built" (Thompson, 2007, p. 8). During the first 5 years of life, much of the significant "blooming and pruning" of neural connections take place in the regions of the brain governing seeing and hearing, language, and higher cognitive functions. "From language ability and communication skills to problem-solving and categorization to capacities for focusing attention and exercising self-control," noted Thompson (2007, p. 8), "later skills are based on the foundational skills established earlier in life."

What this means is that sensitive, attentive caregivers in the course of frequent feeding, soothing, and playing with a baby have a special opportunity to influence the infant's developing neurobiological regulatory system. Put simply, these caregivers contribute to the development of a child's brain, establishing a foundation for the child's ability to learn, exercise self-control, and form positive relationships from then on. In addition, supportive early relationships can buffer the effects of stress on young children. In one study cited by Thompson (2007), for example, temperamentally fearful children who were faced with mildly stressful events exhibited lower physiological stress responses when they were accompanied by mothers to whom they were securely attached in comparison with fearful children who were in insecure relationships.

Of course, the caregiver's influence on the baby's developing brain architecture can be positive or negative. "Chronic experiences of severe stress, especially early in life, can alter the functioning of brain-based stress systems—potentially causing a person to become hyper-responsive even to mild stressors—and can have important effects on physical health, immunological capacity, and psychological well-being" (Thompson, 2007, p. 5).

Human beings are an adaptive species, and it takes a lot to throw a child off a positive trajectory. As long as the child receives some threshold of adequate care, it is likely that she will be okay. But, at a time when, in 70% of couples in the United States, both parents work, providing a period of time to allow parents to get to know and attune and attach to their baby would seem to be a prudent investment in child development. In addition, we know that anything that increases stress on the family increases the likelihood of child abuse, that balancing work and family is stressful, and giving people a respite from that stress for a brief time would be wise. Although neurological research does not directly address the optimal length of time that parents need to focus on their babies before returning to work, it provides another level of support for a range of public policies that empower parents to protect their infants during the period of life when they are least able to protect themselves. Lally argues that, because there is evidence that the quality of early relationships—especially between the mother and baby—influences the development of the brain, paid parental leave should be available to all families with a newborn for at least the first 6 months of life (Lally, 2011).

■ Do children fare worse if their mothers return to work in the 1st year of life, and what about the impact of paternal employment during the first 12 months?

Given that the vast majority of mothers in the United States are at work within the 1st year after giving birth or adopting a baby, the ultimate question is how the timing of return to employment affects children's cognitive and social and emotional development. Analyzing data from the National Longitudinal Survey of Youth–Child Supplement, several studies have indicated that children on average fare better if their mothers do not work full-time in the 1st year of life (Han, Waldfogel, & Brooks-Gunn, 2001; Harvey, 1999; Ruhm, 2004; Waldfogel, 2006). Full-time, early maternal employment during the baby's 1st year of life has been associated with lower cognitive test scores of preschool age children assessed at ages 3, 4 or 5 years, and sometimes persisting to age 7 and 8. For example, one of us (Ruhm, 2004) found that maternal employment during the 1st year of the child's life had a small deleterious effect on the estimated verbal ability of 3- and 4-year-olds, and that the consequences were more harmful when the mother worked long hours.

A more recent study by some of the same researchers, however, provided a degree of reassurance regarding the impact of maternal return to employment during the first 12 months after a baby's birth or adoption. Using data on children from the National Institute of Child Health and Human Development-sponsored Study of Early Child Care, Columbia University researchers Jeanne Brooks-Gunn, Wen-Jui Han, and Jane Waldfogel (2010) found that although early maternal employment has some downsides, it also offers some advantages, such as increasing mothers' income and the likelihood that their children attend high-quality child care. When all factors, such as income and the quality of parenting and child care, were taken into account, the net effect of maternal employment in the 1st year of life was found to be neutral. Consistent with earlier studies, the researchers still found that children fare better if their mothers work part-time (fewer than 30 hours per week) during a baby's 1st year of life. They also caution that their study should not be interpreted to provide grounds for complacency, noting that parents in the United States struggle to meet their children's needs in spite of having only minimal access to public policies—such as paid parental leave and the right to request part-time work hours—that other nations take for granted.

Reviewing the above findings, it is also important to offer some qualifications. First, because it is not ethically possible to randomly assign babies to mothers who return early to work as opposed to those who delay return to employment, most of the applicable research shows a correlation between the timing of return to employment and certain child outcomes, but this is not sufficient to demonstrate causal relationships. Second, because of the nature of the data sources available, many of the findings are too general to address some of the relevant specific policy questions, such as, for example, whether returning to full-time work 6 months, as opposed to 12 months, after the birth or adoption of a baby has a significant impact on cognitive or social development.

Finally, the significant question remains: "What about the dads?" The vast majority of the studies in this area focus only on the effects of maternal employment on children's cognitive or social and emotional development, with little consideration of the extent to which a father's staying at home during a portion of the 1st year might compensate for the mother's earlier return to work. Even pursuing this line of research is challenging at a time of high unemployment, when many fathers of young children may be staying at home but not by choice. Those considerations notwithstanding, although it is possible that mothers provide unique inputs to children's cognitive development, it seems likely that there is at least some substitutability between parents (Ruhm, 2004). In an effort to analyze the National Longitudinal Survey of Youth–Child Supplement data to determine the effect of paternal employment on children's math and reading performance, the economist contributing to this book found a hint that time investments by fathers may substitute for some of those of mothers. Twenty extra hours per week of employment on the part of fathers was associated with small decreases in the math and reading performance of 5- to 6-year-olds (Ruhm, 2004). However, inadequacies in the data and the resulting imprecision of the estimates highlight the need for further study of the impact of paternal employment on young children.

Summary

In this chapter, we have reviewed a large body of research conducted by family physicians, pediatricians, developmental psychologists, psychiatrists, neuroscientists, and economists. We have attempted to address the question of how much time off from employment mothers need to recover from childbirth, how long breastfeeding should continue to promote optimal child health, and how many months of focused attention it takes for a parent to become a responsive caregiver, establishing a pattern that will influence a baby's long-term cognitive, social, and emotional development. Of course, there is no one-size-fits-all answer to these questions, because each child and family is unique, with its own set of special circumstances. A lot depends on the status of the mother's and the child's health, the hours and type of parental employment, and, as we discuss in a subsequent chapter, the quality of nonparental child care available to the family. Yet we find ample evidence from diverse fields of research that families need significant time in the first 4 to 6 months of a baby's life to adjust to being responsible for the care of a new human being, to help get the child off to a healthy start, to form critical relationships, and to accomplish important tasks that will set the stage for the baby's long-term cognitive and social-emotional development.

Here, in summary, are the specific basic lessons we draw from this multidisciplinary review:

- Mothers generally benefit from having at least 6 to 8 weeks off from employment to recover from childbirth; fathers are helped by having at least 2 weeks off.

- Both parents would benefit from working less than full-time during the baby's first 3 months, when few infants sleep through the night.

- Breastfeeding, which has been clearly shown to have multiple maternal and child health benefits, is facilitated when mothers have at least 4 to 6 months off from employment.

- Because it takes at least 4 months for parents and babies to get to know each other, and a minimum of 6 months for them to attach, it is preferable for at least one parent to work no more than part-time during the child's first 6 months of life.

- Mothers typically say they would prefer 6 months' leave, though some would be open to returning to work sooner if they could work part-time and gradually increase their work hours.

- Parents who have a baby born prematurely, with low birth weight or with congenital defects, require more time off from employment to prevent or minimize developmental delays.

References

Ainsworth, M. D. S., Blehar, M. C., Waters, E., & Wall, S. (1978). *Patterns of attachment.* Hillsdale, NJ: Erlbaum.

Ariely, D. (2010). *The upside of irrationality: The unexpected benefits of defying logic at work and at home.* New York: Harper.

BabyCenter. (n.d.-a). *Baby sleep basics: Birth to 3 months.* Retrieved June 25, 2010, from www.babycenter.com/0_baby-sleep-basics-birth-to-3-months_7654.bc

BabyCenter. (n.d.-b). *Body changes after childbirth.* Retrieved August 31, 2010, from www.babycenter.com/body-changes-after-childbirth

Bartick, M., & Reinhold, A. (2010). The burden of suboptimal breastfeeding in the United States: A pediatric cost analysis. *Pediatrics, 125,* e1048–e1056. Retrieved September 1, 2010, from http://pediatrics.aappublications.org/cgi/reprint/peds.2009-1616v1

Brazelton, T. B., & Als, H. (1979). Four early stages in the development of mother-infant interaction. *The Psychoanalytic Study of the Child, 34,* 349–369.

Brigham and Women's Hospital. (2010). *After birth: What to expect after giving birth.* Retrieved June 25, 2010, from www.brighamandwomens.org/patient/CWNParentGuide/inhospital.aspx

Bronfenbrenner, U. (1988). Strengthening family systems. In Zigler, E. & Frank, M. (Eds.) *The parental leave crisis: Toward a national policy* (pp. 143–160). New Haven, CT: Yale University Press.

Brooks-Gunn, J., Han, W. J., & Waldfogel, J. (2010). First-year maternal employment and child development in the first 7 years. *Monographs of the Society for Research in Child Development, 75*(2, Serial No. 296).

Brown, S., Small, R., Faber, B., Drastev, A., & Davis, P. (2002). Early postnatal discharge from hospital for healthy mothers and term infants (Art No: CD002958). *Cochrane Database of Systematic Reviews.*

Buck, P. S. (1931). *The good earth.* New York: The John Day Company.

Calnen, G. (2007). Paid maternity leave and its impact on breastfeeding in the United States: An historic, economic, political, and social perspective. *Breastfeeding Medicine, 2*(1), 34–44.

Centers for Disease Control and Prevention. (n.d.-a). *Breastfeeding among U.S. children born 1999–2007, CDC National Immunization Survey.* Retrieved September 1, 2010, from www.cdc.gov/breastfeeding/data/NIS_data/index.htm

Centers for Disease Control and Prevention. (n.d.-b). *Compressed mortality file 1999–2004.* Retrieved July 20, 2011, from http://wonder.cdc.gov/cmf-icd10.html

Chatterji, P., & Markowitz, S. (2008). *Family leave after childbirth and the health of new mothers* (NBER Working Paper No. 14156). Cambridge, MA: National Bureau of Economic Research. Retrieved July 25, 2011, from www.nber.org/papers/w14156

Cowan, C. P., Cowan, P. A., Heming, G., Garett, E., Coyish, W. S., Curtis-Boles, H., & Boles, A. J. (1985). Transitions to parenthood: His, hers, and theirs. *Journal of Family Issues, 6,* 451–481.

Cunningham, F. G., Leveno, L., Bloom, S., Hauth, J., Rouse, D. J., & Spong, C. Y. (2010). *Williams obstetrics* (23rd ed.). New York: McGraw-Hill Medical.

Curtis, G. B., & Schuler, J. (2002). *Bouncing back from pregnancy.* Cambridge, MA: Perseus.

Dohrenwend, B. S., Krasnoff, L., Askenasy, A., & Dohrenwend, B. P. (1978). Exemplification of a method for scaling life events: The PERI Life Events Scale. *Journal of Health and Social Behavior, 19*, 205–229.

Duitjts, L., Jaddoe, V. W., Hofman, A., & Moll, H. (2010). Prolonged and exclusive breastfeeding reduces risk of infectious disease in infancy. *Pediatrics, 126, e18–e25.* Retrieved September 1, 2010, from http://pediatrics.aappublications.org/cgi/content/abstract/peds.2008-3256v1

Dunst, C. J., & Kassow, D. Z. (2008). Caregiver sensitivity, contingent social responsiveness, and secure infant attachment. *The Journal of Early and Intensive Behavioral Intervention, 5*(1), 40–56. Retrieved August 22, 2010, from www.thefreelibrary.com

Erikson, E. (1950, 1963). *Childhood and society.* New York: W.W. Norton.

Farber, E. A., Alejandro-Wright, M., & Muenchow, S. (1988). Managing work and family: Hopes and realities. In E. Zigler & M. Frank (Eds.), *The parental leave crisis: Toward a national policy* (pp. 161–176). New Haven, CT: Yale University Press.

Farkas, S., Duffett, A., & Johnson, J. (2000). *Necessary compromises: How parents, employers and children's advocates view child care today. A report from Public Agenda.* New York: Public Agenda. Retrieved September 1, 2010, from www.publicagenda.org/files/pdf/necessary_compromises.pdf

Frankman, E. A., Wang, L., Bunker, C. H., & Lowder, J. L. (2009). Episiotomy in the United States: Has anything changed? *American Journal of Obstetrics & Gynecology, 200*, 573.e1–573.e7.

Gjerdingen, D. K., Froberg, D. G., Chaloner, K. M., & McGovern, P. (1993). Changes in women's physical health during the first postpartum year. *Archives of Family Medicine. 2*, 277–283. Retrieved June 19, 2010, from www.archfammed.com

Greenspan, S. (1990). Emotional development in infants and toddlers. In J. R. Lally (Ed.), *Infant/toddler caregiving: A guide to social-emotional growth and socialization* (pp. 15–18). Sacramento: California Department of Education.

Greenspan, S., & Lewis, N.B. (1999). *Building healthy minds: The six experiences that create intelligence and emotional growth.* Cambridge, MA: Perseus Books.

Gruis, M. (1977). Beyond maternity: Postpartum concerns of mothers. MCN: *The American Journal of Maternal/Child Nursing, 2*, 182–188.

Hamilton, B. E., Martin, J. A., & Ventura, S. J. (2009). Births: Preliminary data for 2007. *National Vital Statistics Reports, 57*(12). Retrieved September 1, 2010, from www.cdc.gov/nchs/data/nvsr/nvsr57/nvsr57_12.pdf

Han, W. J., Waldfogel, J., & Brooks-Gunn, J. (2001). The effects of early maternal employment on later cognitive and behavioral outcomes. *Journal of Marriage and Family, 63*, 336–354.

Harrison, M. J., & Hicks, S. A. (1983). Postpartum concerns of mothers and their sources of help. *Canadian Journal of Public Health, 74*, 325–328.

Harvey, E. (1999). Short-term and long-term effects of early parental employment on children of the National Longitudinal Survey of Youth. *Developmental Psychology, 35*, 445–459.

Hawkins, S. S., Griffiths, L. J., Dezateux, C., Law, C., & the Millennium Cohort Study Child Health Group. (2006). The impact of maternal employment on breast-feeding duration in the UK Millennium Cohort Study. *Public Health Nutrition, 10*, 891–896.

Hopper, P., & Zigler, E. (1988). The medical and social science basis for a national infant care leave policy. *American Journal of Orthopsychiatry, 58*, 324–337.

Hyde, J. S., Klein, M. H., Essex, M. J., & Clark, R. (1995). Maternity leave and women's mental health. *Psychology of Women Quarterly, 19*, 299–313.

Kettle, C., & Tohill, S. (2008). Perineal care: Pregnancy and childbirth. *BMJ Clinical Evidence.* Retrieved August 31, 2010, from http://clinicalevidence.bmj.com/ceweb/conditions/pac/1401/1401-get.pdf

Lally, J. R. (2009). The science and psychology of infant-toddler care: How an understanding of early learning has transformed child care. *Zero to Three, 30*(2), 47–53.

Lally, J. R. (2011). The link between consistent caring interactions with babies, early brain development and school readiness. In E. Zigler, W. Gilliam, & W. S. Barnett (Eds.), *The pre-k debates: Current controversies and issues* (pp. 159–162). Baltimore: Brookes.

Martin, J. A., Hamilton, B. E., Sutton, P. D., Ventura, S. J., Menacker, F., Kirmeyer, S., & Matthews, T. J. (2009). Births: Final data for 2006. *National Vital Statistics Reports, 57*(7). Retrieved August 10, 2010, from www.cdc.gov/nchs/data/nvsr/nvsr57/nvsr57_07.pdf

Miller, L. J. (2002). Postpartum depression. *Journal of the American Medical Association, 287*, 762–765.

National Research Council & Institute of Medicine. (2000). *From neurons to neighborhoods: The science of early childhood development.* J. P. Shonkoff & D. A. Phillips, (Eds), Board on Children, Youth, and Families; Commission on Behavioral and Social Sciences and Education. Washington, DC: National Academy Press.

Nelson, C. A., Zeanah, C. H., Fox, N. A., Marshall, P. J., Smyke, A. T., & Guthrie, D. (2007, December 21). Cognitive recovery in socially deprived young children: The Bucharest early intervention project. *Science, 318*, 1937–1940.

Overcoming breastfeeding problems. (2009). Retrieved June 23, 2010, from Medline Plus Web site: www.nlm.nih.gov/medlineplus/ency/article/002452.htm

Parke, R. D., & O'Leary, S. E. (1976). Father-mother-infant interaction in the newborn period: Some findings, some observations and some unresolved issues. In K. Reigal & J. Meacham (Eds.), *The developing individual in a changing world: Vol. 2. Social and environmental issues* (pp. 653–663). The Hague, the Netherlands: Mouton.

Parke, R. D., & Tinsley, B. R. (1982). The father's role in infancy: Determinants of involvement in caregiving and play. In M. Lamb (Ed.), *The role of the father in child development* (pp.429–458). New York: Wiley.

Rauh, V. A., Achenbach, T. M., Nurcombe, B., Howell, C. T., & Teti, D. M. (1988). Minimizing adverse effects of low birthweight: Four-year results of an early intervention program. *Child Development, 59*, 544–553. Retrieved September 30, 2008, from www.jstor.org/stable/1130556

Rossin, M. (2011). The effects of maternity leave on children's birth and infant health outcomes in the United States. *Journal of Health Economics, 30*, 221–239.

Ruhm, C. J. (2000). Parental leave and child health. *Journal of Health Economics, 19*, 931–960.

Ruhm, C. J. (2004). Parental employment and child cognitive development. *The Journal of Human Resources, 39*, 155–192.

Schore, A. (2001). Effects of a secure attachment relationship on right brain development, affect regulation, and infant mental health. *Infant Mental Health Journal, 22*, 7–66.

Schore, A. (2005). Attachment, affect regulation, and the developing right brain: Linking developmental neuroscience to pediatrics. *Pediatrics in Review, 26*(6). 204–217.

Spence, S., Shapiro, D., & Zaidel, E. (1996). The role of the right hemisphere in the physiological and cognitive development of emotional processing. *Psychophysiology, 33*, 112–122.

Stuebe, A. M., Willett, W. C., Xue, F., & Michels, K. B. (2009). Lactation and incidence of premenopausal breast cancer: A longitudinal study. *Archives of Internal Medicine, 169*, 1364–1371.

Tanaka, S. (2005). Parental leave and child health across OECD countries. *The Economic Journal, 115*, F7–F28.

Thompson, R. A., Braun, K., Grossmann, K. E., Gunnar, M. R., Heinrichs, M., Keller, H., et al. (2006). Group report: Early social attachment and its consequences: Dynamics of a developing relationship. In C. S. Carter, L. Ahnert, K. E. Grossmann, S. B. Hardy, M. E. Lamb, S. W. Porges, & N. Sachser (Eds.), *Attachment and bonding* (pp. 351–385). Cambridge, MA: The MIT Press.

Thompson, R. (2007). Testimony at *Improving Head Start for America's children: Hearing before House Committee on Education and Labor, Subcommittee on Early Childhood, Elementary, and Secondary Education,* 110th Cong. (February 28, 2007), pp. 5–12. Retrieved December 28, 2011, from www.eric.ed.gov/PDFS/ED499026.pdf

Tulman, L., & Fawcett, J. (1991). Recovery from childbirth: Looking back 6 months after delivery. *Health Care for Women International, 12*, 341–350.

U.S. Department of Health and Human Services. (2009). *Depression during and after pregnancy.* Retrieved August 31, 2010, from Office of Women's Health Web site: www.womenshealth.gov/faq/depression-pregnancy.cfm

Waldfogel, J. (2006). *What children need.* Cambridge, MA: Harvard University Press.

Zigler, E., Finn-Stevenson, M., & Hall, N. W. (2002). *The first three years and beyond: Brain development and social policy.* New Haven, CT: Yale University Press.

CHAPTER

Infant Care Leave and Quality Infant Care

U se of nonparental child care arrangements for young children has become the norm for working parents in the United States. A paid infant care leave policy would certainly not eliminate the need for supplementary child care, but it would give more families the option to postpone the extensive use of nonparental care during the 1st year of life. Real access to several months of time off with a new baby would also give parents the time to search for child care that meets the temperament of their baby and the unique needs of their family. By reducing the length of time parents need supplemental infant care, a paid leave policy might also help families afford a higher quality of care.

For more than 30 years, there has been an intense debate about the effects of early nonparental care, especially group care, on child development. In our view, much of the debate is off point, focusing on whether parents should use supplemental early care rather than on how to improve the quality of the care. As we discuss below, high-quality, nonparental care has been shown to benefit infants and toddlers, particularly those at high risk because of maternal depression, low birth weight, or low parental income and education; also, there is little evidence that moderate use of good-quality care harms infants from more advantaged families.

However, much of the supplemental care available for infants is not of high quality. Even if such care were widely available and affordable, most families would, for all of the reasons cited in chapter 2, still prefer a period of time primarily at home to get their babies off to a healthy start and to develop patterns of reciprocal interaction that form the foundation for the child's future development. A balanced perspective thus suggests caution regarding significant use of supplemental child care for infants and calls for ensuring that parents have a choice of whether—or at least how soon—to use such arrangements.

In this chapter, we (a) assess the extent to which families in the United States use nonparental care in its various forms during the 1st year of life; (b) review recent research on the effects of supplemental care on child development, health, and safety; (c) discuss the lack of quality care and the cost of care; and (d) suggest the role of infant care leave in a broader public policy on child care.

Use of Nonparental Care for Infants

■ Many infants spend significant hours in one or more forms of supplemental child care.

Although the increase in the early return to employment has slowed since 2000, more than half of the mothers of infants less than 1 year old have been in the labor force every year since 1986, and 41% are back at work within 3 months of giving birth (Han, Ruhm, Waldfogel, & Washbrook, 2008). Moreover, most working mothers in the United States are employed full-time by the 9th month postdelivery. As a result, a large proportion of very young children—sometimes as young as 3 weeks of age—are now in supplemental child care (Zigler, Marsland, & Lord, 2009). According to the Early Childhood Longitudinal Study, half of all children born in 2001 spent some time in nonparental care by 9 months of age (Kreader, Ferguson, & Lawrence, 2005). Between the ages of 3 and 18 months, 37% of children were in child care for more than 30 hours each week (National Institutes of Health [NIH] & National Institute of Child Health and Human Development [NICHD], 2006), and many were in at least two different arrangements during the 1st year of life.

Supplemental child care comes in many forms: in-home care by a relative, care by an unrelated caregiver in the child's home, small group care (commonly referred to as family child care in a caregiver's home), and center-based care. Most infants in nonmaternal care are cared for by grandmothers (34%), fathers (27%), or other relatives (10%), but a significant percentage (36%), amounting to nearly three quarters of a million babies annually, spend at least some time in the care of nonrelatives in out-of-home settings (Laughlin, 2010).[1] Nearly 18% of those in nonparental care are in center-based arrangements, 10% in family child care homes, and 8% in informal out-of-home settings. Finally, about 4% of the infants less than 1 year old with employed mothers have in-home, nonrelative caregivers, and one quarter of the babies are in multiple arrangements (Laughlin, 2010).[2]

---

[1] *Authors' calculation from Table 2 of Laughlin (2010).*

[2] *Because one in four babies is in a multiple arrangement, the total adds ups to more than 100%.*

■ Use of nonparental care and type of care used vary by income level.

Patterns of child care usage for babies in the 1st year of life also vary by income level and whether the care is publicly subsidized. In-home care (by nannies, au pairs, or babysitters) is the most expensive form of infant care and is often preferred by affluent parents (Wrigley & Dreby, 2005). At the other end of the income spectrum, low-income families often rely on care provided by family, friends, or neighbors. On the basis of findings from the National Survey of America's Families in 2002, infants and toddlers in low-income families with employed mothers are generally more likely to be in relative care as opposed to center-based arrangements than are children in higher income families (Kreader et al., 2005). Formal child care is generally less available in low-income neighborhoods, in part because there are not a sufficient number of families present who can afford to purchase it. At the same time, however, babies in very low-income families receiving some form of publicly subsidized child care assistance at 9 months of age are more likely to be in center-based care than are their counterparts whose families are not receiving subsidized care, regardless of family income (Halle et al., 2009). Among low-income families receiving child care assistance, 46% of 9-month-olds are in center-based care.

Impact of Early Nonparental Care on Child Development

Before assessing the implications of child development research on early nonparental care for parental leave policy, we offer some background on the findings, which are highly nuanced and sometimes outright conflicting. Taken as a whole, however, the body of research not only suggests the need for an infant care leave option but also provides some insight on the length of the leave policy needed. We provide some level of detail not only for interested policymakers but also for parents, who often face agonizing decisions regarding whether and when to use supplemental care arrangements for babies, and, if so, what kind.

■ The great debate: Is early child care bad for babies?

For decades, there has been a heated debate among child development experts about the effects of early child care for babies. Early literature cited alleged evidence of the harmful effects of nonmaternal care from studies of environmental deprivation (Spitz, 1945). As discussed in the first author's book with Katherine Marsland and Heather Lord (2009), this early literature confused institutional care (or total separation of the child from parents) with supplemental use of nonparental child care during parents' working hours. Following these negative perceptions of infant child care, the Child Welfare League of America in 1960 recommended no use of nonmaternal care during a baby's 1st year of life. Several highly respected child development experts, such as Mary Ainsworth, T. Berry Brazelton, and Stanley Greenspan, continued to recommend no use of nonparental, out-of-home care during the first 12 months. Perhaps the late Selma Fraiberg (1977) best summed up concerns about early nonparental care when, reflecting on her clinical experience, she worried about "babies ...who are delivered like packages to neighbors, to strangers, to storage houses like Merry Mites" (p. 111) and about what she saw as a resulting increase in the "diseases of non-attachment".

Other experts, such as Bettye Caldwell, Alison Clarke-Stewart, Jerome Kagan, and Henry Ricciuti, argued just as strongly that early child care was benign or that its effects depended on the quality of care, the characteristics of the family, or the temperament of the infant (Zigler et al., 2009). For example, on the basis of a study of children who entered out-of-home care as early as 3 months old, Harvard developmental psychologist Kagan concluded that children in child care were no more or less attached to their mothers than were young children raised exclusively at home (Kagan, Kearsley, & Zelazo, 1977).

In the midst of this debate, some model early intervention programs initiated in the late 1960s and 1970s began to demonstrate that high-quality supplemental care combined with family support activities could benefit infants, at least those from low-income, low-education, or otherwise at-risk families. Longitudinal studies following infants who had participated in the Children's Center associated with the Syracuse Family Development Research Program and a high-quality center in the Abecedarian Project at the University of North Carolina demonstrated that high-quality care could buffer infants against the detrimental effects of maternal depression, prematurity, and poverty (Campbell, Ramey, Pungello, Sparling, & Miller-Johnson, 2002; Cohn, Marias, & Tronick, 1986; Honig, 2004; Lally, Mangione, & Honig, 1988). For example, in an early follow-up study of the Abecedarian Project, where infants from at-risk families entered care as early as 6 weeks old with a median entry age of 4.4 months, program participants showed significant IQ gains through the preschool years. The IQ scores as compared to those of a control group began to even out when the children entered school, but the program participants continued to have higher test scores in early elementary school in reading and math (Ramey & Campbell, 1984). Rather than having a negative impact, therefore, high-quality nonmaternal care was beginning to demonstrate valuable benefits to infants who were likely to be at risk of educational failure.

Nevertheless, the positive findings from these early intervention studies did not put concerns about early child care to rest. In 1987, Jay Belsky, a leading developmental psychologist who had earlier concluded that out-of-home care had no adverse effects on infants, changed his mind, stating that exposing infants to extensive nonmaternal care placed them at risk of developing insecure attachments to their mothers and of experiencing poor social adjustment in childhood. Belsky's dramatic public reversal (1987) prompted vigorous debate within the child development research community (Zigler et al., 2009), with other prominent researchers concluding that the quality of the available research was not sufficient to warrant firm conclusions about the impact of infant child care (Phillips, McCartney, Scarr, & Howes, 1987). In short, the initial wave of child development research on the impact of early nonparental care was often inconclusive and confusing, if not outright contradictory.

Some of the confusion resulted from design problems in the early research. As pointed out in a thoughtful review of the status of early child care research by Deborah Vandell (2004) of the University of Wisconsin, initial research focused on quality or quantity or type of care, making it impossible to separate the purported effects of one factor from another. Another problem was that aside from the research conducted on model programs such as the Abecedarian Project, where it was possible to randomly assign a relatively small sample of participants to the treatment or control group, most of the research was correlational, making it inappropriate to make causal inferences (Vandell). On a broad scale, involving naturally occurring child care experiences, it is far more difficult to randomly assign babies to nonparental and parental care, much less different ages of entry or number of hours of care. Hence, it is difficult to prove that usage of nonparental care causes rather than reflects a particular attribute in child development. For example, does a finding that children who spend many hours in a child care center tend to behave more aggressively in elementary school reflect the impact of the time spent in center-based care on the child, or did the already early troublesome behavior of the child lead the family to place him in more hours of out-of-home care?

■ Recent research attempts to provide more definitive answers.

In response to calls for more rigorous study, the National Center for Clinical Infant Programs (which is now ZERO TO THREE) and the Institute of Medicine of the National Academy of Sciences convened a panel of 16 prominent child care researchers to develop a research agenda to address unresolved questions. The panel, cochaired by the first author and Kathryn Barnard, called for an investment in research to resolve questions regarding the impact of infant and toddler care on child development. Shortly thereafter, the NICHD made a commitment to conduct a national study on infant–toddler child care, coordinated by Henry Ricciuti of Cornell. The resulting study, the NICHD Study of Early Child Care (SECC) initiated in 1991, is the most comprehensive longitudinal study of child care to date in the United States. Conducted by researchers located at leading universities across the nation, the study is following a diverse sample of more than 1,000 children drawn from 10 sites across the country (Brooks-Gunn, Han, & Waldfogel, 2010). More than a fifth of the children live in families defined as poor or near-poor, but the sample is still not nationally representative by statistical standards and may have undersampled lower quality child care settings. NICHD researchers defined child care as any care provided on a regular basis by someone other than the child's mother (even the father) for more than 10 hours a week. Researchers visited children's child care settings, including in-home as well as more formal arrangements, when the children were 6, 15, 24, 36, and 54 months old, and assessed the children at home and at the research site at the same age intervals. The NICHD SECC is ongoing, with follow-up of the children planned until they reach late adolescence.

Unlike much of the previous child development research, the NICHD SECC attempts to examine effects of one attribute of care, such as quality, while controlling for other factors, such as quantity and type of care (NIH & NICHD, 2006). Although the study could not randomly assign children to different types of child care, dates of entry, or hours of care, researchers have used various analytic strategies to minimize the likelihood of selection bias.

The NICHD SECC and other recent studies have allayed some concerns about early infant care and raised others (Zigler et al., 2009). In the following sections, we summarize the most salient findings on three main questions about the use of nonparental care during the first 12 months of life: How does use of early child care relate to parent–child attachment, how does it affect children's social–emotional development, and how does it relate to children's cognitive development? On the basis of the body of research available, we also attempt to distinguish between what is known about the relationships between child outcomes and different types of nonparental care, the quality of the care, and the quantity of the care.

◼ How does early nonparental care relate to parent–child attachment?

Much of the concern about early supplemental care has focused on whether extensive use of nonparental arrangements during the 1st year of life has an adverse effect on the development of parent–child attachment. The NICHD SECC has to date found no evidence that use of nonparental care during the 1st year of life is associated with insecure mother–child attachment. Children in lower quality care were found to be somewhat more likely to be insecurely attached to their mothers, but only if their mothers were lower in sensitivity during interactions with their children (NICHD Early Child Care Research Network, 1997, 1999a, 2002a).

Furthermore, the study has found no association between the level of attachment security and the timing of entry into child care, the continuity of care, the type of care, or even the cumulative amount of supplemental care. Across all outcome measures, the influence of parents appears to be greater than that of nonparental child care (NICHD Early Child Care Research Network, 2005; Zigler et al., 2009). Put simply, parent–child interactions have a much stronger effect on the child's development than does the child's experience in out-of-home care.

■ How does early nonparental care affect children's social and emotional development?

The NICHD SECC findings regarding the relationship between early child care and children's social and emotional development are more complex and troublesome. Specifically, some NICHD findings indicated that extensive time (more than 45 hours per week from 3 to 54 months) in early nonmaternal care is associated with increased aggression, disobedience, and conflict with adults at 54 months of age and in kindergarten (NICHD Early Child Care Research Network, 2003; Vandell, 2004). Other scholars argued that because the increased aggression does not reach clinical levels, it is not a matter of great concern (Zigler et al., 2009). Per usual, further research is needed.

Whereas some follow-up studies have indicated that this negative association with extensive care may no longer be evident by third grade (Newcombe, 2003; Vandell, 2004), one recent study found that more hours of nonmaternal care were associated with greater impulsivity and risk taking at age 15 (Vandell et al., 2010). Contrary to initial findings, the association with increased aggression is no greater with center-based than with other forms of nonmaternal care (Brooks-Gunn et al., 2010). Of particular interest to parents and policymakers considering the amount of supplemental child care that seems to have no adverse effects, children in child care for less than 30 hours a week from age 3 to 54 months did not exhibit a higher rate of behavior problems than did children who were exclusively in maternal care (Vandell, 2004). As noted earlier, even among the children in extensive hours of early care, the behavior problems were not in the clinical range that require special attention or suggest psychopathology.

Recent neurobiological studies may shed some light on the biological reasons for the impact of early nonparental care on social and emotional development (Phillips, 2010). Megan Gunnar and colleagues found elevated cortisol levels in children who experienced out-of-home care in both centers and family child care settings during the 2nd year of life (Dettling, Gunnar, & Donzella, 1999; Gunnar & Quevedo, 2007; Watamura, Donzella, Alwin, & Gunnar, 2003). Cortisol level is used to measure the amount of stress an individual is experiencing. Under normal circumstances, cortisol levels fluctuate throughout the day, gradually decreasing from morning to afternoon. However, under stress, this pattern is reversed, with the cortisol level rising during the day (Zigler et al., 2009). Studies examining such variations are important because exposure to high levels of cortisol can affect early brain development, and some studies suggest that elevated levels lead to "toxic stress," which might trigger fear and anxiety in children, and the type of aggressive behavior described earlier (National Scientific Council on the Developing Child, 2005). Deborah Phillips of Georgetown and coauthor of *From Neurons to Neighborhoods* (National Research Council & Institute of Medicine, 2000) noted that the strongest predictor of elevated stress hormones is "'intrusive-overcontrolling' caregiving ... characterized by adults who are harsh, inconsistent, issue a lot of commands … [and provide] the opposite of sensitive, responsive care" (Phillips, 2010, p. 8). She noted that Gunnar and her colleagues wondered whether the toddler's fledgling attempts to relate to peers in group care, given that these early efforts often prove inadequate, might contribute to the rise in cortisol level. As of this writing, the findings are sufficiently new that we do not know whether the level of stress produced in a typical child care setting for infants and toddlers is enough to impede their development (Zigler et al., 2009).

◼ How does early child care affect the cognitive development of children from disadvantaged backgrounds?

Research on the impact of early child care on disadvantaged children's cognitive development is more positive. High-quality center-based infant care has been linked with promoting the school readiness and success of children at risk of school failure. In the North Carolina Abecedarian Project, where children in the treatment group attended a high-quality program from shortly after birth through 5 years old, while the control group received only nutrition services and pediatric care, the treatment group at age 15 years scored higher in reading and mathematics, were less likely to have been retained in grade, and were less likely to have been placed in special education (Ramey, Campbell, & Blair, 1998). By age 21, the Abecedarian program graduates were 3 times more likely than members of the control group to have attended a 4-year college and significantly more likely to be in a skilled job (Campbell et al., 2002). Indeed, by reducing expenditures for grade retention, special education, and welfare as well as improving participants' health and the mothers' earnings, the program was estimated to generate $2.50 in benefits for every dollar spent on the 5-year investment in the program (Barnett & Masse, 2007). Similarly, in the Infant Health and Development Project, a multisite randomized study that provided high-quality center-based care as part of a comprehensive intervention program aimed at low birth weight, premature infants, children who received a higher dosage (e.g., more days of care) showed cognitive benefits at ages 5 and 8 years (Hill, Waldfogel, & Brooks-Gunn, 2003).

Studies of infant care programs implemented more recently have also demonstrated impacts on children's cognitive and language development. For example, Early Head Start, a federally administered program consisting of home-based (parent education), center-based, and combination models for low-income pregnant women and families with infants and toddlers, is a program that began in 1995 and now serves more than 90,000 children from birth to 3 years old (U.S. Department of Health and Human Services, 2010). Early Head Start has been shown to have significant, favorable, modest-sized impacts on a range of child development and parenting outcomes (Love et al., 2005). It is interesting that the mixed-approach programs, involving both home visitation and center-based care, have shown the most promising results. Even the strictly home-based programs, which serve families through weekly home visits and at least two group socializations per month for each family, have had a surprising impact on children's cognitive and language development (U.S. Department of Health and Human Services, n.d.).

Educare, a high-quality program financed by a private–public partnership spearheaded by the Buffett Early Childhood Fund and the Ounce of Prevention, offers full-day, full-year services to at-risk children from 6 weeks old to kindergarten. Targeted at children from very low-income families, Educare builds on Early Head Start, providing more hours of care by more highly trained staff. A recent study of the program, which is soon scheduled to offer centers in 10 locations across the nation, showed that at-risk children who entered the program between birth and 2 years old actually exceeded the national average on a measure of school readiness (Yazejan & Bryant, 2009).

■ How does early child care affect children from more advantaged backgrounds?

But what significance do these findings have for children from middle-income or more advantaged homes? On the basis of findings from the NICHD SECC, children from a range of backgrounds who experienced good-quality child care showed somewhat better cognitive and linguistic development across the first 3 years of life than did children in lesser quality care (NICHD Early Child Care Research Network, 1999b, 2000b). Children 6 months and older who had more experience in child care centers showed somewhat better cognitive and language development though age 3 years and somewhat better preacademic skills involving letters and numbers at age 4.5 years than did children in other types of nonmaternal care (NICHD Early Child Care Research Network, 2000b, 2002a, 2004). Put simply, good-quality out-of-home care is better than poor quality care.

The best predictor of cognitive and language development up to age 3 years was the amount and complexity of the language used by the caregiver. More stimulation from the caregiver—asking questions, responding to vocalization, and other forms of talking—was linked to somewhat better cognitive and language development (NICHD Early Child Care Research Network, 2000b). Disparities in early vocabulary growth are apparent long before children enter kindergarten. According to a study by Betty Hart and Todd Risley (1995), the typical child of a parent on welfare knows about 400 words by age 3 years, while a child of professional parents at the same age knows 1,200. However, family characteristics such as parents' education, family income, and two-parent family as opposed to single-parent family status, as well as mother's psychological adjustment and sensitivity along with the social and cognitive quality of the home environment, were much stronger and more consistent predictors of children's cognitive outcomes than was the quality of the nonmaternal care (NICHD Early Child Care Research Network, 2002b; NIH & NICHD, 2006). Furthermore, one of the most consistent predictors of the child's cognitive development was the quality of the mother–child interactions. The more responsive, attentive, and cognitively stimulating the mother was during observed interactions, the better the child's outcomes (NICHD Early Child Care Research Network, 1997, 1999a, 1999b, 2003).

◼ What are the implications for parental leave policy?

The preponderance of the evidence indicates that exposure to quality child care—care that is responsive to the temperament of the individual child and provides developmentally appropriate stimulation—promotes both cognitive and linguistic development and may enhance the development of infants and toddlers whose family environments put them at risk of poor educational outcomes (Zigler et al., 2009). And there is little evidence that good-quality supplemental care harms the cognitive development of infants and toddlers from more advantaged backgrounds, although the consistent findings about the benefits of exposure to a responsive, attentive, and cognitively stimulating parent underscore the challenge of finding nonparental care of equal quality.

The findings regarding the impact of early child care on social and emotional development are more mixed, suggesting that more hours of care are associated with less sensitive mother–child interactions and with more behavior problems in children (Vandell, 2004), though researchers still do not know enough about the extent to which the increased aggressive behavior persists into adolescence. Furthermore, it is possible that any negative impact may be offset by benefits, such as a child's developing greater ability to relate to a diverse group of adults or peers, or the advantages that accrue to the child because of increased family income made possible by the parent's or parents' having the freedom to work.

From the standpoint of parental leave policy, it is noteworthy that the most successful child care programs for disadvantaged infants and toddlers combine quality care by trained caregivers with home visitation and other efforts to help the parents themselves learn to better promote their children's cognitive and social and emotional development. Thus, even for the children shown to benefit most from early out-of-home care, it is important for the parents to have enough time off from work or school to participate in the parent education and involvement activities.

To better inform policy on parental leave, further research is needed to separate the possible impact of varying amounts of child care and of different ages of entry. Vandell (2004) proposed an experimental study of paid parental leave in which children are randomly assigned to varying amounts of child care (0–40 hours) and to different entry ages (2–24 months). Although the NICHD SECC provides more information on the association between the timing of entry into care and child development than was previously available, more research is still needed to assess the impact of entering care at 6 weeks, for example, versus 3 months or 6 months.

Impact of Early Nonparental Care on Children's Health and Safety

Much of the child development research has focused on the impact of nonparental care on parent–infant attachment and the child's cognitive and social and emotional development, but parents first and foremost want to make sure that a child care setting will keep their baby healthy and safe. There are two main concerns: protecting babies from communicable disease and protecting them from injury, whether unintentional or deliberate. The NICHD SECC has not addressed issues of health outcomes in depth, so here we rely on public health, medical, and sociological studies.

■ Babies are especially vulnerable to communicable disease in group care settings.

Babies have immature immune systems and have not yet completed the full schedule of recommended immunizations. Moreover, infants are especially vulnerable to communicable diseases because they frequently place objects in their mouths, often spend time crawling on the floor, and wear diapers. In addition, as discussed in chapter 2, babies in supplemental care while their mothers work are less apt to continue to be breastfed and are hence less likely to continue to receive the various health benefits associated with breastfeeding. The American Academy of Pediatrics recommends that babies be fed "human milk" as the exclusive food for the first 6 months of life, and a recent study showed that providing exclusive breast milk even for 4 months and partially thereafter was associated with a significant reduction in respiratory and gastrointestinal illness in infants (Duitjts, Jaddoe, Hofman & Moll, 2010). Infants and toddlers in group out-of-home care are more likely to be exposed to infection than are those cared for at home, and babies in their 1st year of life are most at risk (Aronson & Shope, 2005). Rates of upper respiratory infection, gastrointestinal illnesses, and ear infections are higher among children in center-based or large group settings as contrasted with settings with fewer than six children (Johansen, Leibowitz, & Waite, 1988; Schwartz et al., 1994). Parents with babies in group child care settings interviewed for this book often expressed concerns that "my baby is sick half the time," with the concomitant frustration about missing work because of their babies' illnesses, which often spread to siblings or to the parents as well. Although the escalated exposure to pathogens can help build the baby's immune system, there is no denying that the recurring cycles of illness pose a significant burden for families in the short term.

Assessing the severity of the resulting problems is more complicated. The above–mentioned infections are rarely life-threatening, but relatively minor infections can evolve into more serious illnesses. For example, about 5%–10% of children with otitis media develop chronic middle-ear disease, which can lead to short- or long-term hearing loss (Schwartz et al., 1994).

Center-based care has also been linked to an increased risk of pneumococcal disease, which is an important cause of pneumonia, septicemia, and meningitis (Takala et al., 1995). Center-based care has also been associated with cytomegalovirus infection, a major cause of severe multiple birth defects, which poses a danger to child care workers or mothers who then become pregnant (Dobbins et al., 1994). At the same time, increased early exposure to infectious diseases in center-based care may also have some positive effects on child health, reducing rates of asthma and allergies among children at later ages (Ball et al., 2000; Kramer, Heinrich, Wyst, & Wichmann,1999).

■ Babies are also more vulnerable than older children to injury in nonparental care settings.

Probably the foremost concern about placing a baby in some form of supplemental care is the possibility, albeit fortunately remote, of deliberate or unintentional injury. No government or private agency collects national data on fatalities or serious injuries in child care, and state data are limited. However, sociologists Wrigley and Dreby (2005) conducted a systematic search of national media and legal records, as well as state records of reported incidences in seven states. Overall, they found that fatality rates resulting from violence in child care settings were quite low: Between 1993 and 2003, the overall fatality rate per 100,000 children in child care was less than 0.83; this compares with 2.33 per 100,000 children from abuse and neglect among the population of children at large. Notably, parents, not child care providers, were the perpetrators in 70% of fatalities resulting from child abuse and neglect. However, infants less than 1 year old, because of their dependency, small size, and inability to defend themselves, were much more vulnerable to abuse than older children in child care settings. The overall fatality rate rose to 3 per 100,000 children in child care for children less than 1 year old.

Even more striking were the differences in fatality rates for infants across types of child care. Babies in family child care or home-based settings had a fatality rate resulting from violence 7 times that of those in child care centers. Most infant deaths from violence in the home-based care settings resulted from shaking; it is important to realize that only 20 seconds of vigorous shaking can cause severe brain damage and retinal bleeding (Feldman, Bethel, Shugerman, Grady, & Ellenbogen, 2001; Jenny, Hymel, Ritzen, Reinert, & Hay, 1999; Wrigley & Dreby, 2005). Shaken baby fatalities most often were prompted by the caregiver's frustration at not being able to stop the baby from crying. In a center-based as opposed to home-based setting, coworkers are available to give a stressed caregiver a break.

Fatalities from unintentional injuries in center-based care are quite low, with a decline in injuries as the quality of care improves. However, Wrigley and Dreby (2005) estimated the fatality rate to be 7 times higher in family child care and in-home care by a nanny or babysitter than in a child care center. The greatest difference in rates occurred in fatalities from fires, with centers relatively free of fire risk. Home-based child care settings are much less likely to be regulated or monitored by fire safety inspectors, and state licensing regulations frequently allow one adult to care for far more infants than the provider could transport from the house in case of fire.

Finally, the incidence of sudden infant death syndrome (SIDS) continues to be a concern in child care settings. Overall, the incidence of SIDS has decreased since the "Back to Sleep Campaign," although SIDS still claimed the lives of 2,323 infants less than 1 year old in 2006 (Moon, Kotch, & Aird, 2006). However, based on a retrospective study of SIDS cases in seven states, a fairly high percentage (20%) of SIDS cases occurred in child care settings (Moon, Patel, & McDermott Shaefer, 2000). Of the deaths from SIDS in child care settings, approximately 60% occurred in family child care homes, whether licensed or unlicensed. One third of the SIDS deaths in child care took place during the 1st week of child care, and the average age of the babies who died was about 4 months. The age range of 2–4 months has been identified as the highest risk period for SIDS. Researchers speculate that family child care providers may be less informed about the importance of placing a baby on her back, and that placing the baby on her stomach to sleep, especially when she was not accustomed to that position, may have contributed to the deaths (Moon et al., 2000).

■ How safe or unsafe is nonparental care for babies, and are some types of care settings safer than others?

As with the impact of early child care on social and emotional and cognitive development, the research is complex, and the findings do not all point in the same direction. It is important to provide perspective and not to exaggerate the risks associated with nonparental care of infants and toddlers: Deaths and serious injuries in child care settings make up only a small part of overall mortality and injury in the age group; unintentional injuries are most likely to result from automobile accidents when the baby is in parental care; and infants and toddlers are in general at far greater risk of abuse and neglect by their own parents than in child care settings (Finkelhor & Ormrod, 2001; Wrigley & Dreby, 2005). For babies from abusive or neglectful families, early child care can provide a much higher level of safety than they experience in their own homes.

That said, the dilemma facing parents looking for the safest child care setting for their infant is that there are pros and cons to the various types of care. Family child care or in-home care by a nanny or babysitter poses less of a risk of infectious disease and is often the only feasible option for families who work nonstandard hours. Many families prefer home-based as opposed to larger group settings for infants and toddlers (Schnur & Koffler, 1995; Schulman & Blank, 2007). However, center-based care provides more safeguards against injury, both intentional and unintentional, and center-based providers are more apt than their home-based counterparts, often unregulated, to receive information on the latest pediatric recommendations for infant care. As Wrigley and Dreby (2005) concluded, although fatalities in nonparental care are extremely rare, the risks are higher when the most vulnerable children are placed in the least-regulated or socially controlled forms of care, namely those entirely dependent on the emotional stability of a single caregiver.

In summary, the findings on child health and safety suggest that parents are right to be cautious: Although children on average may be safer in certain respects in nonparental care than in their own homes, this statistical observation is of little comfort to the otherwise well-functioning family whose baby suffers an injury in a child care setting. Contrary to popular perception, centers may offer infants more protection from injury than other types of nonparental care. Taken as a whole, the findings suggest that special caution is particularly in order during the first 4 months of life when most fatalities from SIDS occur. For policymakers interested in determining the optimum length of a paid parental leave policy, the research on the importance of breastfeeding during the first 4 to 6 months of life suggests that access to a leave of this length would significantly reduce the incidence of infection.

What Is the Quality of the Care Available?

Unfortunately, although high-quality infant and toddler care has been linked with positive child outcomes, such arrangements for this age group are often lacking and expensive. Although the availability of child care has certainly increased in recent years, reflecting a roughly 500% increase in licensed centers and a 200% increase in regulated family homes since 1979 (Children's Foundation, 2002), at most 28% of infants with employed mothers are in licensed centers or homes (Laughlin, 2010). As discussed at the outset of this chapter, a majority of infants in nonparental care are in unlicensed settings that are not monitored on a regular basis, and hence information on the quality or even safety of the settings is not routinely available.

■ Fewer quality center-based arrangements are available for infants and toddlers than for preschool children.

Perhaps the most comprehensive assessment of the quality of center-based care for infants and toddlers is the *Cost, Quality, and Child Outcomes in Child Care Centers* study (Helburn, 1995). In this study, Helburn and colleagues observed 401 centers in four states: California, Colorado, Connecticut, and North Carolina. The centers served infants, toddlers, or preschool-age children, or a combination of these age groups, in the spring of 1993. On the basis of observer assessments using the Infant/Toddler Environment Rating Scale (Harms, Cryer, & Clifford, 1990), the study found that across the four states, only one in four infant classrooms met the "good" benchmark (Helburn). Child care at most centers was poor to mediocre, with nearly half of the infant and toddler rooms providing poor quality care. Forty percent of the infant–toddler rooms were observed to endanger children's safety. On average, teachers of infants and toddlers had less experience and less education than preschool teachers, and this difference was reflected in lower scores in infant–toddler classrooms than in preschool classrooms. For example, the combined score on the dimension of Developmentally Appropriate Practices and Appropriate Caregiving was 3.1 out of 7 for the infant–toddler rooms, as compared to a score of 4 for rooms serving preschool-age children on these same dimensions on the Early Childhood Environment Rating Scale (Harms & Clifford, 1980; Helburn).

■ Quality of family child care and relative care for infants and toddlers also found lacking.

The quality of home-based care—the form of care most frequently selected for infants and toddlers—has also been found lacking. In their study of home-based care, Kontos, Howes, Shinn, and Galinsky (1994) observed providers from three states. Using what was then called the Family Day Care Rating Scale (FDCRS; Harms & Clifford, 1989), researchers found high-quality care in only 12% of the family child care home settings and inadequate care in 69% of the relative care settings. Furthermore, researchers found that children from low-income families were in substantially lower quality care than were their more affluent peers. Of course, one might conclude that the FDCRS tool was not totally appropriate to the measurement of care provided by relatives, and that the same instrument used in the child's home to assess the quality of care provided by the child's parents might have provided similar findings. But the study calls into question the popular assumption that care provided by kith and kin is always better for the child than other forms of nonparental care.

More recently, a team of researchers from the University of California, Columbia University, and Stanford University observed the quality of 166 centers and 187 nonparental home settings serving children from low-income families in five cities situated in California, Connecticut, and Florida (Fuller, Kagan, Loeb & Chang, 2004). The most notable finding was the great variability observed across centers and home-based settings. Compared to home-based settings, centers displayed higher quality as measured by provider education and the intensity of structured learning activities but did not consistently display more positive adult–child interactions. Family child care homes had higher FDCRS scores and provider education levels compared to more informal kith and kin settings. Among the study's most troublesome findings was the low quality level—including low level of education—observed among informal home-based settings serving children from already vulnerable, low-income families. Also, the study found that mothers employed for the longest hours per week tended to select the lowest quality home-based providers (Fuller et al., 2004). Given their findings, the researchers were especially troubled by the fact that an increasing portion of public child care funds were being used to subsidize informal care for the most vulnerable children from low-income families.

The NICHD SECC has found similar great variability in the quality of nonparental child care. Child care centers serving infants and toddlers were less apt to meet the standards for adult-to-child ratios, group size, and staff education and training recommended by the American Academy of Pediatrics and the American Public Health Association than were facilities serving preschool-age children (NIH & NICHD, 2006). The study identified *positive caregiving*—that is, sensitive, encouraging, and frequent interactions between the caregiver and the child—as a primary indicator of child care quality. On the basis of this measure, the percentage of children who received a fair amount of positive caregiving (between "poor" and "good") was about 30% across the first 3 years of life. Fewer than 10% of arrangements were rated as providing high-quality child care (NICHD Early Child Care Research Network, 2000a; NIH & NICHD).

What Does Quality Care for Infants Cost?

■ The average fee for infant care exceeds tuition and expenses for a year of college.

Improving the quality of infant care would be far easier were it not for the high price of even mediocre care. According to a study by the National Association of Child Care Resource and Referral Agencies (NACCRRA, 2010), the average annual fees paid for full-time center-based care for an infant in 2009 ranged from $4,560 in Mississippi to $18,993 in Massachusetts. The average annual fee for an infant in center-based care exceeded the average annual cost of a year's tuition and related fees at a 4-year public college in 40 states. Center-based care for an infant cost families more than they spent on food in all states and exceeded their expenditures for rent or mortgage in 18 states (NACCRRA). Center-based care for infants in urban areas costs twice as much as in rural areas. Family child care is less expensive, ranging from $3,550 in South Carolina to $11,900 in Massachusetts. However, the quality is even less certain than that for center-based care, with 24 states allowing providers to care for five children before a license is required (NACCRRA).

■ The price tag for infant care meeting quality standards is much higher.

The cost for infant care that meets nationally recommended quality standards—with high adult-to-child ratios (1:3), small groups, caregivers who are trained in early care and are adequately compensated, and continuity of care—is much higher. For example, in 2008, Google charged its employees $1,425 per month ($17,000 per year) for in-house infant care meeting national accreditation standards, and the Silicon Valley icon was taking surveys to see whether the price could be raised to nearly $2,500 per month ($30,000 per year; Collins, 2009). The cost to operate Educare, a high-quality early learning and care program targeted at disadvantaged children beginning in infancy, was recently estimated at an average cost across all age groups, including preschool as well as infants, of $16,000 to $17,000 in Waterville, ME, and is likely to be substantially higher in Washington, DC, where a new center recently broke ground.[3]

■ **The high cost of formal child care leads many families to use less reliable arrangements.**

Parents at the poverty level may qualify for publicly subsidized care, but only 22% of eligible families receive such subsidies (NACCRRA, 2010). Families at the median income are unlikely to qualify for any form of public assistance other than the federal Child and Dependent Care Credit on taxes. Taxpayers may claim employment-related child care expenses of up to $3,000 annually for one child and up to $6,000 for two or more children. Taxpayers with an adjusted gross income of $15,000 or less get credit for 35% of allowed expenses, for a credit of $1,050 for one child. Taxpayers with an adjusted gross income of $43,000 or more may claim 20%, for a maximum credit of $600 for one child. Clearly these amounts fall far short of the cost of care for infants, whose fees may exceed $1,000 a month. Because many working families cannot afford the cost of licensed care, whether center- or family child care–based, increasing numbers of families tell child care resource and referral agencies that they are turning to the least expensive, but also least reliable, form of nonparental care—informal care (NACCRRA).

Summary: What Is the Role of Paid Leave in a Child Care Policy?

What do babies need during the 1st year of life, and what role does public policy have in promoting the likelihood they will get it? Infants depend on their adult caregivers to meet their basic physical needs and to protect them from harm. Babies also rely on their caregivers for emotional warmth and the social and cognitive stimulation that promotes healthy brain development. Although the responsibility for a baby's care clearly rests primarily with parents, public policy has a role in ensuring that parents have real choices. Nearly 30 years ago, two of us wrote that "current U.S. policy supports neither high-quality infant day care nor alternatives, such as paid leaves for infant care" (Zigler & Muenchow, 1983, p. 91). Today, because of the

---

[3] *Authors' calculation from presentation regarding Educare Center in Waterville. Available at maine.gov/cabinet/educare/documents/revised.*

number of employees not covered by the Family and Medical Leave Act, the absence of wage replacement, and the lack of quality standards for child care, that is still largely true.

On the basis of the body of child development, sociological, and health research available, for at least the first few months of life, families need alternatives to nonparental care. During the first 4 months, babies benefit especially from breastfeeding, and this is the period they are also most vulnerable to SIDS. Given the high cost of infant care and the difficulties in providing safe, healthy care, providing real alternatives, such as a partially paid leave for a portion of the 1st year of a baby's life, looks like both a bargain and a wise investment. Even if paid leave were offered for 3 months at 75% of the median income for a single parent (one quarter of the $28,579 median income in California = $7,145 × 0.75 = $5,359), it would cost no more than the same period of quality center-based care or nanny care in many urban areas.

Parents who can spend more time with their infants in the first months after birth also are in a position to be wiser consumers of, and perhaps even advocates for, improved quality of the out-of-home child care arrangements that their children move into after the parents go back to work. Indeed, as many new parents will attest, searching for the right child care arrangement takes a couple of months of concerted effort and amounts to a job in itself. The more time a parent spends actually observing a prospective child care setting, whether home- or center-based, the more likely the parent is to detect warning signs and to make a good choice.

Even if paid leave for infant care were available, however, most mothers—and fathers—would still elect to return to work sometime during the child's 1st year of life, and access to quality out-of-home care for infants would still be necessary. Furthermore, as discussed above, infants at risk of abuse or educational failure for a variety of factors probably benefit from high-quality early supplemental care. Paid parental leave is best construed as a supplement, not a substitute, for a system of high-quality child care and other family support services. Thus, we also recommend the following:

- *Strengthen efforts to improve quality of child care for infants and toddlers through regulatory requirements, monitoring, and enforcement.* In particular, reinstate federal efforts to develop standards for child care, such as the Federal Interagency Day Care Requirements, to ensure a threshold of quality at least for child care purchased with federal funds. Regulate small group size, and offer more training in how to prevent infectious disease, SIDS, and nonintentional injuries for this most vulnerable group. Even for informal providers, provide public subsidies only to those willing to participate in introductory training on disease and injury prevention.

- *Explore Quality Rating and Improvement Systems as a mechanism to increase consumer information regarding child care settings.* A Quality Rating and Improvement System is a uniform set of ratings, graduated by level of quality, to assess and improve early learning and care programs. Objective ratings help families identify programs, guide providers in making improvements, and give policymakers a basis for providing technical assistance. According to the National Child Care Information and Technical Assistance Center (2009), 23 states are in some stage of implementing these systems, and 20 more are in the planning stages. In addition, some states tie reimbursement rates for subsidized care to quality ratings, thereby providing an incentive for improving the quality of care. One state (Louisiana) provides higher state tax credits to families who select arrangements with higher ratings, providing incentives for middle-income families to select higher quality arrangements.

■ *Train infant and toddler caregivers in relationship-based care.* Practices to support responsive caregiving, secure attachments, identity formation, and attention to developmental trajectories are key to improving the quality of nonparental as well as parental care (Lally, 2009).

■ *Expand home visiting services, making them available to all families with infants on cash assistance.* Exemptions from work for families on cash assistance vary greatly from state to state, from 1 month to 3 years. In our view, families receiving cash assistance should have at least the same length exemption (e.g., 3 or 4 months) as we recommend for paid parental leave. However, continuation of cash assistance during the work exemption period should be provided on condition of the family's willingness to receive a recognized home visiting service, such as Early Head Start or Healthy Families America. According to the Administration for Children and Families (U.S. Department of Health and Human Services, 2010), the cost of home-based Early Head Start is about $9,500, as compared to the cost of a center-based program at $11,000, with a mixed model costing significantly more.

■ *Expand Educare to demonstrate what high-quality care looks like.* According to a study by the Benton Foundation, most people think of child care as a container—a place where one drops off babies to keep them safe and dry all day until the parents pick them up at night. That is, the public makes a distinction between "child care," which they view primarily as a safe place to store children, and "prekindergarten," where children are actually expected to learn something. The benefit of expanding Educare-quality centers is to educate the public, and especially policymakers, about what quality care looks like. In addition, Educare programs can be used to train providers in quality care and provide data on the capacity of high-quality programs to improve disadvantaged children's school readiness and performance.

■ *Pursue models to make good-quality care more affordable.* There are several possible approaches. One, proposed by economists Suzanne Helburn and Barbara Bergmann

(2002), would provide subsidies to all families to pay for care at a level of quality equal to the current national average. They define "affordable" as not costing a family more than 20% of their income above the poverty line. This model would provide free care for poor families and partially subsidized care for low- and middle-income families. An important step toward this goal would be to reauthorize the Child Care and Development Block Grant, which currently only provides subsidized child care to one in seven eligible families. Yet another recommendation is to make the child care tax credit refundable, so that low-income families who do not owe much in taxes can benefit. None of these are new recommendations, but they have the merit of building on existing policy.

■ *Pursue more research on the impact of age of entry into child care and the number of hours of care.* For at-risk children, there is evidence that the earlier the entry into full-time care, provided it is of high quality and includes family support services, the greater the benefits. However, even in many of the model programs that have been the subject of research, babies did not enter care until they were 4 or 6 months old. For the broader population, more research is certainly needed to determine whether there is an optimal age for working parents to transition infants into nonparental care, and whether infants benefit from gradually increased hours over the 1st year of life as opposed to an abrupt entry into full-time care.

In conclusion, we agree with Ron Lally, who noted that

> *The answer to "Should a child under 12 months of age be in care outside the home?" is "It depends." It depends on the interaction of the quality of the child care into which the child is placed, the quality of the home care where the child resides, and the impact on family life of the economic, societal, and personal pressure that family members feel to place their young child in care.... We would love family members to have the choice to stay home, and also the option of high-quality care available to them if they need or desire it* (Lally, personal communication, 2006, as cited in Zigler et al., 2009).

Making sure that parents have alternatives to nonparental care in the first months of life helps to reduce the number of families who have to find care for newborn babies and the length of time they have to purchase this most expensive form of child care. Paid parental leave is not a substitute for expanding access to quality care for infants and toddler, but it would give parents more time to get to know their babies and to find care that matches their needs. Expanding access to paid infant care leave is thus a cornerstone and key foundation of a work–family and child care policy that promotes healthy child development.

References

Aronson, S. S., & Shope, T. R. (2005). Improving the health and safety of children in nonparental early education and child care. *Pediatrics in Review, 26*(3), 86–95.

Ball, T., Castro-Rodriguez, J. A., Griffith, K. A., Holberg, C. J., Martinez, F., & Wright, A. L. (2000). Siblings, day-care attendance, and the risk of asthma and wheezing during childhood. *The New England Journal of Medicine, 343*, 538–543.

Barnett, W. S., & Masse, L. J. (2007). Comparative benefit-cost analysis of the Abecedarian project and its policy implications. *Economics of Education Review, 26*, 113–125. Retrieved July 26, 2011, from www.sciencedirect.com

Belsky, J. (1987). Risks remain. *Zero to Three, 7*(3), 22–24.

Brooks-Gunn, J., Han, W. J., & Waldfogel, J. (2010). First-year maternal employment and child development in the first 7 years. *Monographs of the Society for Research in Child Development, 75*(2). Retrieved July 26, 2011, from www.interscience.wiley.com/journal/118539445/home

Campbell, F. A., Ramey, C. T., Pungello, E., Sparling, J., & Miller-Johnson, S. (2002). Early childhood education: Young adult outcomes from the Abecedarian Project. *Applied Developmental Science, 6*(1), 42–57.

Child Welfare League of America. (1960). *Standards for day care service.* New York: Author.

Children's Foundation. (2002). *The 2000 child care licensing study.* Washington, DC: Author.

Cohn, J. F., Marias, R., & Tronick, E. Z. (1986). Face-to-face interactions of depressed mothers and their infants. *New Directions for Child and Adolescent Development, 34*, 31–46.

Collins, G. (2009). *When everything changed: The amazing journey of American women from 1960 to the present.* New York: Little, Brown.

Dettling, A. C., Gunnar, M. R., & Donzella, B. (1999). Cortisol levels of young children in full-day child care centers: Relations with age and temperament. *Psychoneuroendocrinology, 24*, 519–536.

Dobbins, J. G., Adler, S. P., Pass, R. F., Bale, J. F., Grillner, L., & Stewart, J. A. (1994). The risks and benefits of cytomegalovirus transmission in child day care. *Pediatrics, 94*, 1016–1018.

Duitjts, L., Jaddoe, V. W., Hofman, A., & Moll, H. (2010). Prolonged and exclusive breastfeeding reduces risk of infectious disease in infancy. *Pediatrics, 126*, e18–e25. Retrieved September 1, 2010, from http://pediatrics.aappublications.org/cgi/content/abstract/peds.2008-3256v1

Feldman, K. E., Bethel, R., Shugerman, R. P., Grady, M. S., & Ellenbogen, R. G. (2001). The cause of infant and toddler subdural hemorrhage: A prospective study. *Pediatrics, 108*, 636–646.

Finkelhor, D., & Ormrod, R. (2001, September). Crimes against children by babysitters. *Juvenile Justice Bulletin*. Washington, DC: U.S. Department of Justice, Office of Juvenile Justice and Delinquency Prevention. Retrieved July 27, 2011, from www.ncjrs.gov/html/ojjdp/jjbul2001_9_4/contents.html

Fraiberg, S. (1977). *Every child's birthright: In defense of mothering*. New York: Basic Books.

Fuller, B., Kagan, S. L., Loeb, S., & Chang, Y.-W. (2004). Child care quality: Centers and home settings that serve poor families. *Early Childhood Research Quarterly, 19*, 505–527.

Gunnar, M., & Quevedo, K. (2007). The neurobiology of stress and development. *Annual Review of Psychology, 58*, 145–153.

Halle, T., Hair, E., Nuenning, M., Weinstein, D., Vick, J., Forry, N., & Kinukawa, A. (2009). *Primary child care arrangements of U.S. infants: Patterns of utilization by poverty status, family structure, maternal work status, maternal work schedule, and child care assistance* (OPRE Research Brief No. 1). Washington, DC: U.S. Department of Health and Human Services, Administration for Children and Families, Office of Planning, Research and Evaluation.

Han, W. J., Ruhm, C., Waldfogel, J., & Washbrook, E. (2008). The timing of mothers' employment after childbirth. *Monthly Labor Review, 131*(6), 15–27.

Harms, T., & Clifford, R. M. (1980). *The Early Childhood Environment Rating Scale*. New York: Teachers College Press.

Harms, T., & Clifford, R. M. (1989). *The Family Day Care Rating Scale*. New York: Teachers College Press.

Harms, T., Cryer, D., & Clifford, R. M. (1990). *Infant/Toddler Environment Rating Scale*. New York: Teachers College Press.

Hart, B., & Risley, T. (1995). *Meaningful differences in the everyday parenting and intellectual development of young American children*. Baltimore: Brookes.

Helburn, S. (Ed.). (1995). *Cost, quality, and child outcomes in child care centers* (Public Rep., 2nd ed.). Denver: University of Colorado, Department of Economics.

Helburn, S., & Bergmann, B. (2002). *America's child care problem: The way out*. New York: Palgrave.

Hill, J., Waldfogel, J., & Brooks-Gunn, J. (2003). Sustained effects of high participation in an early intervention for low-birth-weight premature infants. *Developmental Psychology, 39*, 730–744.

Honig, A. S. (2004). Longitudinal outcomes from the Family Development Research Program. *Early Child Development and Care, 174*, 125–130.

Jenny, C., Hymel, K. P., Ritzen, A., Reinert, S. E., & Hay, T. C. (1999). Analysis of missed cases of abusive head trauma. *The Journal of the American Medical Association, 281*, 621–626.

Johansen, A. S., Leibowitz, A., & Waite, L. J. (1988). Child care and children's illness. *American Journal of Public Health, 78*, 1175–1177.

Kagan, J., Kearsley, R., & Zelazo, P. (1977). The effects of infant day care on psychological development. *Educational Quarterly, 1*, 109–142.

Kontos, D., Howes, C., Shinn, M., & Galinsky, E. (1994). *The study of children in family child care and relative care.* New York: Families and Work Institute.

Kramer, U., Heinrich, J., Wyst, M., & Wichmann, H. E. (1999). Age of entry to day nursery and allergy in later childhood. *The Lancet, 353*, 450–454.

Kreader, J. L, Ferguson, D., & Lawrence, S. (2005). *Infant and toddler child care arrangements.* Retrieved July 27, 2011, from Columbia University, National Center for Children in Poverty www.nccp.org/publications/pub_628.html

Lally, J. R. (2009). The science and psychology of infant-toddler care: How an understanding of early learning has transformed child care. *Zero to Three, 30*(2), 47–53.

Lally, J. R., Mangione, P. L., & Honig, A. S. (1988). The Syracuse University Family Development Research Project: Long-range impact of an early intervention with low-income children and their families. In D. R. Powell (Ed.), *Parent education as early childhood intervention: Emerging directions in theory, research, and practice* (pp. 79–104). Norwood, NJ: Ablex.

Laughlin, L. (2010). *Who's minding the kids? Child care arrangements: Spring 2005/summer 2006* (Current Population Report P70-121). Washington, DC: U.S. Census Bureau.

Love, J. M., Kisker, E. E., Ross, C., Constantine, J., Boller, K., Chazan-Cohen, R., et al. (2005). The effectiveness of Early Head Start for 3-year-old children and their parents: Lessons for policy and programs. *Developmental Psychology, 41*, 885–901.

Moon, R. Y., Kotch, L., & Aird, L. (2006). State child care regulations regarding infant sleep environment since the Healthy Child Care America Back-to-Sleep Campaign. *Pediatrics, 118*, 73–83.

Moon, R. Y., Patel, K. M., & McDermott Shaefer, S. J. (2000). Sudden infant death syndrome in child care settings. *Pediatrics, 106*, 295–300.

National Association of Child Care Resource and Referral Agencies. (2010). *Parents and the high cost of child care: 2010 update.* Washington, DC: Author.

National Child Care Information and Technical Assistance Center. (2009). *QRIS and the impact on quality.* Retrieved September 11, 2009, from http://nccic.acf.hhs.gov/poptopics/qrs-impactqualitycc.html

National Institute of Child Health and Human Development Early Child Care Research Network. (1997). The effects of infant child care on infant-mother attachment security: Results of the NICHD Study of Early Child Care. *Child Development, 68*, 860–879.

National Institute of Child Health and Human Development Early Child Care Research Network. (1999a). Child care and mother-child interaction in the first three years of life. *Developmental Psychology, 35*, 1399–1413.

National Institute of Child Health and Human Development Early Child Care Research Network. (1999b). Child outcomes when child care center classes meet recommended standards for quality. *American Journal of Public Health, 89*, 1072–1077.

National Institute of Child Health and Human Development Early Child Care Research Network. (2000a). Characteristics and quality of child care for toddlers and preschoolers. *Applied Developmental Science, 4*, 116–135.

National Institute of Child Health and Human Development Early Child Care Research Network. (2000b). The relation of child care to cognitive and language development. *Child Development, 71*, 960–980.

National Institute of Child Health and Human Development Early Child Care Research Network. (2002a). Early child care and children's development prior to school entry. Results from the NICHD Study of Early Child Care. *American Educational Research Journal, 39*, 133–164.

National Institute of Child Health and Human Development Early Child Care Research Network. (2002b). Parenting and family influences when children are in child care: Results from the NICHD Study of Early Child Care. In J. G. Borkowski, S. L. Ramey, & M. Bristol-Power (Eds.), *Parenting and the child's world: Influences on academic, intellectual and social-emotional development* (pp. 99–123). Mahwah, NJ: Erlbaum.

National Institute of Child Health and Human Development Early Child Care Research Network. (2003). Does amount of time spent in child care predict socioemotional adjustment during the transition to kindergarten? *Child Development, 74*, 976–1005.

National Institute of Child Health and Human Development Early Child Care Research Network. (2004). Type of child care and children's development at 54 months. *Early Childhood Research Quarterly, 19*(2), 203–230.

National Institute of Child Health and Human Development Early Child Care Research Network. (2005). *Child care and child development: Results from the NICHD study of early child care and youth development.* New York: Guilford.

National Institutes of Health & National Institute of Child Health and Development. (2006). *The NICHD Study of Early Child Care and Youth Development: Findings for children up to age 4 ½ years.* Washington, DC: Author.

National Research Council & Institute of Medicine. (2000). *From neurons to neighborhoods: The science of early childhood development.* J. P. Shonkoff & D. A. Phillips, (Eds), Board on Children, Youth, and Families; Commission on Behavioral and Social Sciences and Education. Washington, DC: National Academy Press.

National Scientific Council on the Developing Child. (2005). *Excessive stress disrupts the architecture of the developing brain* (Working Paper 3). Retrieved July 27, 2011, from www.developingchild.net/pubs/wp/Stress_Disrupts_Architecture_Developing Brain.pdf

Newcombe, N. S. (2003). Some controls control too much. *Child Development, 74,* 1050–1052.

Phillips, D. (2010, October). *10 years post-Neurons to Neighborhoods: What's at stake and what matters in child care?* Keynote address at the celebration of the 20th anniversary of Child Care and Development Block Grant, Washington, DC. Retrieved December 22, 2011, from www.irle.berkeley.edu/cscce/wp-content/uploads/2010/12/DeborahPhillips_Keynote_CCDBG20thCelebration_10-19-10.pdf

Phillips, D., McCartney, K., Scarr, S., & Howes, C. (1987). Selective review of infant day care research: A cause for concern! *Zero to Three, 7*(3), 18–21.

Ramey, C. R., & Campbell, F. A. (1984). Preventive education for high-risk children: Cognitive consequences of the Carolina Abecedarian Project. *American Journal of Mental Deficiency, 88,* 515–523.

Ramey, C. T., Campbell, F. A., & Blair, C. (1998). Enhancing the life-course for high-risk children: Results from the Abecedarian Project. In J. Crane (Ed.), *Social programs that really work* (pp. 163–183). New York: Sage.

Schnur, E., & Koffler, R. (1995). Family child care and new immigrants: Cultural bridge and support. *Child Welfare, 74,* 1237–1248.

Schulman, K., & Blank, H. (2007). *State strategies to support family, friend and neighbor care.* Washington, DC: National Women's Law Center.

Schwartz, B., Giebink, G. S., Henderson, F. W., Reichler, M. R., Jereb, J., & Collet, J. P. (1994). Respiratory infections in day care. *Pediatrics, 94,* 1018–1020.

Spitz, R. A. (1945). Hospitalism: An inquiry into the genesis of psychiatric conditions in early childhood. *Psychoanalytic Study of the Child, 1,* 53–74.

Takala, A. K., Jero, J., Kela, E., Ronnberg, P.-R., Koskenneiemi, E., & Eskola, J. (1995). Risk factors for primary invasive pneumococcal disease among children in Finland. *Journal of the American Medical Association, 273,* 859–865.

U.S. Department of Health and Human Services. (2010). *Head Start Program fact sheet fiscal year 2010.* Retrieved July 25, 2011, from Administration for Children and Families http://eclkc.ohs.acf.hhs.gov/hslc/Head%20Start%20Program/Head%20Start%20Program%20Factsheets/fHeadStartProgr.htm

U.S. Department of Health and Human Services. (n.d.). *Early Head Start benefits children and families: Research to practice.* Washington, DC: Author. Retrieved December 22, 2011 from Administration for Children and Families, Early Head Start Research and Evaluation Project www.acf.hhs.gov/programs/opre/ehs/ehs_resrch/index.html

Vandell, D. L. (2004). Early child care: The known and the unknown. *Merrill-Palmer Quarterly, 50,* 387–414.

Vandell, D. L., Belsky, J., Burchinal, M., Steinberg, L., Vandergrift, N., & NICHD Early Child Care Research Network. (2010). Do effects of early child care extend to age 15? Results from the NICHD Study of Early Child Care. *Child Development, 81,* 737–756.

Watamura, S. E., Donzella, B., Alwin, J., & Gunnar, M. R. (2003). Morning-to-afternoon increases in cortisol concentrations for infants and toddlers in child care: Age differences and behavioral correlates. *Child Development, 74,* 1006–1020.

Wrigley, J., & Dreby, J. (2005). Fatalities and the organization of child care in the United States, 1985–2003. *American Sociological Review, 70,* 729–757.

Yazejan, N., & Bryant, D. M. (2009). *Promising early returns: Educare implementation study data, March 2009.* Chapel Hill: Frank Porter Graham Child Development Institute, University of North Carolina at Chapel Hill.

Zigler, E., Marsland, K., & Lord, H. (2009). *The tragedy of child care in America.* New Haven, CT: Yale University Press.

Zigler, E., & Muenchow, S. (1983). Infant day care and infant-care leaves: A policy vacuum. *American Psychologist, 38,* 91–94.

The Economics of Paid Leave for Infant Care

Previous chapters have shown that parental leave may enhance child health and development by providing parents with the time to attach to their newborn or newly adopted infant and attune to the child's specific cues. In this chapter, we explain why, from an economist's perspective, public policies providing parents with rights to at least some paid leave following the arrival of a new baby are desirable. To do so, we first summarize the various potential economic benefits of paid parental leave for children, families, and employers, whether provided voluntarily by employers or mandated by government. We then suggest why, on the basis of economic theory, broad access to paid parental leave is unlikely to become available through privately negotiated labor market arrangements alone. Finally, we discuss the public policy options for addressing the apparent market failure that comes into play with respect to paid parental leave. From the outset, it is important to stress that "the devil is in the details," by which we mean that the potential benefits (or costs) of various possible paid parental leave policies are likely to depend critically on their precise structure. We do not delve far into these details here, reserving most of this discussion for the specific policies we propose in chapter 7.

Potential Economic Benefits of Paid Parental Leave

■ What are the benefits of paid parental leave for children?

As discussed in some depth in chapter 2, the evidence indicates that paid parental leave benefits the health and developmental outcomes of children. The key reason is that the leaves are likely to provide parents with additional time to invest in their newborns. In the 1960s, Nobel prize-winning economist Gary Becker, a pioneer in the field of family economics, emphasized the role of parental time investments in children. Specifically, child outcomes (and other household goods and services) are produced using inputs of purchased goods and time (Becker, 1965). For instance, meals may be produced by combining food purchased at the grocery store with time in preparing, cooking, and cleaning up after eating. A clean house is produced using purchased inputs, such as a vacuum cleaner, and the housecleaner's time.[1]

In the same way, purchased products—such as books and computers—are combined with parental time to produce human capital in children. For instance, toddlers' cognitive abilities are enhanced when parents read to them. Indeed, parental time is likely to be a particularly important input for many child outcomes. For example, language development is likely to be enhanced when parents talk to their children, an activity that takes large amounts of time and little else. As we discussed in chapter 3, the typical child of parents who are professionals knows 3 times as many words by the time he is 3 years old as does the child of a parent on cash assistance (Hart & Risley, 1995). Moreover, there is good reason to believe that such time investments are particularly important when they occur very early in life and that paid leave may therefore provide parents with additional time to spend with their infants during a critical period.

There is a substantial body of research emphasizing the role of the early child environment in producing long-term outcomes (National Research Council & Institute of Medicine, 2000; Zigler, Finn-Stevenson, & Hall, 2002). Indeed, what is often referred to as the "Barker hypothesis" after early research by David Barker and his colleagues (Barker, Winter, Osmond, Margetts, & Simmonds, 1989) indicates that even prenatal conditions may have lasting effects.[2] Some of these consequences may be purely biological; however, there is substantial evidence that brain development itself is influenced by the type of stimulation received during the earliest years of life. In particular, as we discussed in chapter 2, neural pathways are being rapidly formed during the first months of life as a result of the types of cognitive stimulation received; more positive environments result in favorable development in a variety of areas including emotional control and language development (Schore, 2001, 2005; Spence, Shapiro, & Zaidel, 1996; Thompson, 2007; Zigler et al., 2002).

---

[1] *Before products such as vacuum cleaners or washing machines were available, these same household services were produced using less sophisticated purchased inputs (such as brooms) and greater amounts of time. As market goods such as prepared meals become cheaper and more readily available, the time required to produce specified household products falls.*

[2] *Barker's work did not carefully distinguish the effects of the prenatal environment from those of subsequent confounding factors. However, recent research has shown that the early environment has lasting effects even after carefully accounting for other factors. For example, van den Berg, Lindeboom, and Portrait (2006) showed that Dutch infants born in boom years live around 2 years longer than those born during a subsequent recession; Almond (2006) found that in utero exposure to the 1918 flu epidemic reduced subsequent education and was associated with less favorable labor market outcomes and reduced social and economic status.*

Studies of brain development have been complemented by economic research examining how parental inputs influence child development. Probably most important are theoretical and empirical analyses conducted by Nobel prize-winning economist James Heckman and several coauthors (Cunha & Heckman, 2007; Heckman, 2000). Heckman emphasized three key features in the production of child outcomes: *self-productivity, dynamic complementarity,* and *critical or sensitive* periods. Self-productivity refers to the idea that (cognitive and noncognitive) skills obtained at one age create additional skills at later ages. Thus, skills are self-reinforcing and cross-fertilizing. For instance, emotional maturity and security foster the future development of cognitive abilities. Dynamic complementarity implies that human capital obtained at one age increases the returns to investments in skills occurring later in life. Sensitive periods exist if, all else being equal, investments in human capital have higher returns in some stages of life than in others.[3] The combination of dynamic complementarity and self-productivity implies that investments are likely to be particularly productive when they occur early in life, an effect that is further strengthened if the biology of brain development makes this a sensitive period. Figure 4.1, adapted from what is often called "Heckman's curve" (2008, p. 311), provides evidence of higher returns to investments occurring at young ages—prior to school entry—than for those taking place after the preschool years.

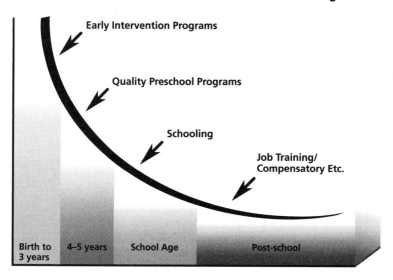

Figure 4.1. Adapted from "Schools, Skills, and Synapses" by J. J. Heckman, 2008, *Economic Inquiry, 46*, p. 311.

---

[3] *There is a critical period if investments are only effective at one stage of life.*

Although Heckman's work does not directly examine parental leave, there is good reason to suspect that returns to investments are particularly high during the infancy period. Consistent with this possibility, careful recent analyses of the effects of maternal employment suggest that work during the 1st year of the child's life is associated with small negative effects on future cognitive and emotional development, whereas jobs held subsequently have a neutral or positive impact (Bernal & Keane, 2010; Hill, Waldfogel, Brooks-Gunn, & Han, 2005; Ruhm, 2004; more neutral results have been obtained by Brooks-Gunn, Han, & Waldfogel, 2010). As discussed in chapter 2, one reason is that it is often difficult for working mothers to breastfeed or offer only their own milk during the baby's 1st year of life. Thus, their babies may not realize the substantial benefits to health and development associated with breastfeeding, such as reductions in acute and chronic diseases and small gains in cognitive test scores (Gartner et al., 2005). A second reason, as discussed in chapter 3 and elsewhere at length by the first author (Zigler, Marsland, & Lord, 2009), is that the average quality of child care is relatively low in the United States, and it may be especially poorly suited to meeting the needs of infants. For instance, careful observation of the quality of care in nine states between 1996 and 1999 revealed that just 9% of 15- to 36-month-old children in nonparental settings generally received positive caregiving, while 61% rarely or never did (National Institute of Child Health and Human Development Early Child Care Research Network, 2000).

Given the limitations on parental leave presently available in the United States, we cannot be sure whether the rights to relatively short durations of paid time off work that we advocate will yield the kind of child health benefits described in earlier chapters. As we discuss in chapter 5, Canada and many European nations provide more extended durations of leave (a year or more in many cases), partly because of the belief that doing so confers advantages to children. Such lengthy leaves are not realistic in the context of the United States at the present time, but we believe that even relatively brief amounts of time at home (measured in weeks or months) with infants may yield advantages. For example, the Canadian extension of parental leave rights from 6 months to 1 year, occurring in 2000, increased the duration of breastfeeding and was associated with reductions in chronic conditions, asthma, allergies, and ear infections later in the 1st year (Baker & Milligan, 2008). Similarly, as discussed in chapter 2, U.S. mothers remaining off work for more than 12 weeks after giving birth breastfeed more than their counterparts returning to jobs more quickly, and their babies receive more well-baby visits and immunizations (Berger, Hill, & Waldfogel, 2005). Finally, two studies from Europe showed that short-to-moderate durations of parental leave reduce infant and early childhood mortality (Ruhm, 2000; Tanaka, 2005).

■ What are the benefits of paid parental leave for mothers?

Women, who now compose nearly half of the U.S. workforce, would realize immediate economic benefits from paid parental leave, whether provided voluntarily by employers or mandated by government.[4] One striking feature of the labor market in the United States and most other industrialized countries is the disparity in the pay of men and women. The average earnings of women are somewhat less than those of men, but with some convergence of wages over time (Blau, 1998). However, whereas earnings generally rise or stay relatively constant for men when they become fathers, most women experience a large wage reduction—or family wage gap—when they become mothers, relative to either their childless counterparts or men. For instance, Waldfogel (1998b) summarized research indicating that mothers earned 10% to 15% less than childless women. Former *New York Times* economics journalist Ann Crittenden (2001, p. 88) called this wage gap the *mommy tax*: "a heavy personal tax levied on people who care for children, or for any other dependent family members." Citing economists Gita Sen and Shirley Burggraf, she projects the "price of motherhood" at well over a million dollars in the case of a college-educated woman and concludes that dependent care is an important factor contributing to poverty for less-educated women. Given that four out of five women in the United States eventually become mothers, according to the U.S. Census Bureau, (Infoplease, n.d.), a majority of the gender may experience the wage penalty.

There are many reasons why motherhood may be associated with a decline in relative earnings. Some women may simply be more interested (than men) in engaging in household activities, including child care, and so may choose to work fewer hours, take jobs offering more flexibility, or temporarily leave the labor force when their children are young.[5] These gender disparities could be related to biology, cultural influences, or combinations of the two that are difficult to disentangle, and many of these differences may be unaffected by the presence or absence of leave policies.

However, entitlements to paid leave may address other sources of the family wage gap. Probably most important is that sufficiently generous leave rights may allow some women to continue working for their employer after having a child. To the extent paid leave eliminates the time otherwise needed to find a new job, the policy increases labor market experience, generally yielding a payoff in the form of higher pay. Even more significant is that the continuity of employment may protect what economists refer to as *specific human capital* and *employer–employee match quality*.

Specific human capital refers to investments in training and skill development that are specific to the employer, industry, or occupation (for an early discussion, see Oi, 1962). Consider the example of "Jane," who has worked for the previous 10 years in the human resources department of a large manufacturing company providing other employees with training on

---

[4] *See Lester (2005) for an in-depth discussion of the impact of paid leave on women's place in the workforce.*

[5] *For instance, Skyt Nielsen, Simonsen, and Verner (2004) showed that the family gap in Denmark is overestimated by failing to account for the disproportionate self-selection of mothers into relatively low-paid public sector jobs.*

aspects of the firm's operations. The company benefits from offering this training, and Jane's experience allows her to supply the instruction more quickly and effectively than a newly hired employee. As a result, Jane's earnings have risen over time (as she has become more effective at her job), and her employer has benefited as well. Assume that Jane is forced to quit her job upon giving birth, to make time available to spend with her baby, because her company does not offer leave. When she is ready to return to work, she has to accept a different type of position with her employer or find another employer. As a result, she will need to start over, and her specific human capital will have been diminished.

A similar result occurs, for employers as well as employees, when good job matches are lost. In the example above, assume that Jane is particularly effective not because of her experience per se but rather because she is a natural teacher—by which we mean that she has an unusual instinct and understanding of how to effectively communicate in a learning environment. Jane may have held a number of jobs while she (and her employers) learned the areas where she was exceptionally proficient. Having found such a good match, both she and her employer have an incentive to retain it. Once again, however, if she has to change jobs after giving birth, it is quite likely that her new position will not be as well suited as her old one to her capabilities, interests, and qualifications—the new job will not be as good a match.[6] For example, economic conditions may be such that positions in human resources departments are hard to find and, even if such employment is available, the companies hiring may provide training in ways less well suited to Jane's teaching style. Also, potential employers will not be able to directly observe Jane's abilities and so may not offer such positions to her, even when the match quality would be high.

Good match quality and specific human capital investment will often go together, because companies may be more willing to provide training to individuals they think have a natural aptitude for the job (or future positions into which the employee may be promoted). Workers, in turn, will be more willing to make costly human capital investments when they like and have natural ability for the job. Thus, parental leave benefits may help to retain good job matches and specific human capital by raising the probability that mothers continue in the same job (or with the same employer) after giving birth.

Some might argue that the rights currently granted under the Family and Medical Leave Act (FMLA) are sufficient to avoid these problems; however, there are at least two reasons to doubt this. First the FMLA does not cover a large proportion (approximately half) of workers, particularly those in small companies. Second, many mothers cannot afford the unpaid leaves the law requires to be made available to eligible workers. The data strongly indicate that this issue is salient. For example, research by Han, Ruhm, and Waldfogel (2009) showed that rights to (mostly unpaid) leave in the United States increased leave-taking among college-

---

[6] *See Jovanovic (1979) for early research on the labor market consequences of job matching.*

educated mothers but not among those with less schooling. Similarly, such entitlements raise the use of leave for married mothers but not their unmarried counterparts.

The evidence, although not fully conclusive, suggests that the increased job continuity permitted by paid leave entitlements has the potential to reduce the family wage gap. For instance, Waldfogel (1998a) found that the family gap was largely eliminated for British and U.S. mothers who used parental leave and eventually returned to their employers. Such results need to be interpreted with caution because they refer to a period prior to enactment of the FMLA, when leave was provided only on a voluntary basis by employers. As a result, mothers obtaining such leaves were not randomly selected but instead were likely those who would have had relatively small family wage gaps, even in the absence of leave.

■ What are the benefits of paid parental leave to employers?

By raising the probability that mothers continue in the same job (or with the same employer) after giving birth, paid parental leave helps employers as well as employees. Employers benefit from the increased productivity that results from retaining good job matches and specific human capital. As discussed in chapter 1, to the extent that parental leave, paid or unpaid, reduces employee turnover, it may benefit employers as much as employees. Major accounting firms calculated that the cost of hiring and training a new employee can be 1.5 times a departing worker's annual salary (Greenhouse, 2011). Even the unpaid FMLA seems to have strengthened the ties of the best educated, most highly trained mothers to the workforce, with the vast majority back at work 9 months after giving birth and 83% returning to their prebirth employer (Johnson, 2008). The FMLA, as shown in previous analyses, while enabling parents to take off time in the short term, actually promotes higher work participation in the medium term (Han et al., 2009).

Private Labor Markets and Paid Parental Leave

Given that both employers and employees can share in the gains of the resulting higher productivity, one might normally expect workers and firms to construct voluntary arrangements whereby at least some paid leave is available. That is, if offering certain employee benefits helps employers attract and retain good employees, and employees want these benefits enough to bargain for them, employers will offer those benefits voluntarily. Economists generally consider voluntary arrangements between employers and employees as desirable, and government intervention as undermining efficiency.

However, economists identify a variety of situations, broadly described as *market failures*, where government intervention provides potential benefits. (These potential benefits will not automatically be realized, and there are many situations in which the costs of government intervention will exceed the gains, even in the presence of market failures.) Succinctly, a market failure is defined as a situation where the market fails to distribute resources efficiently. An outcome is economically efficient if no one can gain from a reallocation without someone else losing. It is inefficient if a reallocation would allow at least one individual or party to gain without anyone's losing. Two sources of potential market failure are particularly important when considering rights to paid leave: externalities and asymmetric information.

■ Externalities reduce the likelihood of privately negotiated leave arrangements.

One of the reasons why employers and employees are unlikely to negotiate paid parental leave benefits on a broad scale is, as suggested earlier, that some of the anticipated benefits are external to the labor market. Economists define externalities as "indirect effects of consumption or production activity, that is, effects on agents other than the originator of such activity which do not work through the price system" (Laffont, 2008). Thus, as we discussed earlier, for leave benefits, potential externalities include improvements in parental health and child health and development that are not fully taken into account by working parents or their employers when negotiating labor market arrangements. For example, better health provides externalities because most health care costs are paid for either by the government or other third parties (e.g., private insurance plans) and, hence, any reduction in health care costs not only benefits the private decision makers (e.g., parents electing to take leave) but also the external parties involved in paying for the health care. Access to paid leave might also be expected to reduce the percentage of workers who, in the absence of such leave benefits, resort to public assistance to finance time off for care of babies or other family members (Lester, 2005). The resulting reduction in public expenditures for public assistance would represent another benefit to external parties, in this case taxpayers, but would not immediately or directly benefit employers. Even many of the benefits deriving from the improvement in child health and development would be external, contributing to improvements in the quality or productivity of the future workforce as well as the productivity of current employees.

Other long-term benefits to society from paid parental leave might include, for example, more educated individuals who in turn commit fewer crimes or develop new technologies, and these gains would be widely dispersed.[7] And even if that were not the case, there may be strong equity arguments for making leave more available to disadvantaged families. As already mentioned, less educated and sole-parent families currently find it relatively difficult to afford the unpaid leaves granted under the FMLA, and it seems grossly unfair that their children

---

[7] *Computing the net gains to society is complicated. For instance, highly educated individuals tend to have lower medical costs in a given year, but they live longer, with potentially offsetting effects on lifetime health care costs.*

should be denied the benefits of such leaves, even if these gains are completely private. Parental leave may also favorably affect the health of mothers. For example, Chatterji and Markowitz (2005) estimated that state leave mandates enacted prior to the FMLA increased maternity leave use by around 1 week and were associated with reductions in postpartum depressive symptoms and physician visits to address health problems. Gains in maternal health provide additional external benefits, by reducing the costs of medical care financed through government programs such as Medicaid, as well as through private insurance plans that pool risks across broad groups of individuals (usually on the basis of employment status).

■ Asymmetric information represents another source of potential market failure.

Another key reason why private arrangements are unlikely to result in desired levels of paid (or unpaid) leave is that asymmetric information may prevent this from occurring (in economically efficient amounts). Asymmetric information "deals with the study of decisions in transactions where one party has more or better information than the other. This creates an imbalance of power in transactions which can sometimes cause the transactions to go awry" (*Information asymmetry*, n.d.). Research during the 1960s by the economists George Akerlof (1970), Michael Spence (1973), and Joseph Stiglitz (Rothschild & Stiglitz, 1970), which led to their being awarded the Nobel Prize in 2001, highlighted the importance of such unequal information in creating a variety of situations in which markets would not yield desired outcomes.

In the context of parental leave, asymmetric information creates problems because workers typically know more about their probability of having children and using leave than do their employers. Consider the following situation. Half of the labor force consists of "Type A" workers who have a 30% probability of taking paid parental leave (over some specified period of time), while the other half are "Type B" workers who have a 10% chance of using leave. Further assume that the cost to employers of providing paid leave to any given employee is $500, while the benefits to the employee (from being able to take leave after the birth of a child) are $750. In this situation, it would be economically efficient for all workers to receive rights to leave, given that the benefits exceed the costs, and, in the absence of asymmetric information, voluntary arrangements would lead this to occur.

To better understand the impact of asymmetric information, consider the case in which there is complete (and symmetric) information about probabilities of future leave use. Type A workers, who have a 30% chance of using leave, would accept a wage reduction of up to $225 (0.3 × $750), while their employers would be willing to provide the leave as long as wages were lowered by at least $150 (0.3 × $500). Similarly, Type B workers would voluntarily receive up to $75 (0.1 × $750) less for jobs providing leave, while employers would be happy to provide them with leave as long as by doing so wages were reduced by $50 (0.1 × $500) or more. Thus, all workers would be willing to agree to larger wage reductions to obtain rights to future leave than it would cost firms to provide it to them, and there are no barriers to this occurring.

Next consider the more realistic situation in which workers know their type (i.e., the probability of using leave in the future) but employers do not. If the firm understands the fraction of Type A and B workers in the labor force and the probability that each type will use leave (strong assumptions already), they could calculate that the expected cost of providing paid leave rights to the average worker would be $100 ([0.5 × 0.3 × $500] + [0.5 × 0.1 × $500]).[8] However, consider what would happen if they made this offer to their (current or potential) employees. Type A individuals would view this offer as an excellent deal, because they would have been willing to accept up to a $225 wage decrease to obtain leave benefits, and so they will happily work for the firm. However, Type B persons would not find the offer attractive, because the maximum amount they would have been willing to pay for the leave rights was $75.[9] Therefore, these persons will choose a wage package that does not provide for paid leave, even though it would be economically efficient for them to have it.

This is not the end of the story. Now that Type B workers have opted out of leave benefits—probably by choosing to work for a different employer, because most firms provide relatively uniform fringe benefits to similar employees—all of the workers taking jobs offering leave will be "high-risk" Type A individuals. If the firm continued to provide the leave benefit in exchange for a $100 wage reduction, they would now lose money, because the expected costs for Type A workers, the only employees now in these jobs, would be $150. Recognizing this change in the pool of employees, the employer would reduce wages by at least this amount, and only type A workers would receive leave benefits (for a comprehensive discussion of many of these issues, see Summers, 1989).

These concerns are not hypothetical. Only a small fraction of workers have access to paid family leave in the United States. To show this, Table 4.1 summarizes data from the National Compensation Survey, which provides information on the frequency with which establishments provide various employment benefits, including paid and unpaid family leave (i.e., time off for childbirth as well as for personal or family health problems). The figures in the table overstate the fraction of employees with leave rights, because employers can make these available to some but not all employees (e.g., by imposing job tenure or work hour requirements).

---

[8] *This is simply a weighted average of the cost of providing leave to the two groups of workers, where the weights are the shares in each group. Having more than two groups would complicate the mathematical calculation but not change the overall conclusion.*

[9] *Actually, they might be willing to pay a bit more for the benefit because it provides a form of insurance against a somewhat unknown probability of having a child. However, accounting for this does not change the basic market failure created by asymmetric information.*

Table 4.1: Private Sector Workers in Establishments Providing Family Leave, 2010 (%)

	Paid Leave	*Unpaid Leave*
All Private Sector Workers	10	85
Occupation		
Management/Professional	17	90
Service	6	79
Sales/Office	11	86
Construction/Natural Resources	7	77
Production/Transportation	5	85
Full-Time	12	88
Part-Time	5	76
Wage Percentile Within Broad Industry		
Lowest 10%	3	72
Highest 10%	18	91
Industry		
Goods Producing	8	86
Services Providing	11	84
Establishment Size (No. of Workers)		
1–49	7	77
50–99	9	89
100–499	10	92
500 or more	17	96

Note. From U.S. Department of Labor, Bureau of Labor Statistics (2010). Data refer to private sector nonagricultural workers in March 2010 and exclude those working in private households or who are self-employed. Percentages refer to establishments offering leave benefits to some (but not necessarily all) workers. Some establishments provide both paid and unpaid leave, so that the sum of these two categories can exceed 100%.

Unpaid family leave is offered fairly frequently, in part because it is often required under the FMLA, but paid family leave is not. As Table 4.1 indicates, just 10% of nonagricultural private sector employees were in establishments providing any formal paid family leave, while 85% offered unpaid leave to at least some workers.[10] The table further shows that leave is relatively frequently supplied to highly paid persons and those who are in professional or managerial jobs, working full-time, or in large firms. However, even in these cases, less than one fifth of employees work for establishments offering formal paid family leave.

Such low rates of paid leave provision could be explained in two ways. First, for the sake of argument, it is possible that workers may simply not be interested in paid leave—perhaps

---

[10] *These statistics refer to specific rights to family leave. Some employees will also use accrued vacation or sick leave to cover a period off work with young children. Paid or unpaid leave may also sometimes be offered on an informal basis. These statistics exclude private household workers and the self-employed.*

because they do not want their pay to be reduced by the expected cost (to employers) of the leaves. In that case, private markets would be providing efficiently low levels of leave. Second, and what we think more likely, is that workers would prefer the option for leave in at least some situations, but private employers do not provide desired amounts because of the problem of adverse selection under asymmetric information.

Public Policy Options for Promoting Rights to Paid Parental Leave

■ Mandating employers to provide paid leave versus publicly supported leave.

Given a situation in which rights to paid leave benefits are economically efficient and desired by employees but are not being provided in privately operating labor markets, how can parental leave be made universally available? One possibility is to impose an "employer mandate"—that is, a requirement for firms to offer and pay for specified amounts of leave. Such mandates have some attractive characteristics, the most obvious being that the costs are not directly borne by the government (and taxpayers indirectly). On the other hand, mandates are likely to face particularly fierce political opposition by employers. In addition, they may lead to large wage reductions among groups likely to use the benefits (e.g., 20- to 40-year-old women), which may be viewed as inequitable. Also, if there are institutional barriers to such group-specific wage reductions, the employment of these workers may fall.[11] This last point is especially salient because mandates may provide employers with strong incentives to avoid hiring groups of workers with high use of parental leave, particularly if they are unable to pass along the costs by reducing wages.

The other alternative, the one we favor, is to require employers to allow their workers to take leave during the period surrounding childbirth but with wage replacement coming directly from the government rather than companies. We refer to this as "public provision," while recognizing that employers (along with employees) may still bear some portion of the associated costs (e.g., the expense of covering staffing requirements during the leave period and possibly of continuing health insurance payments). In the extreme (and unrealistic) case where paid leave is completely costless to firms, issues related to asymmetric information or incentives to avoid employing high-use groups are completely circumvented. However, the leave rights must be paid for somehow, and the method of doing so may introduce other distortions. For instance, paid leaves are often financed through payroll taxes levied exclusively on employees

---

[11] *Gruber (1994) provided a careful and comprehensive analysis of this issue in the context of mandated health insurance coverage for maternity-related expenses; see Ruhm (1998) for discussion specific to parental leave benefits.*

(e.g., this is done for California's paid leave program). Such taxes decrease the net (after-tax) wage, which may reduce the incentive to work. However, such employment disincentives are likely to be fairly small because the total cost of leave benefits would not be that great and these expenses would be spread over the entire workforce.[12] On the other hand, if the payroll tax is paid only up to an income ceiling threshold, as currently occurs for Social Security but not Medicare, the tax may be extremely regressive—constituting a larger share of the income of low than high earners.

Probably the fewest distortions would be imposed by paying for parental leave benefits out of general tax revenues. This has several advantages. First, it is the broadest based source of funding and provides the fewest incentives to discriminate against high-use groups. Second, financing comes from unearned as well as earned sources of income, implying that work disincentives are minimized. Finally, this explicitly recognizes the idea that parental leave benefits represent a social investment in children and families, and a responsibility that should be widely shared. However, despite all of these advantages, public financing out of general revenues would likely face particularly strong political opposition, particularly in an era of large budget deficits and a general lack of support for federally funded social programs.

Additional Considerations

▓ How long a leave is feasible?

Even an agreement that paid parental leave should be provided, and that the costs for financing it should be shared by the public, would leave open the question of the desired leave duration. Leaves that are very short are likely to provide insufficient time off work to increase job continuity because many mothers will quit their jobs so as to be able to spend a longer period of time at home with their children. On the other hand, extremely lengthy leaves may have their own problems, in particular the depreciation of human capital occurring during the period away from the job. Consider the case of "Tina," who previously worked programming software for Internet-related applications and who receives a year of paid leave following the birth of her new child (an unheard of amount of time off work in the United States but common in some European countries). The industry may be changing so rapidly that when she is ready to return to work, her skills have become obsolete, possibly making it difficult or impossible for her to assume the same responsibilities she had prior to taking leave.[13] The loss

---

[12] *The situation is more complicated if employers and employees each pay a share of payroll taxes (as they do for Social Security and Medicare). In general, the employer share of the tax will be passed through to employees, in the form of lower wages, but again this burden is spread across all workers and so will not adversely affect groups most likely to use the leave. However, there may also be employment reductions for groups (e.g., minimum wage workers) for whom wage rates cannot fall.*

[13] *Even when leaves are "job-protected," workers will frequently not return to their old position but rather to one that is technically defined as being "equivalent."*

of human capital may be even more severe if she has a second child a short while later and again takes leave, or if she does not return to work during the period between the two births. It is also likely to be particularly costly for employers to accommodate such lengthy leaves, and even more so if there is uncertainty about the likelihood that the mother will eventually wish to return to the old job. One response of employers may be to limit "high-risk" groups to jobs where such flexibility is less costly, probably resulting in occupational segregation.

■ What about fathers?

Up to this point, we have referred only to mothers. What about fathers? One obvious option is to make the leave rights available to either parent, except possibly for that portion providing medical benefits to mothers in dealing with the rigors of childbirth. In practice, however, leave that is available to both parents is used almost exclusively by mothers (Organization for Economic Cooperation and Development, 2010). Conventionally, economists would favor letting families make whatever voluntary arrangements they desire, and so economists would support having most or all leave taken by women, if that is freely chosen by families. On the other hand, if norms regarding who invests time with children are socially determined (at least in part), it may be viewed as desirable to "lean against the wind" by providing explicit encouragement for fathers to use at least some of the leave. The case for doing so may be further strengthened if these choices are influenced by employer-imposed constraints or expectations. For instance, if employers tend to restrict women of childbearing age to positions where leave-taking is less costly, families who would otherwise choose to have mothers and fathers use leave more equally might find it in their interest to have women take most of the time off work, because the mother's position will usually pay less. Reserving a portion of the leave for fathers may partially offset these employer expectations and may provide a countervailing force to counterbalance other factors leading to gender-based norms in the work–family arena.

■ Why can't families finance the leave themselves?

If parental leave is so important for children, one might ask why families cannot finance the time off for care of newborn or newly adopted infants themselves. As Lester (2005, p. 15) phrased the question in an extensive article on paid family leave policy, why can't workers "simply borrow money or save for predictable interruptions in wage income due to the birth of a child?" The short answer, as we discussed in chapter 2, is that many workers with higher incomes do take unpaid family leave following the birth or adoption of a child, presumably supported by spousal income or joint savings. However, for many other families, obstacles include the timing of the birth or adoption of children, which in most families takes place in the parents' early career years, when salaries are relatively low and opportunities to set aside earnings for savings are more limited. Were parents able to postpone childbearing until they were 50, they might be in a better financial position to take leave—although too tired to manage the follow-up child rearing. As for borrowing, Lester stated wryly, the option of securing loans against future earnings is not widely available in private markets.

■ Should parental leave be mandatory?

One might also ask why we advocate rights to paid time off from work rather than requiring such work absences. This issue is not hypothetical. As we discuss in chapter 5, maternity leave was compulsory in the initial implementation of many European leave programs, justified on the basis of protecting the health of mothers, and in some countries a portion of the time off work remains compulsory. However, there are at least four reasons why we oppose mandatory leave. First, we have a philosophical preference for voluntary arrangements whenever these are possible and believe that compulsory leaves require a higher burden of proof on the evidence of benefits than currently exists. Second, arrangements within households are diverse, creating problems with applying a single solution to all situations. For instance, some households may be able to coordinate work arrangements between husbands and wives so as to have one or both parents with the infant at all or most times, even without the use of parental leave. Third, it is not obvious to what extent leaves that are obligatory, rather than being voluntarily taken, increase time investments in children or yield the other gains discussed in this and earlier chapters. Finally, as a practical matter, enforced leaves seem more likely to be required of mothers than fathers, quite possibly resulting in a more gendered set of workforce arrangements than currently exists. We view this to be undesirable.

Summary

In this chapter, we have presented an economic case for paid parental leave for care of newborn or newly adopted infants. Although there is evidence that paid parental leave for a few months of infant care would benefit children, women, families, and ultimately the public at large, it is unlikely to occur through private market negotiations alone. Employers who offer paid leave benefits voluntarily may attract a disproportionate number of employees likely to take paid leave. Moreover, many of the benefits of paid parental leave would be indirect or extend beyond the immediate workforce. Hence, from the standpoint of economics, some type of public policy is needed to make paid parental leave more available. Subsequent chapters explore the impact of leave policies in other nations and in the one state, California, that has offered paid family leave for some time. In the final chapter, we offer our own recommendations for parental leave policy.

References

Akerlof, G. A. (1970). The market for lemons: Quality uncertainty and the market mechanism. *Quarterly Journal of Economics, 84*, 488–500.

Almond, D. (2006). Is the 1918 influenza pandemic over? Long-term effects of in utero influenza exposure in the post-1940 U.S. population. *Journal of Political Economy, 114*, 672–712.

Baker, M., & Milligan, K. (2008). Maternal employment, breastfeeding, and health: Evidence from maternity leave mandates. *Journal of Health Economics, 27*, 871–887.

Barker, D. J., Winter, P. D., Osmond, C., Margetts, B., & Simmonds, S. J. (1989). Weight in infancy and disease from ischemic heart disease. *The Lancet, 334*, 577–580.

Becker, G. S. (1965). A theory of the allocation of time. *The Economic Journal, 75*, 493–517.

Berger, L., Hill, J., & Waldfogel, J. (2005). Maternity leave, early maternal employment and child health and development in the US. *The Economic Journal, 115*, F29–F47.

Bernal, R., & Keane, M. P. (2010). Quasi-structural estimation of a model of childcare choices and child cognitive ability production. *Journal of Econometrics, 156*, 164–189.

Blau, F. D. (1998). Trends in the well-being of American women, 1970–1995. *Journal of Economic Literature, 36*, 112–165.

Brooks-Gunn, J., Han, W. J., & Waldfogel, J. (2010). First-year maternal employment and child development in the first 7 years. *Monographs of the Society for Research in Child Development, 75*(2, Serial No. 296).

Chatterji, P., & Markowitz, S. (2005). Does the length of maternity leave affect maternal health? *Southern Economic Journal, 72*, 16–41.

Cunha, F., & Heckman, J. (2007). The technology of skill formation. *American Economic Review, 97*(2), 31–47.

Crittenden, A. (2001). *The price of motherhood: Why the most important job in the world is still the least valued.* New York: Henry Holt.

Gartner, L. M., Morton, J., Lawrence, R. A., Naylor, A. J., O'Hare, D., Schanler, R. J., & Eidelman, A. I. (2005). Breastfeeding and the use of human milk, *Pediatrics, 115*, 496–506.

Greenhouse, S. (2011, January 8). The retention bonus? Time. In accounting, firms find flexible hours pay dividends. *The New York Times*, p. B1.

Gruber, J. (1994). The incidence of mandated maternity benefits. *American Economic Review, 84*, 622–641.

Han, W. J., Ruhm, C., & Waldfogel, J. (2009). Parental leave policies and parents' employment and leave-taking. *Journal of Policy Analysis and Management, 28*(1), 29–54.

Hart, B., & Risley, T. (1995). *Meaningful differences in the everyday parenting and intellectual development of young American children.* Baltimore: Brookes.

Heckman, J. J. (2000). Policies to foster human capital. *Research in Economics, 54*(1), 3–56.

Heckman, J. J. (2008). Schools, skills, and synapses. *Economic Inquiry, 46*(3), 289–324.

Hill, J., Waldfogel, J., Brooks-Gunn, J., & Han, W. J. (2005). Towards a better estimate of causal links in child policy: The case of maternal employment and child outcomes. *Developmental Psychology, 41*, 833–850.

Infoplease. (n.d.). *Women by the numbers.* Retrieved May 24, 2011, from www.infoplease.com/spot/womencensus1.html

Information asymmetry. (n.d.). Retrieved November 9, 2010, from Wikipedia Web site: http://en.wikipedia.org/wiki/Asymmetric_information

Johnson, T. D. (2008). *Maternity leave and employment patterns of first-time mothers: 1961-2003* (Current Population Reports, P70–113). Washington, DC: U.S. Census Bureau.

Jovanovic, B. (1979). Job matching and the theory of turnover. *Journal of Political Economy, 87*, 972–990.

Laffont, J. J. (2008). Externalities. In S. N. Durlauf & L. E. Blume (Eds.), *The New Palgrave dictionary of economics online.* Retrieved December 11, 2011, from www.dictionaryofeconomics.com/article?id=pde2008_E000200

Lester, G. (2005). A defense of paid family leave. *Harvard Journal of Law & Gender, 28*, 1–83.

National Institute of Child Health and Human Development Early Child Care Research Network. (2000). Characteristics and quality of child care for toddlers and preschoolers. *Applied Developmental Science, 4*, 116–135.

National Research Council & Institute of Medicine. (2000). *From neurons to neighborhoods: The science of early childhood development.* J. P. Shonkoff & D. A. Phillips, (Eds), Board on Children, Youth, and Families; Commission on Behavioral and Social Sciences and Education. Washington, DC: National Academy Press.

Oi, W. Y. (1962). Labor as a quasi-fixed factor. *Journal of Political Economy, 70*, 538–555.

Organization for Economic Cooperation and Development. (2010). *OECD family database: Use of childbirth-related leave by mothers and fathers.* Retrieved July 25, 2011, from www.oecd.org/els/social/family/database

Rothschild, M., & Stiglitz, J. E. (1976). Equilibrium in competitive insurance markets. *Quarterly Journal of Economics, 90*, 629–649.

Ruhm, C. J. (1998). The economic consequences of parental leave mandates: Lessons from Europe. *Quarterly Journal of Economics, 113*, 285–317.

Ruhm, C. J. (2000). Parental leave and child health. *Journal of Health Economics, 19*, 931–960.

Ruhm, C. J. (2004). Parental employment and child cognitive development. *The Journal of Human Resources, 39*, 155–192.

Schore, A. (2001). Effects of a secure attachment relationship on right brain development, affect regulation, and infant mental health. *Infant Mental Health Journal, 22*, 7–66.

Schore, A. (2005). Attachment, affect regulation, and the developing right brain: Linking developmental neuroscience to pediatrics. *Pediatrics in Review, 26*(6), 204–217.

Skyt Nielsen, H., Simonsen, M., & Verner, M. (2004). Does the gap in family-friendly policies drive the family gap? *Scandinavian Journal of Economics, 106,* 721–724.

Spence, A. M. (1973). Job market signaling. *Quarterly Journal of Economics, 87,* 355–374.

Spence, S., Shapiro, D., & Zaidel, E. (1996). The role of the right hemisphere in the physiological and cognitive development of emotional processing. *Psychophysiology, 33,* 112–122.

Summers, L. H. (1989). Some simple economics of mandated benefits. *American Economic Review, 79,* 177–183.

Tanaka, S. (2005). Parental leave and child health across OECD countries. *The Economic Journal, 115,* F7–F28.

Thompson, R. (2007). Testimony on *Improving Head Start for America's children: Hearing before House Committee on Education and Labor, Subcommittee on Early Childhood, Elementary, and Secondary Education,* 110th Cong. (February 28, 2007), First Session, Serial No. 110-6. Retrieved December 28, 2011, from www.eric.ed.gov/PDFS/ED499026.pdf, pp. 5–12.

U.S. Department of Labor, Bureau of Labor Statistics. (2010). *National Compensation Survey: Employee benefits in the United States, March 2010.* Washington, DC: Author.

van den Berg, G. J., Lindeboom, M., & Portrait, F. (2006). Economic conditions early in life and individual mortality. *American Economic Review, 96,* 290–302.

Waldfogel, J. (1998a). The "family gap" for young women in the United States and Britain: Can maternity leave make a difference? *Journal of Labor Economics, 16,* 505–545.

Waldfogel, J. (1998b). Understanding the 'family gap' in pay for women with children. *Journal of Economic Perspectives, 12,* 137–156.

Zigler, E., Finn-Stevenson, M., & Hall, N. W. (2002). *The first three years and beyond: Brain development and social policy.* New Haven, CT: Yale University Press.

Zigler, E., Marsland, K., & Lord, H. (2009). *The tragedy of child care in America.* New Haven, CT: Yale University Press.

CHAPTER

Parental Leave Policies in Europe and Canada

The United States is quite unusual in providing such limited support for mothers and fathers with young children. As discussed in chapter 1, under the Family and Medical Leave Act (FMLA), some (but not all) parents are entitled to 12 weeks of unpaid leave following the birth of a child or for a variety of other reasons. Some states supplement the FMLA with more generous unpaid leave, or in a few cases, paid time off work, and many employers also offer some type of parental leave benefits. Nevertheless, most new parents have no rights to paid leave (other than by using sick leave or accrued vacation), and a large minority do not have legislated rights even to unpaid time off the job.

The lack of paid leave following childbirth or adoption in the United States contrasts sharply with the patterns in most other countries. The first maternity leave entitlements were provided more than a century ago, and these are currently offered in as many as 173 nations (Heymann, Earle, & Hayes, 2007). During the last 3 decades, maternity leave rights—which cover the period immediately before and after childbirth—have increasingly been supplemented with entitlements to brief paternity leaves for fathers, usually beginning immediately after childbirth and lasting for a relatively short amount of time. In addition to maternity and paternity leave, in many nations, relatively lengthy periods of parental or child care leaves are available to mothers, fathers, or both. In this chapter, we use the general term *parental leave* to refer to all of these entitlements but also sometimes to distinguish between them. Parental leave is also tightly integrated with the social insurance systems of many countries with regard to family and individual income maintenance, the provision of child care for toddlers, and insurance against sickness and medical care.

Understanding the ways in which other countries support families is useful not because the policies will necessarily transfer directly to the United States—with its different and sometimes unique traditions—but rather because knowing provides some sense of the solutions that have been implemented and seem to work well in many of these nations. For example, providing rights to a year or more off work following the birth of a child, with a substantial degree of wage replacement, might seem extreme and unworkable in the United States because such a policy would represent such a large departure from our current system. Yet, such an arrangement would not be at all unusual in most industrialized countries and, indeed, would be viewed as quite limited in many. Conversely, mandating that mothers have the right to take 3 months off from work, with job protection and at least partial wage replacement, is likely to be viewed as a substantial policy change by many in the United States, even though this would be considered to be extremely restrictive throughout most of Europe. Even Canada, our neighbor to the north who shares many of our cultural and economic traditions, supplies rights to leave that considerably surpass those existing or proposed for the United States—and that are far beyond those that we suggest in chapter 7.

We begin with a brief review of the history of parental leave policies, and then we describe the current parental leave policies in Western Europe and Canada, as well as a policy recently enacted in Australia.[1] We compare provisions in terms of eligibility, duration, and overall generosity of leave benefits. We also assess the relative costs of the various parental leave benefits and the impact on employers and the overall economy. Finally, we review what is known about the consequences of the parental leave policies in Europe and Canada: Do these policies help parents balance their work and family responsibilities, how have they affected women's position in the labor market, and do they enhance maternal and child health and development?

A Brief History of Parental Leave Policies in Western Europe

■ The initial policy impetus was protectionist.

Europe has a long tradition of providing rights to maternity leave. Germany adopted the first such law in 1883, as part of Bismarck's social insurance system, followed by Sweden in 1891 and then France in 1928 (Ruhm & Teague, 1997). These entitlements were linked to sick leaves and initially ranged between 4- and 12-week durations with limited lump sum or flat rate payment benefits (Kamerman, 2006). In 1919, the International Labor Organization (ILO) adopted its first convention related to maternity protection; it provided that a woman working

---

[1] *This chapter focuses on Western European nations because they have the longest tradition of providing maternity or parental leave. In addition, along with Canada and Australia, their institutions and economies are relatively more similar to the United States than those of other countries. For a discussion of leave policies in developing nations, see Pizzo (1988).*

in industry or commerce "shall not be permitted to work during the six weeks following her confinement; shall have the right to leave her work if she produces a medical certificate stating that her confinement will probably take place within six weeks; shall ... be paid benefits sufficient for the full and healthy maintenance of herself and her child" (ILO, 1919). By World War I, 13 countries provided paid maternity leave, with eight more offering unpaid leave; all major Western European countries supplied rights to paid leave by the beginning of World War II (Kamerman, 2006).

The terminology of ILO conventions related to maternity "protection" is not coincidental. The early policies were paternalistic in their concern for health of the child and mother. Some or all of the leave period was typically compulsory, job protection was infrequently provided, and many of the leave policies had a pronatalist and nationalistic orientation (Frank & Lipner, 1988).

The situation began to change after the end of the second World War, as reflected in the 1952 revision of the ILO Maternity Protection Convention, which widened the groups of women covered to include those in nonindustrial and agricultural occupations, extended the period of maternity leave to 12 weeks (with at least 6 weeks after birth remaining compulsory), and with cash payments of not less than two thirds of previous earnings provided from social insurance or other public funds and not from the employer (ILO, 1952).

Policies evolved to include job reinstatement and paternity leave.

The 1960s ushered in a period of rapid change—parental leave policies evolved from prohibitions on employing women before and after birth to periods of time away from work, with job protection, to care for infants and toddlers (Ruhm & Teague, 1997). During this period, many nations previously mandating compulsory leave added provisions ensuring job reinstatement when the leave ended. Other countries provided entitlements to job-protected leave for the first time, and durations of the leave period began to be extended by the implementation of parental leave provisions that were, at least in principle, available to mothers or fathers and occurred after the end of the maternity leave period (Brocas, Cailloux, & Oget, 1990; Kamerman, 2006).

These changes are reflected in a European Union Council Directive from 1996 (Directive 96/34/EC) that required all European Union members except for Great Britain to provide a minimum of 3 months of parental leave to mothers and fathers, with the right to return to the same job or, if that is not possible, an equivalent or similar job. The amount of payment during the leave period is not specified, but the directive states that the previous work requirement to qualify for the leave shall not exceed 1 year, and the leave provisions are individual rights, meaning that fathers, as well as mothers, have entitlements to time off from work.

This last provision reflected the increasing concern in many European countries that parental leave policies be designed in ways that are gender-neutral and that encourage fathers to take leave and be involved in raising children.[2] Such concerns reflected the reality that although many European countries had implemented extended periods of parental leave by the 1990s, in most countries take-up was almost exclusively restricted to women, raising the possibility that the policies might have the effect of reducing, rather than increasing, gender equity in the allocation of work and family responsibilities. For example, Bruning and Plantenga (1999) cited evidence that less than 1% of Austrian fathers and between 1% and 2% of German fathers used parental leave during the mid-1990s, compared to 96% of corresponding mothers. Even in Finland, Norway, and Sweden, where a majority of men take some parental leave, the vast majority of total time off work is taken by women (see also Organization for Economic Cooperation and Development, 2008, for more recent evidence).

Current Parental Leave Policies in Western Europe and Canada

◼ Paid maternity leave is a given.

The range and structure of current European parental leave policies exhibit substantial variation but also some common elements.[3] Table 5.1 (see p. 106) summarizes important elements of these systems, across countries, by providing separate information for mothers and fathers on leave durations and sources and amounts of payment during the period off from work. Several points need to be kept in mind when interpreting the information in the table. First, all European nations—indeed all industrialized countries other than the United States— provide mothers with paid maternity leave during the period surrounding childbirth. Typically, the period is between 14 and 20 weeks, with between 70% and 100% of previous wages paid during the leave period (a few countries, such as Austria, Iceland, Norway, and Sweden, do not have separate maternity leave but rather subsume it into their system of parental leave). The option for time off work usually begins a few weeks before birth and continues after it. A portion of this maternity leave is compulsory in some countries, reflecting the initial protective motivations of many of the policies.

Most countries also provide for corresponding paid paternity leave, but generally for a considerably shorter amount of time. Beyond maternity and paternity leave, most nations

---

[2] *However, some policy changes also continue to be motivated by other considerations. For instance, the 2007 replacement in Germany of a means-tested parental leave benefit with one that depended on previous wages was implemented in the hope that it would simultaneously increase female labor force participation and fertility rates, particularly for high-income families (Spiess & Wrohlich, 2008).*

[3] *Although Western European nations have the longest traditions of providing maternity or parental leave, some innovations developed elsewhere, such as paid child-rearing leaves in Central and Eastern Europe.*

provide for an often lengthy amount of parental leave, either as a family benefit—which can be used by either mothers or fathers—or as an individual benefit—which is allocated separately to mothers or fathers and cannot be transferred between them without special circumstances. Because transferable parental leave benefits are almost always used by women, the column in the table showing the "maximum amount" of leave available to mothers includes the entire duration of parental leave that is available to them. Conversely, the "total leave" available to fathers is limited to periods of paternity and parental leave that are restricted to men. The leave durations listed refer to those available to eligible persons and do not reflect the additional entitlements sometimes obtained by special classes of individuals (e.g., government workers) or extra rights obtained under collective agreements. The entitlements also refer to "normal" births. Many countries allow additional time off work for multiple births, medical complications, or other situations (such as for second or later children).

The second point to keep in mind when reading the table is that the payment amounts often are subject to a variety of restrictions or qualifications. For example, benefits during the maternity and paternity leave periods, and for some portion of parental leave, are often specified as a percentage of previous earnings, but these may be subject to ceiling amounts or minimum payment levels, and with less generous coverage for groups such as self-employed workers. Some countries allow individuals to choose a more limited period of leave at a high replacement rate or a longer duration at lower pay. Some portion of the leave is also often paid at a flat rate, which again varies across countries but generally corresponds to a relatively low replacement rate.

Countries offering particularly long periods of time off from work often do not provide explicit payment for some portion of the time taken, although the integration of parental leave with the broader social insurance system implies that child-based family allowances are sometimes available (independent of previous employment status of qualification for parental leave). When the leave is unpaid, its most important component is job protection (although credit for time in the social insurance system may be included). The job protection can refer to the right to return to the specific job previously held or to a generally similar position, with the precise terms sometimes depending on the length of leave taken.

Third, it is noteworthy that the vast majority of leave payments are financed by a combination of payroll taxes (on employers and employees) and general government revenues, rather than being directly paid by employers. This approach is consistent with ILO and European Union standards and is motivated by the desire to spread the costs widely so as not to burden specific employers as well as to reduce the likelihood that companies will discriminate against workers most likely to use the leave.

Table 5.1: Parental Leave Provisions in Europe and Canada, 2008

Country	Source of Payment	Leave Available to Mothers*			Leave Exclusive to Fathers			Comments
		Maximum Amount	Paid Leave	Payment Amount	Total Leave	Paid Leave	Payment Amount	
Austria	Payroll taxes, government	2 years	2 years	16 weeks (100%), flat rate	None	None	None	Higher flat rate for shorter parental leave periods
Belgium	Payroll taxes	28 weeks (9 weeks required)	28 weeks	4 weeks (82%), 11 weeks (75%), flat rate	13 weeks (3 days required)	13 weeks	100% (3 days), 82% (7 days), flat rate	3 months of leave can be doubled for part-time work
Canada	Payroll taxes	52 weeks (8 weeks required)	50 weeks	55%	None	None	None	2-week waiting period prior to leave payments; more generous leave in Quebec
Denmark	Government	50 weeks (2 weeks required)	48 weeks	50%–90% (22 weeks), 30%–54% (32 weeks)	2 weeks	2 weeks	50%–90%	Higher payment rates for manual than nonmanual workers; employers pay first 2 weeks of maternity leave
Finland	Payroll taxes, government	37 months (4 weeks required)	37 months	90% (9 weeks), 75% (5 weeks), 70% (29 weeks), flat rate	4 weeks	4 weeks	70%	Includes 2 "bonus" weeks of leave to fathers taking final 2 weeks of parental leave
France	Payroll taxes, government	37 months (2 weeks required)	42 weeks	100% (16 weeks), flat rate	14 days	14 days	100%	For more than 1 child, longer period of full paid leave, and flat rate continues until child's 3rd birthday
Germany	Payroll taxes, government	37.5 months (8 weeks required)	15.5 months	100% (14 weeks), 67% (12 months)	2 months	2 months	67%	Paid leave can be spread over 24 months part-time work
Greece	Payroll taxes, government	50 weeks (17 weeks required)	43 weeks	100% (33 weeks), flat rate	28 weeks	2 days	100%	Longer leave entitlements for public sector employees
Iceland	Payroll taxes, government	6 months (2 weeks required)	6 months	80%	3 months	3 months	80%	Flexibility in timing of leave, through 18 months after birth

Table 5.1: Parental Leave Provisions in Europe and Canada, 2008 (continued)

Country	Source of Payment	Leave Available to Mothers*			Leave Exclusive to Fathers			Comments
		Maximum Amount	Paid Leave	Payment Amount	Total Leave	Paid Leave	Payment Amount	
Ireland	Payroll taxes, government	56 weeks	6 months	80%	14 weeks	None	None	
Italy	Payroll taxes, government	46 weeks (20 weeks required)	46 weeks	80% (20 weeks), 30% (26 weeks)	5 months	None	None	Leave can be taken until child's 8th birthday but no payment after age 3
Netherlands	Private insurance, payroll taxes	42 weeks (4 weeks required)	42 weeks	100% (16 weeks), flat rate	26 weeks	26 weeks	100% (2 days), flat rate	
Norway	Payroll taxes, government	90 weeks (3 weeks required)	48 weeks	100%	60 weeks	6 weeks	100%	Flat rate available during period without payment if children not in publicly funded child care
Portugal	Payroll taxes	31 months	7 months	100% (4 months), 33%	4.7 months (4 weeks required)	4.7 months	100% (1.67 months), 33%	Portion of leave can be used until child's 6th birthday
Spain	Payroll taxes, government	3 years (6 weeks required)	16 weeks	100%	3 years	15 days	100%	Specific (general) job protection for 1 year (3 years); employers pay first 2 days of paternity leave
Sweden	Payroll taxes	21.5 months (2 weeks required)	21.5 months	78% (20 months), flat rate	18 months	14 weeks	78% (2 weeks), flat rate	Great flexibility in use of leave, through child's 8th birthday
Switzerland	Payroll taxes	14 weeks (8 weeks required)	14 weeks	80%	None	None	None	More generous leave in Bern
United Kingdom	Payroll taxes, government	65 weeks (2 weeks required)	39 weeks	90% (6 weeks), flat rate	15 weeks	2 weeks	Flat rate	Unpaid parental leave limited to 4 weeks per year

*Leaves to mothers include time that can be taken by either parent. Leave to fathers is limited to periods exclusively available to fathers. Payment amounts are often subject to ceilings and often come with lower benefits for self-employed persons. Flat rate amounts last for remaining period of paid leave. Social security system credit often continues during periods of unpaid leave. Leave durations can sometimes be extended by lowering payment rates for complicated or multiple births or child illnesses. Many countries also provide child-based "family allowances" independent of leaves or employment. From Moss (2009), Ray (2008), and Social Security Administration (2008a, 2008b).

■ Parental leave policies vary more widely.

Although paid maternity leave policies in Europe have many common elements, there are much larger disparities in the period following the end of maternity leave. Three years or more of job-protected time off work are provided in Finland, France, Germany, and Spain, while mothers in Austria, Norway, and Sweden are entitled to be home for between 1.5 and 2 years. However, these total durations can be somewhat misleading because in several of these countries (e.g., Austria, France, and Spain), only a fraction of the leave is accompanied with pay at high replacement rates. Conversely, nations such as Denmark and Italy offer somewhat shorter periods of leave but at relatively high rates of pay, so that their overall provisions may actually be more generous, an issue to which we return later.

Paternity leave is less common and of shorter duration. All but 2 of the 17 European nations detailed in Table 5.1 provide fathers with entitlements to at least some time off work following the birth of a child, but payment at a rate of at least two thirds of previous pay is provided exclusively to fathers for at least 3 weeks in just five countries (Finland, Germany, Iceland, Norway, and Portugal), whereas others offer only a few days of highly paid leave (Greece and the Netherlands) or none at all (Austria, Ireland, and Italy). In many of these nations, longer periods off work, often with pay, are available to fathers if mothers choose not to take leave or to explicitly transfer the entitlement to their husbands. However, as discussed earlier, families rarely exercise this option. Lengthy periods of leave, whether paid or unpaid, occur because some countries provide individual (nontransferable) rights to fathers or some type of "bonus" arrangement to encourage fathers to take time off work. For example, in 2000, Iceland introduced a 3-month period of paid leave available only to men—"the fathers' quota"—designed to increase the take-up of leave among fathers (Pétursdóttir & Einarsdóttir, 2008), and Finland offers 12 "bonus days" to fathers who take the last 2 weeks of parental leave (Salmi, Lammi-Taskula, & Takala, 2008).

Eligibility requirements to qualify for parental leave are generally not harsh. In many countries, all employed parents are eligible for leave with pay, although a service requirement of around 6 months is not uncommon. Some countries also require a slightly longer period of prior work or social insurance contributions to qualify for the full period of paid parental leave. Self-employed persons may also have different qualification conditions or higher social insurance contribution rates, and there are occasionally additional qualification conditions for fathers (e.g., residing with the child's mother).

As a measure of the generosity of a country's leave rights, Moss and Deven (2009) suggested computing the total number of months that mothers and fathers can be on leave (through maternity, paternity, or parental leave) at a wage replacement rate of at least two thirds of previous earnings. This analysis indicated that the most generous leaves are provided by

Germany (15 months) and the five Nordic countries: Sweden (13 months), Norway (13 months), Denmark (12 months), Finland (11 months), and Iceland (9 months). Conversely, the United Kingdom offers less than 2 months of highly paid leave, and seven nations (Austria, Belgium, France, Greece, the Netherlands, Spain, and Italy) provide around 4 months off work at this rate of pay.[4]

Ray, Gornick, and Schmitt (2008) calculated the maximum amount of "full-time equivalent" (FTE) paid leave as the duration of leave multiplied by the average wage replacement.[5] This approach differs from that of Moss and Deven (2009) because leave provided at low rates of pay will add to the FTE measure—for instance, 20 weeks at a 30% replacement rate would be counted as 6 FTE weeks. Despite these differences in measurement, the overall findings are fairly similar. Sweden offers the highest number of FTE weeks (47 weeks), followed by Norway (44 weeks), Germany (42 weeks), Greece (34 weeks), and Finland (33 weeks). The least generous provisions are in Switzerland (11 weeks), the United Kingdom (12 weeks), Austria (16 weeks), the Netherlands (16 weeks), and Belgium (18 weeks).[6]

Although this chapter focuses specifically on parental leave entitlements, because these are most relevant to the discussion of changes proposed for the United States, it is important to note that in many European countries these are integrated with the provision of child care, with different choices being made across nations in this regard. For instance, among the Nordic countries, where these interrelationships have the longest history, Finland has chosen a system that combines long durations of highly paid parental leave with minimal support for publicly financed child care, whereas Denmark combines shorter parental leave with particularly high rates of child care coverage for infants and toddlers (Datta Gupta, Smith, & Verner, 2008).

▪ Leave policy costs are relatively low.

Despite long durations and relatively high wage replacement rates in many European countries, total costs of the parental leave programs are fairly modest. Gornick and Meyers (2003) estimated that in 1998, costs in the most generous Nordic countries ranged from 0.5% to

---

[4] *Three Eastern European countries, which are not discussed in this chapter, also provide particularly generous leaves: Hungary (25 months), Estonia (15 months), and Slovenia (13 months). Switzerland, which is not included in the Moss and Deven (2009) study, supplies less than 4 months of paid leave.*

[5] *These calculations incorporated a number of simplifying assumptions. First, replacement rates for flat rate benefits were estimated as the benefit level divided by the average wage rate. Second, when mothers have the choice between short leaves at high replacement rates or lengthier absences at lower rates, the shorter leaves were used in the calculations. Third, when benefits were offered on a sliding scale, the lowest benefit amount was used.*

[6] *Information for Iceland is not provided. The one disparate finding is for Greece, where Moss and Deven (2009) indicated a relatively short period of leave, and Ray et al. (2008) a fairly long one. The main difference is that Moss and Deven did not appear to include the value of child care leaves that can be taken either in the form of a 2-hour per day paid reduction in the mother's work hours during the child's first 2 years of life, and a 1-hour per day reduction during the 3rd and 4th years, or an equivalent number of hours in a single 4-month block following the end of maternity leave.*

0.7% of gross domestic product (GDP), while the expenses in other European countries varied from as little as 0.07% of GDP to between 0.3% and 0.4% in France and Germany. Despite increases in the generosity of the programs, these figures had changed only slightly by 2002, according to Datta Gupta et al. (2008)—with costs ranging between 0.5% and 0.8% of GDP in the Nordic countries and from 0.1% to 0.2% of GDP in seven other Western European nations (Austria, Germany, Ireland, the Netherlands, Portugal, Switzerland, and the United Kingdom).[7] It seems likely that the expenses of programs on a scale that might be considered for the United States would be at the lower end of these ranges.

■ Leave policies allow some flexibility.

European countries offer flexibility in the use of parental leave (but typically not maternity leave) over a variety of dimensions. For instance, parents in Belgium, Germany, Portugal, and Sweden can choose to use a portion of their leave entitlement at any point until the child reaches a specified age, while those in Austria, Denmark, Germany, and Norway have the option of longer leaves at lower benefit rates versus shorter absences with higher levels of wage replacement (Moss & Deven, 2009). Many nations allow parents to take reduced leave while working part-time (and Portugal provides incentives for them to do so), although the laws generally do not provide a specific right to part-time work (Ray et al., 2008). Finally, some countries (e.g., Portugal and Spain) allow parents to reduce their workday or take specified breaks from work to facilitate breastfeeding, and many countries allow parents with young children to limit work schedule changes or refuse overtime if this conflicts with family responsibilities (Hegewisch & Gornick, 2008).[8]

Leave Policies in Canada and Australia

■ Canada represents a midtier nation in its parental leave benefits.

Parental leave provisions in Canada are of particular interest because the country shares many institutions with the United States and is an important trading partner. Like the United States, Canada operates as a federalist system, and there are substantial differences in laws across provinces, although for parental leave these are generally not large. As recently as 1970, only three provinces offered any job-protected maternity leave. However, entitlements increased relatively rapidly thereafter, with all but two provinces mandating at least 12 weeks of leave

---

[7] *Publicly provided child care was much more expensive: 1.1% to 2.7% of GDP in the Nordic countries in 2002, and 0.2% to 0.9% of GDP in the other European nations examined (Datta Gupta et al., 2008).*

[8] *The United Kingdom also provides employees with children less than 18 years old the right to request flexibility in employment hours or the location of work. Employers are not required to grant this flexibility but are obligated to consider the application and can refuse it only if there is a clear business reason for doing so (ACAS, 2011).*

in 1977 and all provinces providing entitlements to 15 or more weeks off work in 1981, at least 17 weeks in 1990, and 52 weeks in 2001 (Baker & Milligan, 2008a). By 2008, Canadian parents were entitled to between 52 and 54 weeks of leave in all provinces except Quebec, where the duration is 70 weeks. The leave is paid at a rate of 55% of average insured earnings, up to a ceiling, with a higher replacement rate in Quebec. There is no explicit right to paternity leave (except in Quebec), although parental leave (after the end of the 15 to 18 weeks of maternity leave) can be taken by either mothers or fathers.

Canada is somewhat unusual in that the leave system is administered at the provincial (rather than national) level, and leave payments are administered through the Employment Insurance system, financed by employee and employer premiums (Ray, 2008). To qualify for the leave, individuals must have worked at least 600 hours in the prior 52 weeks and paid Employment Insurance premiums during that time. Following parental leave, the employee must be returned to a position providing equal or greater pay and benefits, and some provinces require parents on leave to receive pay increases they would have obtained had they not been on leave.

Compared to policies in most European nations, Canadian parental leave provisions are less generous, with lower wage replacement rates during the maternity leave period and stricter eligibility criteria. On the other hand, the total duration of paid leave (or FTE weeks of leave), while not equal to paid leaves in Germany or the Nordic countries, considerably exceeds those in nations such as Switzerland, the United Kingdom, Austria, Belgium, and Ireland. Thus, in the European context, Canada can be viewed as a midtier country in terms of its parental leave benefits, while being unusual in administering these through the employment/unemployment rather than sickness benefit/social insurance system.

■ Australia is the newcomer in parental leave policies.

Australia is also instructive because it shares a common language with the United States and was, until recently, the only other industrialized country that did not provide entitlements to paid leave, although the primary caregiver was entitled to 12 months of unpaid leave (and 24 months in some cases, subject to employer agreement). However, effective January 1, 2011, Australia began providing 18 weeks of paid leave to qualifying primary caregivers (usually mothers), with these rights being transferable to other caregivers (usually fathers) if the mother returned to work prior to receiving the full entitlement (Commonwealth of Australia, 2009). Payment is at the federal minimum wage, which corresponds to around half of average full-time female earnings, with eligibility requiring (a) 330 hours of work during a 10-month period ending 3 months before birth and (b) a salary less than a threshold equal to about 2.7 times average full-time female earnings (Alexander, Whitehouse, & Brennan, 2010).

Consequences of Parental Leave Entitlements

Now that we have described the provisions of parental leave policies in Europe, Canada, and Australia, along with the associated expenditures, we need to look at how well these policies work. The primary motivations for providing rights to parental leave are to enable parents to more easily balance the competing demands of work and child rearing, to enhance the labor market position of women, and to improve child health and development. Parental leave has also sometimes been structured in an effort to increase fertility and improve gender equity, by reducing the "family gap" in wages between men and women and by increasing the involvement of fathers in the lives of their young children.

As discussed in chapter 4, one clear benefit of parental leave is that it allows women (and men) time off from work after the birth or adoption of a child, without having to change jobs. By removing the need to search for new employment, the leave policy might be expected to help parents retain skills or knowledge specific to the prebirth employer, thereby potentially contributing to the employee's chances for career advancement and higher earnings. However, in the case of very long leave rights (e.g., a year or more), we might expect these effects to be reversed, because human capital may depreciate during the time away from work, making the individuals less productive in market employment. Extended entitlements might also result in employers being less inclined to employ persons who are likely to take extensive time off from work or to structure employment so as to minimize the costs of these absences (such as by providing less training for employees likely to take extended leaves).

Europe and Canada provide an excellent laboratory for examining the impact of leave policies, and considerable research has recently been conducted on these issues, particularly in the Nordic countries and Germany. The remainder of this chapter summarizes what we have learned from these investigations, with a special focus on analyses occurring during the last decade, because these typically used better data and more sophisticated methods than were employed in earlier studies.

▪ Leave entitlements of short or intermediate duration appear to have positive effects on job continuity and employment.

Although hard to measure precisely, the available evidence has suggested that rights to paid maternity and parental leave are extensively used, with virtually all mothers taking leave in some countries (Moss, 2010). Unpaid leave is less utilized, and fathers use much less leave than mothers, although their leave-taking has increased in countries that provide father-only leave or that increase the total leave period if some is taken by fathers.

Most evidence suggests that leave entitlements, particularly of short or intermediate duration, have positive effects on job continuity and employment. In a study conducted by one of the authors (Ruhm, 1998) of nine European countries between 1969 and 1993, paid leave rights were associated with increased female employment, with fairly comparable effects for brief and lengthy leaves. The latter finding suggests that much of the employment benefit may be due to the increased job continuity permitted by relatively short leaves, relative to no paid leave rights. Baker and Milligan (2008a) supplied direct evidence that leave entitlement enhanced job continuity in Canada, as did Waldfogel (1998) for mothers in Britain. Once again it appears that fairly brief paid leaves (17–18 weeks) are effective in this regard. Conversely, extending existing rights to highly paid leave slows the postbirth reemployment of mothers. Indeed, data from a wide variety of jurisdictions—including Canada, Britain, Germany, and Scandinavia—showed that many women return to jobs precisely at the time paid leave ends (Burgess, Gregg, Propper, & Washbrook, 2008; Dustmann & Schönberg, 2008; Hanratty & Trzcinski, 2009; Rønsen & Sundström, 2002). Because one explicit aim of the policies is to encourage and support parents in spending more time at home with their young children, the leave-induced employment delays should presumably be viewed as a desirable consequence.

A more important question is whether leave entitlements raise or lower maternal employment in the long run. The answer is not obvious because the net effect might depend on the relative strength of offsetting factors such as greater job continuity (which raises employment) versus lost human capital during the leave period (which probably reduces it). The previously mentioned research by Ruhm (1998) provided evidence of favorable employment effects, but the period examined ended in 1993, when durations of European paid leave were typically much below current levels (e.g., mothers in 1993 were entitled to 28, 16, 14, and 48 weeks of paid leave in Denmark, France, Ireland, and Italy, respectively, compared to 48, 42, 26, and 46 weeks in 2008). The same issue applies to Carneiro, Løken, and Salvanes's (2011) finding that the Norwegian extension of paid leave from 12 to 18 weeks in 1977 had no effect on longer-term employment. Conversely, Ondrich, Spiess, Yang, and Wagner's (1999) investigation of five German leave expansions, occurring between 1986 and 1993, indicated small negative employment effects, and Schönberg and Ludstek's (2008) examination of German data for a longer period (1975–1991) revealed no labor supply impact. These studies included quite lengthy leave extensions (up to 3 years, although not all with pay).

■ Lengthy leave entitlements may reduce women's wages and limit their advancement.

Most investigations have found either no effect or small positive consequences of short or moderate durations of leave on female wages. Research by one of the authors (Ruhm, 1998) indicated that earnings are unaffected by brief leaves, but there is a small penalty associated to rights to a lengthier time at home. Similarly, Albrecht, Edin, Sundström, and Vroman (1999) found that female earnings were not affected by the multiple changes in leave entitlements occurring in Sweden between 1966 and 1993, nor did Dustmann and Schönberg (2008) uncover effects for Germany or Lalive and Zweimüller (2009) for Austria. Rasmussen (2010) indicated that the Danish leave expansion from 14 to 20 weeks actually raised mothers' wage incomes for several years, although the increases were not permanent.

On the other hand, there is reason to think that lengthy leave entitlements may reduce the wages of women, at least for a time. Datta Gupta and Smith (2002) found that Danish women taking lengthy leaves received lower earnings because they were not accumulating human capital during the period away from the job; however, the wage penalty disappeared by the time the women were about 45 years old. Nielsen (2009), also using data from Denmark, found negative long-term effects on the careers of women, as measured by wages and promotions. Consistent with this, Puhani and Sonderhof (2008) indicated that the German expansion of parental leave rights from 18 to 36 months in 1992 reduced the training that employers provided women of childbearing age, which seems likely to have restricted their long-run labor market prospects.

A particular concern is that generous leave rights may result in occupational segregation and a "glass ceiling" that limits the advancement of women. There is evidence that such concerns are justified. Albrecht, Björklund, and Vroman (2003) tested for glass ceiling effects by estimating male/female wage differences at various points in the earnings distribution, with the hypothesis that a glass ceiling would be manifested by larger gender differentials higher in the distribution. Their results suggested that there was no glass ceiling in Sweden in 1968 but that one had emerged by the early 1980s and strengthened in the 1990s, corresponding to periods of rapidly expanding parental leave rights.[9] They further indicated that occupational segregation increased during the period the glass ceiling emerged and that the returns on investment in education were higher for men than women, particularly at the top of the distribution. Using similar methods in analyzing data for 11 European countries from 1994 through 2001, Arulampalam, Booth, and Byran (2007) showed that glass ceilings were more severe in countries with high values on the Organization for Economic Cooperation and Development work/family reconciliation index, of which parental leave is an important component (other components include the percentage of young children in formal child care, flexible work policies, and extra-statutory leaves provided by firms).

---

[9] *Sweden provided 16 weeks of paid, job-protected leave in 1969, 52 weeks in 1985, and 64 weeks in 1993 (Ruhm, 1998).*

■ Paid parental leave is associated with child health and developmental benefits.

Proponents of parental leave entitlements believe that, in addition to improving the labor market position of women and their work–family balance, these policies will enhance the health and long-term development of children. These issues are challenging to study, because many potential benefits are difficult to measure and may not be strongly manifested until many years after birth. Also, in the countries where these studies are being conducted, fairly generous parental leave policies have been in place for so long that the questions most salient in the United States, such as the impact of no paid leave versus a 3- to 6-month partially paid leave, can no longer be addressed. Rather, the studies in Europe, and even in Canada, are assessing whether there is an added value to increasing parental leave benefits to a year or more. That said, previous research does provide evidence of health benefits associated with the provision of parental leave, but with less indication of gains in the area of children's educational outcomes.

Ruhm's (2000) study of 16 European nations over the 1969–1994 period demonstrated that paid parental leave entitlements were associated with reductions in infant and young child mortality, with the largest decreases occurring in postneonatal deaths (those occurring between the 2nd and 12th month of life), which is where parental involvement might be anticipated to have the strongest effect. Mortality rates are predicted to be minimized at rights to around 40 weeks of paid leave, with little or no benefit associated with unpaid leave, and smaller gains from either shorter or longer paid leave entitlements. A follow-up study by Tanaka (2005), which expanded the sample to 18 nations and the time period through 2000, found similar results and also indicated that leave rights might reduce low-weight births. This analysis also indicated that for rights to paid leave to have beneficial effects, they must be accompanied by job protection. Finally, Baker and Milligan (2008b) showed that the 2000 extension of Canadian leave rights from roughly 6 months to a year led to longer periods of breastfeeding; they also provided some evidence of reductions in asthma, chronic conditions, allergies, and ear infections at 7 to 12 months old, although they expressed concern about the robustness of these findings. In a follow-up study, Baker and Milligan (2010) showed that the leave expansions increased the time that Canadian parents spent at home by around 3 months and reduced use of nonparental child care. However, they found little evidence of changes in child development at 7 through 12 or 13 to 24 months old. Such results, suggesting that the short-term benefits of parental leave on child development may be limited, should be interpreted with caution when considering changes in U.S. policies, for several reasons. First, their analysis excluded children in single-parent households, where time at home may be of greatest importance. Second, the proposed extensions of U.S. leaves cover a period during the first 6 months of the child's life, when Canadian parents already (even before the 2000 extension) had rights to time off from work. Finally, developmental benefits may manifest at later child ages than were examined in the Canadian study.

Particularly innovative research has been conducted using administrative data from several European countries to examine how leave entitlements are associated with child educational or labor market outcomes much later in life. Carneiro et al. (2011) found that the 1977 expansion of paid parental leave in Norway from 12 to 18 weeks had positive effects on child education (dropout rates, college attendance, and years of education), particularly for girls and children born to less educated parents. On the other hand, Dustmann and Schönberg (2008) generally found no effect on the educational attainment or future wages of German children, with some possibility that extensions of already lengthy entitlements (i.e., 6 months or more) might have negative effects on schooling. Similarly, Rasmussen (2010) failed to uncover an effect on child educational outcomes of the 1984 extension of Danish leave rights from 14 to 20 weeks, while Liu and Nordström Skans (2010) indicated that the 1988 increase in Swedish leave duration from 12 to 15 months did not affect the subsequent average school performance, measured at 16 years old, but with possible gains for the children of highly educated mothers.

▮ Leaves of limited duration are unlikely to affect fertility.

Parental leave entitlements have also sometimes been expanded in an effort to increase fertility (or at least to halt its decline). They may have achieved some success in this regard, particularly in Scandinavian countries, where the combination of substantial female labor force participation and relatively high fertility rates are believed to be related to the constellation of family-friendly policies, of which parental leave is probably the most important (Datta Gupta et al., 2008). For example, Björklund (2006) attributed some of the relatively high fertility rate in Sweden to its generous leave policies (relative to those of other European nations), and Lalive and Zweimüller (2009) found that the 1990 expansion of Austrian leave durations from 12 to 24 months substantially raised future births.

Fertility increases, although attractive in the European context, might be considered undesirable in the United States, with its higher birth rates and relatively rapid population growth. However, it seems unlikely that the relatively modest leave entitlements that we advocate, or that might be realistically considered for this country, would have such effects. Indeed, in both the Swedish and Austrian studies cited above, the increased fertility largely results from a "speed premium" whereby eligibility for leave benefits can be extended (to up to twice its original length) by having an additional child prior to the expiration of the original period of leave. To allow parents the time to plan for and have another child in time to claim the extended benefit, the original period of leave would have to exceed 1 year.[10] Thus, the type

---

[10] It is interesting to note that Lalive and Zweimüller (2009) found that fertility did not decline when Austria subsequently reduced leave entitlements from 24 to 18 months (in 1996), suggesting that the minimal planning period is greater than 12 but less than 18 months.

of limited paid parental leave (e.g., a few months) under consideration in the United States seems unlikely to have much effect on the country's fertility rates.

Conclusion

The United States is unique among industrialized countries in the absence of any entitlement to paid leave, for either mothers or fathers, following the birth of a child. This chapter summarizes the leave rights available in our closest neighboring nation—Canada—and in major Western European nations as well as Australia. These countries currently provide mothers with a minimum of 3 to 4 months of paid leave, with most supplying at least 6 months, and many offering a year or more of paid time off work. These are often supplemented by substantial rights to unpaid leave, and much of the entitlement can be shared by either mothers or fathers. Indeed, one trend in many nations has been to make leave a family right— that can be used interchangeably by either parent—or to mandate a portion of time off from work that can be used only by fathers.

Parents (particularly mothers) generally do take the full period of highly paid leave that is available, indicating that such policies do help to ease issues of work–family balance. Entitlements to short or moderate durations of leave (e.g., 9 months or less) also appear to have largely beneficial effects on the labor market outcomes of women and the health and development of children. For lengthier leaves, the situation becomes more ambiguous, with some research suggesting benefits but also with greater potential costs. For instance, human capital will not be accumulated and may depreciate during lengthy time away from jobs, and employers may reduce the training provided to persons likely to take such extended leaves. Companies may also segregate groups likely to use lengthy entitlements into jobs or occupations where the costs of prolonged job absences are minimized. More generally, leave entitlements exceeding 1 year, particularly if provided with job protection, will place greater burdens on employers, raise costs to the government (assuming that the leaves are publicly financed) and may increase fertility, which might be desirable in Europe but less so in the United States.

References

ACAS. (2011). *The right to apply for flexible working: A short guide for employers, parents and careers.* London: Author. Retrieved from www.acas.org.uk/CHttpHandler.ashx?id=1076&p=0

Albrecht, J., Björklund, A., & Vroman, S. (2003). Is there a glass ceiling in Sweden? *Journal of Labor Economics, 21,* 145–177.

Albrecht, J. W., Edin, P., Sundström, M., & Vroman, S. B. (1999). Career interruptions and subsequent earnings: A reexamination using Swedish data. *The Journal of Human Resources, 34,* 294–311.

Alexander, M., Whitehouse, G., & Brennan, D. (2010). Australia. In P. Moss (Ed.), *International review of leave policies and related research 2010* (Employment Relations Research Series 115, 42–50). London: University of London.

Arulampalam, W., Booth, A. L., & Byran, M. (2007). Is there a glass ceiling over Europe? Exploring the gender pay gap across the wage distribution. *Industrial and Labor Relations Review, 60,* 163–186.

Baker, M., & Milligan, K. (2008a). How does job-protected maternity leave affect mothers' employment? *Journal of Labor Economics, 26,* 655–691.

Baker, M., & Milligan, K. (2008b). Maternal employment, breastfeeding, and health: Evidence from maternity leave mandates. *Journal of Health Economics, 27,* 871–887.

Baker, M., & Milligan, K. (2010). Evidence from maternity leave expansions of the impact of maternal care on early child development. *The Journal of Human Resources, 45,* 1–32.

Björklund, A. (2006). Does family policy affect fertility? *Journal of Population Economics, 19,* 3–24.

Brocas, A., Cailloux, A., & Oget, V. (1990). *Women and social security: Progress towards equality of treatment.* Geneva, Switzerland: International Labour Office.

Bruning, G., & Plantenga, J. (1999). Parental leave and equal opportunities: Experiences in eight European countries. *Journal of European Social Policy, 9,* 195–209.

Burgess, S., Gregg, P., Propper, C., & Washbrook, E. (2008). Maternity rights and mothers' return to work. *Labour Economics, 15,* 168–201.

Carneiro, P., Løken, K., & Salvanes, K. G. (2011). *A flying start? Maternity leave benefits and long-run outcomes of children.* Institute for the Study of Labor (IZA) Discussion Paper No. 5793, retrieved December 2, 2011 from http://ftp.iza.org/dp5793.pdf

Commonwealth of Australia. (2009). *Australia's paid parental leave scheme: Supporting working Australian families.* Retrieved June 4, 2011, from www.deewr.gov.au/Department/Publications/Documents/PPLBooklet.pdf

Datta Gupta, N., & Smith, N. (2002). Children and career interruptions: The family gap in Denmark. *Economica, 69,* 609–629.

Datta Gupta, N., Smith, N., & Verner, M. (2008). The impact of Nordic countries' family policies on employment, wages, and children. *Review of Economics of the Household, 6*(1), 65–89.

Dustmann, C., & Schönberg, U. (2008). *The effects of expansions in maternity leave coverage on children's long-term outcomes* (IZA Discussion Paper No. 3605). Bonn, Germany: Institute for the Study of Labor.

Frank, M., & Lipner, R. (1988). History of maternity leave in Europe and the United States. In E. F. Zigler & M. Frank (Eds.), *The parental leave crisis toward a national policy* (pp. 3–22). New Haven, CT: Yale University Press.

Gornick, J. C., & Meyers, M. K. (2003). *Families that work: Policies for reconciling parenthood and employment.* New York: Russell Sage Foundation.

Hanratty, M., & Trzcinski, E. (2009). Who benefits from paid leave? Impact of expansions in Canadian paid family leave on maternal employment and transfer income. *Journal of Population Economics, 22,* 693–711.

Hegewisch, A., & Gornick, J. C. (2008). *Statutory routes to workplace flexibility in cross-national perspective.* Washington, DC: Institute for Women's Policy Research.

Heymann, J., Earle, A., & Hayes, J. (2007). *The work, family, and equity index: How does the United States measure up?* Project on Global Working Families, Institute for Health and Social Policy. Montreal, Quebec, Canada: McGill University. Retrieved December 2, 2011, from www.mcgill.ca./files/ihsp/WFEIFinal2007Feb.pdf

International Labor Organization. (1919). C3 Maternity Protection Convention, retrieved December 2, 2011, from www.ilo.org/ilolex/cgi-lex/convde.pl?C003

International Labor Organization. (1952). C103 Maternity Protection Convention (revised), Retrieved December 2, 2011, from www.ilo.org/iloex/cgi-lex/convde.pl?C103

Kamerman, S. B. (2006). *A global history of early childhood education and care: Background paper prepared for the Education for All Global Monitoring Report 2007: Strong foundations: Early childhood care and education.* Paris: United Nations Educational, Scientific and Cultural Organization.

Lalive, R., & Zweimüller, J. (2009). How does parental leave affect fertility and return to work: Evidence from two natural experiments. *Quarterly Journal of Economics, 124,* 1363–1402.

Liu, Q., & Nordström Skans, O. (2010). The duration of paid parental leave and children's scholastic performance. *The B. E. Journal of Economic Analysis and Policy, 10*(1).

Moss, P. (Ed.). (2009). *International review of leave policies and related research 2009* (Employment Relations Research Series 102). London: University of London.

Moss, P. (Ed.). (2010). *International review of leave policies and related research 2010* (Employment Relations Research Series 115). London: University of London.

Moss, P., & Deven, F. (2009). Country notes: Introduction and main findings. In P. Moss (Ed.), *International review of leave policies and related research 2009* (Employment Relations Research Series 102, pp. 77–99). London: University of London.

Nielsen, H. S. (2009). *Causes and consequences of a father's child leave: Evidence from a reform of leave schemes* (IZA Discussion Paper No. 4267). Bonn, Germany: Institute for the Study of Labor.

Ondrich, J., Spiess, C. K., Yang, Q., & Wagner, G. G. (1999). Full time or part time? German parental leave policy and the return to work after childbirth in Germany. *Research in Labor Economics, 18,* 41–74.

Organization for Economic Cooperation and Development. (2008). OECD *family database*. Retrieved from www.oecd.org/els/social/family/database

Pétursdóttir, G. M., & Einarsdóttir, T. (2008). Making parental leave parental: Fathers on leave in Iceland. In P. Moss, P. Korintus, & M. Korintus (Eds.), *International review of leave policies and related research 2008* (Employment Relations Research Series No. 100, pp. 85–89). London: Department for Business, Enterprise and Regulatory Reform.

Pizzo, P. (1988). Uncertain harvest: Maternity leave policies in developing nations. In E. Zigler, & M. Frank (Eds.), *The parental leave crisis: Toward a national policy* (pp. 276–290). New Haven, CT: Yale University Press.

Puhani, P. A., & Sonderhof, K. (2008). *The effects of maternity leave extension on training for young women* (IZA Discussion Paper No. 3820). Bonn, Germany: Institute for the Study of Labor.

Rasmussen, A. W. (2010). Increasing the length of parents' birth-related leave: The effect on children's long-term educational outcomes. *Labour Economics, 17,* 91–100.

Ray, R. A. (2008). *A detailed look at parental leave policies in 21 OECD countries*. Washington, DC: Center for Economic Policy Research.

Ray, R., Gornick, J. C., & Schmitt, J. (2008). *Parental leave policies in 21 countries: Assessing generosity and gender equity*. Washington, DC: Center for Economic Policy Research.

Rønsen, M., & Sundström, M. (2002). Family policy and after-birth employment among new mothers—A comparison of Finland, Norway and Sweden. *European Journal of Population, 18*(2), 121–152.

Ruhm, C. J. (1998). The economic consequences of parental leave mandates: Lessons from Europe. *Quarterly Journal of Economics, 113,* 285–317.

Ruhm, C. J. (2000). Parental leave and child health. *Journal of Health Economics, 19,* 931–960.

Ruhm, C. J., & Teague, J. L. (1997). Parental leave policies in Europe and North America. In F. D. Blau & R. G. Ehrenberg (Eds.), *Gender and family issues in the workplace* (pp. 133–156). New York: Russell Sage Foundation.

Salmi, M., Lammi-Taskula, J., & Takala, P. (2008). Finland. In P. Moss & M. Korintus (Eds.), *International review of leave policies and related research 2008* (Employment Relations Research Series No. 100, pp. 184–199). London: Department for Business, Enterprise and Regulatory Reform.

Schönberg, U., & Ludstek, J. (2008). *Maternity leave legislation, female labor supply, and the family wage gap* Institute for the Study of Labor (IZA) Discussion Paper No. 2699. Retrieved December 2, 2011, from http://ftp.iza.org/dp2699.pdf

Social Security Administration. (2008a). *Social security programs throughout the world: The Americas, 2007* (SSA Publication No. 13-11804). Washington, DC: Author.

Social Security Administration. (2008b). *Social security programs throughout the world: Europe, 2008.* Washington, DC: Author.

Spiess, C., & Wrohlich, K. (2008). The parental leave benefit reform in Germany: Costs and labour market outcomes of moving towards the Nordic model. *Population Research and Policy Review, 27,* 575–591.

Tanaka, S. (2005). Parental leave and child health in OECD across countries. *Economic Journal, 15* (501), F7–F28.

Waldfogel, J. (1998). The family gap for young women in the United States and Britain: Can maternity leave make a difference. *Journal of Labor Economics, 16* (3), 505–545.

CHAPTER

Paid Family Leave: Lessons From California

With Sami Kitmitto

Introduction

In 2002, California became the first state in the nation to enact paid family leave legislation. The state's Paid Family Leave (PFL) law, coupled with earlier statutes providing protection for women during pregnancy and the postpartum period, allows eligible workers to claim time to recover from childbirth or bond with a new child without suffering termination of employment or full loss of compensation. California's PFL legislation is a groundbreaking law (by U.S. standards) and forms a critical piece in a total package of leave policies. The state's experience thus provides an important look at how paid family leave combined with job protection might change the landscape of balancing work and family in the United States.

At the outset, it is important to clarify that California's PFL law, like the federal Family and Medical Leave Act (FMLA), covers more conditions than the care of a newborn or adopted infant. The term *family leave* refers not only to paid time off for purposes of getting to know or bond with a new infant but also time off to care for a seriously ill family member, which we refer to as *family medical care leave*. Because the focus of this chapter is on infant care leave, our discussion is largely limited to the provisions of PFL and other related statutes that help families obtain time off to recover from childbirth and to care for a new baby or newly adopted child. The provisions allowing time off from work to care for an ill family member, although important, extend beyond the scope of this book.

Over the past decade, major reform in family leave law has taken place primarily at the state level, with California leading the way. As first described in chapter 1, the FMLA provides some workers with job protection but offers far from universal coverage and no wage replacement.

Since 1978, a handful of states (including California) with existing temporary disability insurance (TDI) programs have provided wage replacement for women on pregnancy leave shortly preceding or following childbirth. In more recent years, efforts to expand paid leave benefits for family leave to cover time to care for a new baby or newly adopted child (and ill family members) have had some success in three states, one being California and the other two being Washington and New Jersey.

California's PFL legislation went into effect in July 2004 and offers up to 6 weeks of paid leave for bonding with a new child or to care for an ill family member. The program, funded entirely by a payroll tax on employees, expanded California's existing state disability insurance (SDI) program (formerly called TDI). In addition to the previous coverage for women for "pregnancy disability," the law now offers partial wage replacement (55%) to virtually all workers for family leave. Together, the pregnancy disability leave and the PFL can offer up to 3 months of paid leave to a mother following the birth of a new baby. Meanwhile, families may be eligible for job protection during and beyond their paid leave through other federal and state legislation.

In 2009, New Jersey enacted a paid family leave program which is similar to California's in that it is constructed on the foundation of the state's TDI and financed solely by employee payroll taxes. Like California's PFL, New Jersey's Family Leave Insurance also provides 6 weeks of partial wage replacement. The wage replacement rate in New Jersey, however, is higher (approximately 66%) than California's 55% rate.

In 2007, the state of Washington passed a Family Leave Insurance law, thereby breaking ground in a state that did not have an existing disability insurance infrastructure. In addition to providing workers with up to $250 per week for 5 weeks, Washington's law is designed to protect workers' jobs while they are using the Family Leave Insurance program (Economic Opportunity Institute, 2008). However, because Washington had no preexisting disability insurance system to implement the paid family leave program, the state projected it would need nearly $10 million for the first 3 years to set up an infrastructure to administer the program (Washington State Employment Security Department, 2008). During the financial crisis that gripped the nation in the fall of 2008, the state postponed implementation of the family leave program, initially scheduled to begin in 2009, until at least 2012 (Economic Opportunity Institute, 2008, 2009).

In 2010, 10 additional states—Arizona, Hawaii, Massachusetts, Missouri, New Hampshire, New York, Oregon, Pennsylvania, Texas, and Vermont—introduced, though did not enact, paid family leave laws (Walsh, 2011). Most offered 4 to 6 weeks of part-paid leave.

In this chapter, we focus on paid family leave and related statutes in California. This state, with the longest experience with paid family leave in the United States, offers the most information on how a comprehensive parental leave policy for infant care might work on a national scale. We first review the separate statutes that together offer job protection and wage replacement for many (although still not all) working families with new babies or newly adopted children. Second, we provide some examples of how families can piece together the job protection and wage replacement benefits afforded by multiple statutes to obtain an infant care leave of relatively substantial duration. Finally, we examine state administrative data and recent reports to assess the impact of the PFL law in California on the time taken off from employment for infant care. With several years of history now available since the enactment of PFL, access to administrative tables on the program, and a recent survey by Eileen Appelbaum and Ruth Milkman (2011) of California workers and employers in 2009 and 2010, it is possible to explore a number of questions relevant for policymakers interested in the infant care leave aspect of this pioneering PFL program:

- Has partial wage replacement led to greater access to parental leave for infant care? In particular, has it succeeded in making parental leave available to relatively low-income workers?

- Has partial wage replacement affected the duration of leave taken by new parents?

- How has the law affected patterns of leave usage by men and women?

- How important is job protection? Are employees of small business who are not eligible for job protection under the FMLA nonetheless claiming the paid leave?

- How has California's PFL law affected employers and productivity?

- How much has the program cost?

In short, for purposes of promoting time off for new parents to spend with their newborn or newly adopted children, what is the added value of paid family leave over unpaid, job-protected leave, and how does the addition of wage replacement affect California families and businesses?

California's PFL law evolved from a set of circumstances that might be difficult to replicate in other states. Not only was California one of the few states with an existing TDI structure onto which the paid family leave could be added, but also there was a strong advocacy base for the legislation. A coalition of community groups headed by the Labor Project for Working Families adopted paid leave as a legislative goal, obtained a planning grant from the David and Lucile Packard Foundation, and worked with both a legislature and a governor supportive of paid family leave rights (Labor Project for Working Families, 2003; Wisensale, 2006).[1] As one might expect from a policy constructed over time with no single architect or blueprint, there are

---

[1] *Marie B. Young served as the Packard Foundation program officer for the planning project for the paid leave program, thereby helping to ensure that the coalition was broad enough to move forward with the concept.*

gaps in the job protection extended to new parents by the various statutes, and many families may also be unaware of how best to maximize the wage replacement available under the disparate pieces of legislation. Nonetheless, taken together, the PFL, combined with other California and federal statutes, offers an important example of how a relatively modest paid parental leave program for infant care might function nationwide. The lessons learned from California may also be of interest to other states.[2]

Statutes Affecting Pregnancy and Infant Care Leave in California

California's PFL program is a pioneering piece of legislation, but it is hardly the first or the only statute in the state affecting access to leave for pregnancy, childbirth, or newborn care. On the contrary, several separate though intersecting laws adopted over the past 65 years set the stage for PFL, and together they provide a package of job protection, or wage replacement, or both. The relevant statutes can be grouped into two main categories—those addressing pregnancy disability leave and designed to allow for the mother's preparation for and recovery from childbirth, and those providing parental leave for care of a new or newly adopted child, with both men and women eligible for the latter type of leave. We begin with an overview of laws pertaining solely to women during pregnancy and recovery from childbirth. Then we move to a discussion of statutes that apply more broadly to new fathers as well as adoptive parents with a new child.

■ Rights to maternity leave had been developing in California for some time.

Legislation in California addressed wage replacement for women on leave for pregnancy or recovery from childbirth before it addressed job protection. The foundation for paid pregnancy leave in California is the TDI program enacted in 1946. As mentioned above, California is one of five states (the others are Hawaii, New Jersey, New York, and Rhode Island) that have TDI programs (Wisensale, 2006). Ironically, when the state enacted the program in 1946, pregnancy was specifically excluded from consideration as a temporary disability. However, once the state decided to add pregnancy as a temporary disability, it had the infrastructure (now housed at the Employment Development Department [EDD]) in place to collect payroll taxes and administer payments at little additional cost. In 1973, the California legislature

---

[2] *In 2008, the Obama presidential campaign proposed $1.5 billion in incentives for states to develop their own approaches to paid family leave. After the election, the administration's proposal was substantially reduced to $50 million to help states with start-up costs and, as of this writing, has not been included in a budget enacted by Congress. However, using federal policy to encourage state development of paid family leave policies may still hold traction, as evidenced in Rep. Lynn Woolsey's (D-CA) "Balancing Act of 2011" which is described in chapter 7.*

extended TDI benefits to "abnormal" pregnancies and, in 1976, to disabilities accompanying "normal" pregnancies for 3 weeks before and 3 weeks following delivery (Appelbaum & Milkman, 2011). Finally, in 1979, the program was again amended to provide the same benefits to disabled pregnant employees as to workers with any other type of disability.

As a result of the above amendments to the state's TDI programs, women who lose wages because they take time off related to pregnancy and childbirth are considered temporarily disabled and hence eligible to apply for SDI benefits. Although the payment level depends on earnings, there is no minimum prior work requirement, and benefits are not limited to employees working for establishments with a set number of employees. The program replaces approximately 55% of lost wages and is funded by an employee payroll tax. The length of leave is not stipulated in the law but is set by recommendation of the employee's doctor. A temporary disability leave for a normal pregnancy typically begins up to 4 weeks before the expected delivery date and typically ends up to 6 weeks after the actual delivery, with around 2 additional weeks typically recommended for recovery from a cesarean section (California EDD, n.d.-a).

Other state statutes affecting the rights of pregnant women and new mothers include the amendments to the State Fair Employment Practices Act of 1978. Both this law and the federal Pregnancy Discrimination Act enacted the same year mandate that employers providing benefits to a temporarily disabled person must supply those same benefits to women temporarily unable to work because of pregnancy or recovery from childbirth.[3] That is, the law requires that employer-provided benefits (e.g., adjusted job tasks and schedules, job protection, maintenance of fringe benefits, and paid and unpaid leave) afforded to other sick or disabled employees must apply equally to pregnant employees and women who have recently undergone childbirth. Further, California's State Fair Employment and Housing Act legislation was also amended in 1978 to provide job-protected leave of up to 4 months for women temporarily disabled by pregnancy, childbirth, or both while working at businesses with five or more employees (Appelbaum & Milkman, 2011; California Office of the Attorney General, 1998). These provisions are now part of the Fair Employment and Housing Act and known as California's pregnancy disability leave.

In summary, the various statutes described above, which are applied to protect women who are pregnant or have recently delivered babies, together function something like maternity leave policies in other nations. The California requirement that a physician verify the woman's temporary inability to work may be unusual, and the very use of the term *disability* may be off-putting to some women or interpreted, albeit incorrectly, to apply only to those experiencing something other than the normal course of pregnancy and childbirth. That said, most pregnant

---

[3] *The Pregnancy Discrimination Act applies only to employers with 15 or more employees; the California law covers employers with 5 or more employees.*

women in California have for some time had access, at least theoretically, to a largely job-protected leave of up to 16 weeks (4 months) and partially paid leave of typically 10 to 12 weeks. These provisions are only slightly less generous than those in many Western European nations.

◼ Prior state statutes also had begun to provide parental leave for infant care.

Prior to the passage of PFL, California already had some legislation providing job-protected leave for getting to know or bond with a new baby or newly adopted child. Unlike the pregnancy disability protections, which by definition are offered only to expectant or new mothers, this group of California laws gradually began to expand rights to leave benefits for infant care and made them available to fathers and adoptive parents as well as biological mothers.

The California Family Rights Act (CFRA), enacted in 1992 a year before the nearly identical FMLA, provides job protection for bonding with a newborn, newly adopted, or newly placed foster child. Employees are allowed up to 12 weeks of unpaid, job-protected leave in any 12-month period for any of the covered reasons. For a new child, the leave must be taken within 12 months of the delivery or placement. One limitation of these laws is that only employers with 50 or more employees within a 75-mile radius of the job site are covered. In addition, there are work requirement criteria for individual eligibility: The employee must have worked for the same employer for more than a year and must have worked more than 1,250 hours in the past 12 months (California Department of General Services, 2000; U.S. Department of Labor, 2010). The one difference between the CFRA and the FMLA is that CFRA protection is coordinated with the other California job protection statute, pregnancy disability leave, so that if pregnancy disability leave is being used, CFRA protection will not become effective until the pregnancy disability leave ends. Together, pregnancy disability leave and CFRA provide up to 26 weeks of job protection for eligible pregnant women. FMLA job protection, in contrast, will run concurrently with pregnancy disability leave such that it would not provide any extra protection if 12 or more weeks of pregnancy disability leave were used.

Thus, by 1992, and prior to the passage of the FMLA, California law already provided up to 28 weeks of job protection for pregnant women and mothers recovering from childbirth: Pregnancy disability leave provided 16 weeks (4 months) of job-protected leave for pregnancy and recovery from childbirth, and the CFRA provided 12 weeks for parental leave. In addition, because of amendments to the state's TDI program, most employed pregnant women in California were eligible for 4 weeks of partially paid leave before giving birth and 6 to 8 weeks following the delivery.

■ PFL has added value.

What PFL added, beginning in 2004, was an additional 6 weeks of partially paid time off from employment for care of a new baby or newly adopted child, or for care of a seriously ill family member. Moreover, fathers and domestic partners, as well as mothers, can claim the leave. Collectively, then, both parents can claim up to 6 weeks of partially paid leave any time in the first 12 months after the birth or adoption of a child. Furthermore, PFL is available to workers regardless of employer size. Small business employees are eligible, and self-employed workers can elect to participate if they pay into the program. As shown in Table 6.1, PFL is thus a critical piece (but only one piece) of a patchwork of legislation that together can be used to provide maternity and parental leave for infant care.

Table 6.1: Summary of California Pregnancy Leave and Parental Leave Laws

Law		Job Protection	Wage Replacement
Pregnancy Disability Leave	Statute	California pregnancy disability leave	California State Disability Insurance (SDI)
	Details	16 weeks (4 months)	55% replacement; duration by doctor's orders (typically 4 weeks prior to and 6 weeks after birth)
	Eligibility	Workplace > 5 employees	All employees
Parental Leave	Statute	California Family Rights Act (CFRA)	California Paid Family Leave (PFL)
	Details	12 weeks	55% replacement for 6 weeks
	Eligibility	Workplace >50 employees in 75 miles radius and more than 12 months with employer and more than 1,250 hours with employer in last year	All employees

A Closer Look at California's PFL

As with most legislation, advocates of the PFL law had to make some significant compromises to ensure its passage. First, the maximum length of paid benefits was reduced from the initially proposed 12 weeks to 6. Second, in the original proposal the payroll tax was to be shared equally by employers and employees but the final legislation required all of the taxes to be paid by employees. Third, a provision was added allowing employers to require employees to take up to 2 weeks of accrued vacation time before enrolling in paid leave. Finally, the final legislation did not provide job protection beyond that available from other laws (Labor Project for Working Families, 2003; Wisensale, 2006). One result is that employees of small businesses or those who do not meet FMLA work history requirements may not have job-protected leave.

Provisions of PFL

As stated earlier, California's EDD administers the PFL as an extension of the SDI program. The temporary disability payments for pregnancy and childbirth recovery and the family leave payments are funded by a single tax on employee wages (1.20% in 2011) and pay the same benefits (approximately 55% of wages). In addition, they are designed to work seamlessly: Toward the end of leave taken for pregnancy and childbirth recovery, a recipient is mailed a form by EDD to request an extension of benefits as paid family leave. The maximum wages taxed in 2011 were $93,316, and the corresponding maximum benefits were $987 per week. There is a 7-day, unpaid waiting period before receiving benefits, and workers must have had at least $300 in gross earnings in the "base" quarter (California EDD, n.d.-b).[4] Benefits are not taxed by the state, but the Internal Revenue Service has determined that family leave benefits are subject to federal taxes while temporary disability benefits are not. Under PFL, a worker may choose to work part-time while claiming the partial pay for the time not worked (California EDD, n.d.-b).[5] Weekly benefits are reduced such that a worker's combined income from employment and from the PFL program is not greater than his or her base period weekly pay.

■ How PFL works in practice.

Here we offer two hypothetical examples of how families can piece together the provisions of the various statutes affecting time off related to the birth or adoption of a child in California. These examples underscore how PFL coupled with other statutes that provide job protection can assist families in a variety of circumstances following the birth or adoption of a child. At the same time, the examples illustrate complications associated with a leave policy patched together from multiple statutes, as well as some possible weaknesses in the statutes.

A full-time working couple is able to maximize the leave benefits.

Pam was pregnant with her first child. Because she had worked full-time for several years at a company employing well over 50 people, she easily met the requirements for unpaid, job-protected leave, as well as the less stringent requirements for paid leave. As recommended by her doctor, Pam stopped working roughly 4 weeks before her due date. She completed her waiting period of 7 unpaid days and submitted a claim to the EDD. For the next 4 weeks, Pam's job was protected under both California and federal law, and she was eligible for wage

---

[4] *The base quarter is the 3-month period with the highest earnings occurring during the 12-month period spanning approximately 5 to 17 months prior to the claim start date. Only earnings for which the employee has paid the SDI payroll tax count for calculating eligibility and benefits. Almost all workers pay the SDI tax. The exceptions are self-employed individuals who can elect not to pay into SDI, some unionized state government employees, and those working for an employer who self-insures to provide equivalent benefits.*

[5] *Workers are prohibited from receiving money from the SDI program, unemployment insurance, or workers' compensation at the same time that they are receiving PFL benefits. PFL recipients are permitted to receive sick leave benefits from their employer.*

replacement under California's temporary disability program. During the base period for calculating benefits, her highest quarterly earnings were $15,700, and her weekly benefit amount was $665, or $95 per day.

Pam's baby was delivered nearly 2 weeks after the anticipated due date, by cesarean section. The doctor recommended that Pam not return to work for roughly 8 weeks. For the 6 weeks of leave she took prior to giving birth, plus the 8 weeks of rest and recovery prescribed by her doctor following the delivery, she received a total of $8,360 in partial wage replacement payments covered by California's disability insurance, or approximately 55% of her quarterly earnings of $15,700, minus 7 unpaid waiting days.

Immediately after the baby was born, Pam's husband, Robert, also took time off from work to help his wife recover from the cesarean and to help care for and spend time with their newborn daughter. For the next 6 weeks, both Pam and Robert were at home with their new baby, with Pam receiving benefits under disability insurance and Robert receiving benefits under PFL. At the end of the 6 weeks, when his benefits ran out, Robert returned to work.

Near the end of Pam's disability insurance period, the EDD mailed her a form to request PFL. Pam promptly completed and returned the form, and she continued to receive the same level of wage replacement during her paid parental leave as under her preceding TDI claim. Because she worked for an employer with more than 50 workers at her job site, she was also eligible for 12 additional weeks of job protection during her parental leave.

Pam's story represents a best-case scenario in which the employee is well-informed about the law and meets the eligibility requirements necessary to use the maximum possible benefits. In total, relying on the coverage afforded by the multiple statutes, Pam was able to take 26 weeks of job-protected leave, with 20 of those weeks partially paid (6 weeks of pregnancy disability leave before the birth, 8 weeks of pregnancy disability leave for recovery from the birth, and 6 weeks as part of PFL). Her husband was able to obtain 6 weeks of partially paid leave through the PFL program, all of which was job-protected by the FMLA (as well as the CFRA). If Pam and Robert had lived in most other states, they would each only have been eligible for a total of 12 weeks of job-protected leave under the FMLA with no wage replacement, unless provided by their employers.

■ A small-business employee can claim leave for an adopted baby.

Joe worked part-time, 30 hours a week, for a small business when he and his wife suddenly learned that their application for the adoption of a baby girl had been approved. Because Joe's wife worked long hours for a small start-up software company that offered no benefits, the couple decided that Joe would take the first weeks off from work to spend with their new baby. Because Joe worked for a business with fewer than 50 employees, he was not eligible for federal or state job-protected leave. Fortunately, his employer agreed to hold his job for him while he took 6 weeks off work. Joe was eligible for paid family leave, although, per California law, his employer requested that he first use up accumulated vacation time before beginning his leave.

After the adopted baby was officially placed in the couple's home, Joe took the next 8 business days as paid vacation time. After using up his accrued vacation, he turned to California's paid leave. Because Joe's "vacation" lasted more than 7 calendar days, the program's required waiting period was fulfilled. Based on his highest quarterly payroll earnings of $9,100 in the 12-month base period, his maximum weekly benefit was calculated as $385, roughly 55% of his average weekly wage. For the first 2 weeks, Joe did not work at all; however, in the third week, there was an emergency at work, and he decided to work 3 days, while his wife took time off to care for their baby. For this week, the PFL program compensated Joe for the days he did not work. The program's flexibility allowed him to respond to needs at his job while still on leave to spend time with his new baby.

In all, Joe was able to take 6 weeks of partially paid leave. Although he would have liked more time off work, Joe felt he could not afford to take unpaid leave. In addition, even if money were not an issue, he would have been worried about asking his employer to hold his job for a longer period. After he returned to his regular part-time schedule, he was still able to spend a few hours during the day with the baby. In addition, his wife was sometimes able to obtain a day per week off from work to stay home, although her schedule was too irregular for her to bother with the process of applying for PFL.

Joe's experience presents a case in which taking time off from work for a newly adopted child might not have been possible without the PFL program. It also highlights a component of the program that many parents find invaluable: the flexibility to fluidly move in and out of work while still being eligible for leave payments. At the same time, the case shows why the lack of job protection in the paid leave program limits the time off some employees may take and why the application requirements, such as the 7-day waiting period, may be too cumbersome for employees wishing to take shorter or irregular leaves.

Assessing the Impact of California's PFL

We turn now to assess the impact of the PFL on bonding with a new or newly adopted child, the duration of leave taken by new parents, patterns of leave usage by men and women, and access to leave for low-income employees and those working in small businesses. In addition, we highlight some issues that may impede usage of PFL, such as lack of job protection and insufficient public awareness of who is eligible and how to claim the maximum benefits for which one is eligible. Finally, we discuss the cost of the PFL program and what is known about the law's impact on employers and productivity.

Our primary source of data was the California EDD, which administers the PFL program. The EDD publishes monthly expenditures and claims and other summary data on the TDI and PFL programs on its Web site (www.edd.ca.gov). In addition, we used nonpublic data tables on the first few years of the program that the EDD prepared at the request of California's Senate Research Office; these provide breakdowns of claims by income, duration, and employer size for selected years. We also considered PFL claims as a proportion of the total births and eligible workers, using supplementary information from two external data sources: *National Vital Statistics Reports* (www.cdc.gov/nchs/products/nvsr.htm), published by the Centers for Disease Control and Prevention, and the American Community Survey (www.census.gov/acs/www/) produced by the U.S. Census Bureau. In an attempt to determine how the pattern of paid leave claims in California compared with the use of unpaid leave under the FMLA, we turned to a 2000 survey of employees (Cantor et al., 2001), although we recognize that the difference in time periods analyzed makes these comparisons inexact. Finally, we supplemented our own analysis with findings from the previously cited survey by Appelbaum and Milkman (2011) of 253 private employers and 500 employees in 2009 and 2010.

■ To what extent is PFL used for "bonding" with a new baby or newly adopted child?

From its implementation in 2004 until the recession near the end of the decade, California's PFL program grew steadily, from approximately 151,000 claims in the 2004–05 state fiscal year (SFY; July 1–June 30) to nearly 191,000 in SFY 2008–09 (see Table 6.2). Over the first 4 years, claims increased 7% to 10% annually, before decelerating to a 2.7% growth rate in 2008–09 and declining by 3.5% during the last year of the decade, probably in response to the severe economic downturn. Of particular interest, the vast majority (86%–88%) of PFL claims have been for parental leave rather than family medical care, with more than 94% of these being for bonding with a newborn child and about 1% for a new adoption or foster placement. The remaining approximately 5% of claims were made for care of children by stepparents, a legal guardian, or other person who acted as the child's legal guardian.[6] It is interesting that a similar pattern has emerged in the use of the paid family leave legislation in New Jersey, where 82% of claims in the first 11 months of 2011 were for bonding with a newborn or adopted child (New Jersey Department of Labor and Workforce Development, n.d).

Although it would be interesting to consider how the use of California's PFL compares with that of unpaid leave under the federal FMLA, differences in the data about the two programs do not facilitate such a direct comparison. Because PFL is a program that requires application

---

[6] *For the purposes of paid family leave, "child" is defined as a biological, adopted, or foster child, a stepchild, a legal ward, a son or daughter of a domestic partner, or a child of a person standing in loco parentis.*

Table 6.2. Paid Family Leave (PFL) Claims in California by State Fiscal Year

Claims	Fiscal Year					
	2004–05	2005–06	2006–07	2007–08	2008–09	2009–10
Total claims	150,514	160,988	174,838	192,494	197,638	190,743
Increase/decrease from previous year		10,474	13,850	17,656	5,144	–6,895
% increase/decrease from previous year		7.0%	8.6%	10.1%	2.7%	–3.5%
Average weekly benefit	$409	$432	$439	$457	$472	$488
Average weeks per claim	4.84	5.35	5.37	5.35	5.39	5.37
Parental claims	129,764	141,319	153,120	168,594	175,406	167,523
% of total claims	86.2%	87.8%	87.6%	87.6%	88.8%	87.8%
Breakdown of parental claims						
Biological	98.5%	97.9%	93.7%	94.4%	94.4%	94.8%
Adoption/foster	1.5%	1.1%	0.9%	0.8%	0.7%	0.7%
Other		1.0%	5.4%	4.8%	5.0%	4.6%
Family care claims	21,543	19,669	21,718	23,900	22,232	23,220
% of total claims	14.3%	12.2%	12.4%	12.4%	11.2%	12.2%

Note. Figures reported in the table are for California fiscal years, which run from July 1 through June 30. Parental claims = claims for leaves for a new child. Family care claims = claims for leaves to care for a sick family member. From EDD PFL Program data (http://www.edd.ca.gov/About_EDD/Quick_Statistics.htm).

to a state agency to obtain benefits, detailed administrative data that are collected by the state can be used for analysis. In contrast, the FMLA provides workers with rights but does not require application to, or reporting by, a central agency. Given the absence of administrative data related to FMLA usage, we relied on a 2000 survey of employees related to FMLA leave-taking.[7] According to that survey, only about one third of FMLA-covered leaves taken by employees were for purposes of providing parental care.[8]

To estimate the proportion of eligible individuals who applied for PFL leave in California, we calculated the number of births in each calendar year from Vital Statistics data and then compared this to total claims filed during the calendar year (by averaging claims during the two fiscal years included in the calendar year). These calculations, detailed in Table 6.3, show that there were 30 paid leave claims for every 100 births in California in 2008 and 2009. This almost certainly understates the proportion of eligible parents filing claims, because some new

---

[7] *Several caveats should therefore be kept in mind when considering the analysis that follows. First, the comparison data are primarily national in scope, and the California experience may differ somewhat from that of the rest of the country in ways that we do not account for. Second, the survey data were from 2000, whereas the California paid leave data are from 2004–05, raising the possibility of changes in leave-taking patterns over time that we did not capture. Third, persons not returning to their jobs after taking leave are excluded from the 2000 survey data and thus are not included in the numbers reported. Fourth, the 2000 survey does not clearly distinguish between FMLA leave to recover from childbirth and that which is for bonding with the child, and so the two types of leave are likely to be combined, to some extent, in our analysis. By contrast, bonding leaves are precisely distinguished from pregnancy leaves in the California administrative data.*

[8] *This calculation is based on Tables 2.3 and 3.8 from Cantor et al. (2000).*

Table 6.3: Paid Family Leave (PFL) Claims Filed and Number of Live Births by Calendar Year

Claims	2004 (July–Dec)	2005	2006	2007	2008	2009
Total claims filed	74,405	154,425	169,373	183,347	200,105	187,916
Increase/decrease from previous year		5,615[c]	14,948	13,974	16,758	–12,189
% increase/decrease from previous year		7.5%[c]	9.7%	8.3%	9.1%	–6.1%
Estimated % of claims that are for newborn bonding[a]	84.9%	85.4%	84.0%	82.4%	83.2%	83.5%
Estimate of biological parental claims	63,185	131,929	142,269	151,023	166,548	156,950
Live births	272,421[b]	548,882	562,440	566,414	551,592	527,011
% increase/decrease from previous year		4.3%[c]	-3.4%	-0.2%	-2.6%	-4.5%
Total claims per 100 live births	23	24	25	27	30	30

Note. From EDD PFL program data (www.edd.ca.gov/About_EDD/Quick_Statistics.htm) and National Vital Statistics Reports (Hamilton, Martin, & Ventura, 2010; Martin, Hamilton, Sutton, Ventura, Matthews, Kirmeyer, & Osterman, 2010; Martin, Hamilton, Sutton, Ventura, Matthews, & Osterman, 2010; Martin et al., 2006, 2007, 2009).

[a] For 2004, this is the state fiscal year (SFY) 2004–05 percentage of claims that were for parental leave multiplied by the percentage of parental claims that were for newborns; for 2005, the multiplication is performed for SFY 2004–05 and SFY 2005–06 rates and then the average of the two is used, and so on.

[b] This number is one half the 2004 calendar year figure, which was 544,843.

[c] These numbers have been adjusted to annual rates based on the fact that PFL was only implemented for the second half of 2004.

mothers or fathers did not meet the employment or earnings conditions required to qualify for PFL. However, assuming that eligibility remained reasonably constant over time, the ratio of claims to births provides perspective on the increased use of the program. Although the number of claims rose rapidly until 2008, the number of births actually trended downward. Hence, the estimated number of parental leave claims rose from 23 to 30 per 100 births between 2004 and 2008, with the largest increase from 2007 to 2008, making it likely that the use of paid parental leave has increased over time and exceeds the proportion of FMLA-covered leaves used to care for or bond with infants.

■ How has the PFL program affected the duration of leaves in California?

Workers claiming paid parental leave are taking nearly the maximum amount of leave for which they are eligible. Furthermore, the duration of parental leave taken under California's paid leave law appears significantly longer than that reported in prior national studies of FMLA usage where there was legislated job protection but not wage replacement. To reach this conclusion, we compared national data from the 2000 Survey of Employees to durations of paid parental leave in California during 2004–05, as estimated using administrative data from

Figure 6.1: Duration of California Paid Family Leaves (PFLs) and National Family and Medical Leave Act (FMLA) Leaves

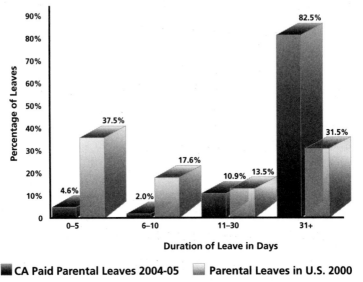

Note. California PFL leave durations refer to the number of days taken for each leave; FMLA duration refers to duration of the longest leave reported by the survey respondent. From EDD PFL Program internal data and Cantor et al. (2001).

the state.[9] The results, summarized in Figure 6.1, show that more than four fifths of the California paid leaves extended longer than 1 month (in 2004–05), compared to fewer than one third in the national data on FMLA leave duration (for 1999 and 2000).[10] Also, the duration of all PFL claims (for parental and family care) has been relatively steady, after the 1st year, averaging 5.37 weeks in 2009–10 out of a maximum of 6 weeks.[11]

From an analysis by Han, Ruhm, and Waldfogel (2009) drawn from the June 2004 Current Population Survey (CPS),[12] we find further evidence that the average leaves of more than 5 weeks claimed under the California PFL program may be longer than those covered only by the FMLA. Although 63% of mothers (and 3% of fathers) were on (FMLA-protected) leave during the CPS survey week of the child's 1st month of life, just 34% of women (and less than

---

[9] Data on the duration of leaves used to make this comparison was only available for 2004–05.

[10] The differences in our analysis are probably understated by this comparison for two reasons. First, the duration of California paid leaves excludes the 7-day unpaid waiting period, meaning that all of these leaves are actually 7 days longer than reported. Second, the national data identify only the longest FMLA leave taken; including the excluded brief leaves would skew the estimates toward even shorter durations.

[11] More detailed nonpublic data tables obtained from the California Senate Research Office and available for SFY 2004–05 showed that 82.4% of women and 34.5% of men (74.2% combined) took the maximum amount of leave.

[12] One again, these statistics are from detailed supporting data provided by the authors of this article.

1% of men) were still away from the job for "other" reasons 1 month later. Given the structure of the CPS, these later figures approximately correspond to the average child's being 1 month old when the mother returns to work, indicating that FMLA job-protected leaves are typically shorter than PFL leaves in California.[13]

Although most parental claims under California's PFL were for close to the maximum duration, there is some indication that better compensated women managed to take more time off for new children than did their lower paid counterparts. For instance, in Appelbaum and Milkman's (2011) survey of workers, women in high-quality jobs (those with wages greater than $20 per hour and employer-provided health care) who used PFL took longer leaves than those who did not (18 weeks vs. 12 weeks), whereas similar effects were not found for those in low-quality jobs (paying $20 per hour or less or without employer-provided health insurance).

■ Has PFL increased the proportion of fathers taking parental leave?

One of the most interesting aspects of paid leave, beyond its potential contribution to child development, is its impact on gender roles. Although some countries have separate policies for maternity and paternity leave, California's paid leave program is gender-neutral. Women still claim the majority of PFL in California, but the share of PFL leaves taken by men has been increasing over time—from less than one fifth of the total in 2004–05 to more than one quarter in 2009–10. However, the gender disparity grows when calculated by the number of days of leave rather than number of claims, because women take longer leaves than men. For instance, Figure 6.2 shows the breakdown of claims by gender and duration in fiscal year 2004–05. The most interesting fact is that more than four out of five women who used PFL for a new child took 40 or more of the maximum 42 days available, compared to around one third of men.[14] By contrast, men were nearly 4 times more likely than women (17.2% vs. 4.5%) to take paid leaves of 10 days or less. Appelbaum and Milkman (2011) similarly found that women take longer PFL leaves than do men (median durations of 12 and 3 weeks, respectively).[15] Even though men take shorter paid leaves than women in California, there is evidence that the availability of PFL increased their leave durations quite dramatically:

---

[13] *CPS surveys typically occur in the 3rd week of the month. Because the average child will be born in the middle of the month (around the end of the 2nd week), the average child will be around 1 week old in the survey week of the birth month and 5 months old in the survey week of the next month. Labor force status refers to the week prior to the week of the survey (the reference week), implying that children will typically be around 1 month old in the reference week of the month after birth.*

[14] *California's PFL program counts 7 days in a week for paying benefits; thus, 6 weeks is equivalent to 42 days.*

[15] *As mentioned above, less than 1% of fathers surveyed in the June 2004 CPS were absent from work for "other" reasons in the month after birth (Han et al., 2009), suggesting that leaves lasting longer than 1 month were rare for men outside of California during this time period.*

Figure 6.2: Duration (in Days) of Paid Family Leave (PFL) Claims by Gender, State Fiscal Year 2004–05

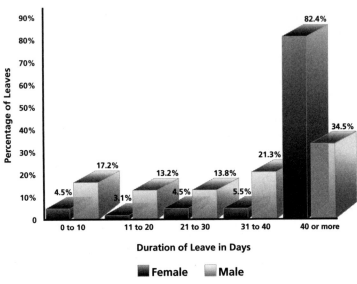

Note. From EDD PFL program internal data.

Appelbaum and Milkman found that men who used PFL took leaves that were twice as long as the leaves taken by men who did not use PFL.

■ Are low-income employees accessing California's PFL program?

As discussed in chapter 1, the FMLA appears to disproportionately benefit employees with high incomes; less advantaged employees may not be as able to take unpaid time off (Han et al., 2009; Klerman & Leibowitz, 1994). According to national data from 2000, three fourths of FMLA-eligible workers who needed but did not take a leave indicated that they could not afford the loss of wages (Cantor et al., 2001). Given that usage of FMLA leaves (per worker) increases with income, it is important to determine whether California's PFL has reduced the disparity in access by helping relatively low-income workers afford to take time off to care for new or newly adopted children.

Figure 6.3 shows the distribution of paid parental leave claims for 2005–06 by earnings category, where the latter is defined by the annual salaries used to establish the PFL claim.[16] The figure shows that claims per 10,000 workers were relatively low for persons in both the

---

[16] *Because there are not equal numbers of workers in each earnings category, we used data from the American Community Survey to estimate the number of employees in each category, so that we could report the number of claims per 10,000 workers.*

Figure 6.3: Parental Leave Claims per 10,000 California Workers, by Household Income, State Fiscal Year 2005–06

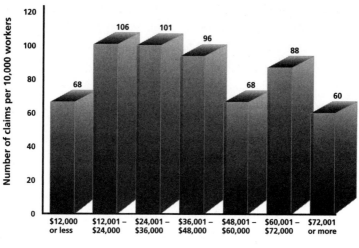

Note. From EDD PFL program internal data and author calculations from the 2005 *American Community Survey* (U.S. Census Bureau, n.d.).

lowest group (less than $12,000) and highest group (greater than $72,000). Disregarding the first category, however, usage of paid parental leave in California was highest among low- to middle-income workers (with annual incomes between $12,000 and $48,000), with usage declining as income increased. Conversely, Cantor et al. (2001) obtained the opposite pattern for FMLA leaves that were unaccompanied by wage replacement.[17] This suggests that the wage replacement provided in California's PFL program does indeed help lower income workers take leave.[18]

■ Are eligible women claiming both pregnancy disability leave and PFL?

As described earlier, most pregnant working women in California are eligible for two types of paid leave: pregnancy disability leave (typically 6 to 8 weeks following delivery) and an additional 6 weeks of PFL anytime during the 1st year after the birth. Comparing Vital Statistics data on live births for 2004 and 2005, and California administrative data on leave utilization

---

[17] *In 2000, 2.2% to 2.6% of workers with family income categories below $50,000 took a leave for care for a new child; for incomes between $50,000 and $75,000, the rate was 3.5%; for $75,000 to $100,000, it was 4.3%; and for family incomes over $100,000, it was 7.4% (Cantor et al., 2001).*

[18] *The pattern of California PFL usage, however, does differ by gender. For lower earning categories up to $48,000, males' usage rates increase with income. For males, rates then drop for those with earnings over $72,000.*

for fiscal year 2004–05, we find that neither type of leave was claimed for 68% of births. Some of these pregnant women were not working and hence were ineligible for leave, but it still seems likely that a substantial number were eligible but did not claim leave. On the other hand, nearly two thirds of pregnant women who received temporary disability insurance also obtained paid parental leave, suggesting that the application process for moving from one type of leave to the other is working relatively well.[19]

■ What is the public's level of awareness of the PFL program?

One potential issue with any new law is that it may take time for the public to become aware of it. Usage of California's PFL has been lower than predicted,[20] suggesting that public awareness of the program may be limited. Public awareness of PFL increased during its first full year, when the state had funds to publicize the program, but leveled off between 2005 and 2007 when publicity was curtailed (Appelbaum & Milkman, 2004; Milkman, 2008). In addition, Schuster et al. (2008) indicated that, 18 months after PFL took effect, knowledge of the program was low, with only 18% of working parents with chronically ill children having heard of it.[21]

Appelbaum and Milkman (2011) delved into the topic of awareness in more detail. Among workers surveyed in 2009 and 2010 who had a recent eligible event (bonding with a new child or care of an ill family member), only 51.4% knew about the PFL program. Furthermore, certain subpopulations (such as low-income families, Latinos, and immigrants) had the lowest awareness of the program. Those respondents earning $15 per hour or less knew about the program far less frequently (35.5%) than those earning over $15 per hour (54.3%).

Even families who are aware of the program may be confused about its specific requirements and provisions because of the complex interrelationships between the various policies. For instance, pregnant working women may not realize that pregnancy disability leave is available for normal as well as abnormal pregnancies and recoveries from childbirth, or they may be reluctant to ask their physicians to verify the length of leave they need. Families may also be bewildered by the requirement to use a few days of vacation first and about the level of payment they will receive. In addition, they may be confused about which portion of the leave

---

[19] *Mothers almost never obtain paid parental leave without first claiming temporary disability benefits.*

[20] *Actual claims for parental leave (175,406 in 2008–09) slightly exceeded the "low" estimate (146,149) that economists Arindrajit Dube and Ethan Kaplan (2002) made prior to passage of the legislation. However, actual claims for family medical care, highest in 2007–08 at 23,900, were far below even the economists' "lower estimate" of 186,632.*

[21] *The parental leave provisions may have been better publicized than other portions of the law. Physicians and hospitals routinely inform expectant and new parents about the program, according to Lilian Miwa Maher, PFL outreach coordinator for the Legal Aid Society-Employment Law Center in San Francisco (personal communication, October 21, 2009), as do child care resource and referral agencies in the state.*

(if any) provides job protection as well as wage replacement. Such complexity may discourage some eligible parents from applying for leave or limit the amount they actually use. When asked to discuss potential weaknesses of California's family leave laws, Netsy Firestein of the Labor Project for Working Families commented that the intersecting laws are so complicated that "people just don't get it!" (personal communication, October 21, 2009).

■ Is the lack of job protection undermining PFL utilization?

California's PFL legislation makes family leave more accessible to low-income workers by providing wage replacement, but it lacks job protection. Almost all women receiving wage replacement during pregnancy under SDI also obtain job protection under the pregnancy disability leave statutes. But this protection stops when the pregnancy-related "disability" ends. The jobs of workers taking paid leave under California's PFL are protected only if they are covered by the federal FMLA or corresponding CFRA; this coverage is not universal, being limited to employees who work in businesses with 50 or more employees (in a 75-mile radius), and with other restrictions on eligibility. Hence, we might expect to see different patterns of leave-taking by workers at businesses with fewer than versus 50 or more employees.

The available California data allow us to analyze claims by employer size for the first quarter of 2006 (although parental and family care claims are combined). Figure 6.4 reports the number of claims per 100,000 workers by employer size. Claim rates are relatively low for workers in small businesses (under 50 employees) when compared to those that are larger.

Figure 6.4: Number of Paid Family Leave (PFL) Claims per 100,000 Workers by Employer Size, 2006

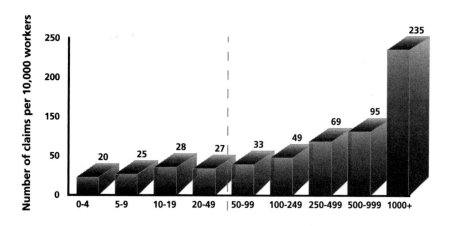

Note. The annualized rate is obtained by multiplying claims during January through March of 2006 by 4. From EDD PFL Program internal data.

Immediately below and above the 50-employee threshold, there is a slight, but not dramatic, 22% increase in claims per worker: 27 versus 33. This threshold does not exactly define eligibility for job protection, because the legislation refers to number of employees within a 75-mile radius, not the total number working at the company, implying that some workers in the 50–99 category will not receive job protection because the company's employees are geographically dispersed. These data also do not control for differences in fertility rates or in the prevalence of males and females in each employer size category, nor are the data broken down by type of claim. These caveats notwithstanding, we interpret the data as raising the possibility that lack of job protection may play a role in influencing use of the paid leave program. However, this is unlikely to be the entire explanation for differences in claims rates. For instance, claims are much more common for persons working in the largest companies (1,000 or more employees) than for those in the next biggest category (500–999 employees), even though both are likely to be eligible for job-protected leave.

Appelbaum and Milkman (2011) investigated why some workers who knew about the PFL program elected not to use it. Among those workers, nearly a quarter (23.9%) cited fear of losing their job as one of the reasons they chose not to claim leave. Although Appelbaum and Milkman did not break down results by eligibility for job protection, one could reasonably guess that such responses would be more prominent among workers without job protection. Overall, 36.9% of those respondents cited at least one concern regarding their status in the workplace (i.e., upsetting their employer, hurting their chances for advancement, or losing their job) as a factor in not using PFL.

■ How does PFL affect breastfeeding and child care?

As discussed in previous chapters, breastfeeding provides multiple maternal and child health benefits. According to Appelbaum and Milkman (2011), the use of PFL increased the duration of breastfeeding among both employees in "high-quality jobs" and "low-quality jobs." Use of PFL roughly doubled the number of weeks of breastfeeding among both groups, from 5 to 11 weeks for mothers in better compensated positions and 5 to 9 weeks for those in less advantaged employment.

For working parents, finding child care once the parents return to work is also an important concern. As one parent interviewed for background material for this book commented, "Looking for quality child care was like a full-time job in and of itself, and I never would have been able to devote the time to that without the paid leave." Here, Appelbaum and Milkman (2011) found that PFL was particularly beneficial to parents in "low-quality jobs": Nearly three fourths of those who used PFL reported that their leave had a positive effect on their ability to arrange child care, while only half of those who took a leave but did not use PFL reported the same.

How has the leave program affected employers?

As with the FMLA, major business organizations, such as the California Chamber of Commerce and the California Manufacturers and Technology Association, along with hundreds of individual businesses, adamantly opposed California's PFL bill (Broyles, 2002). Allan Zaramberg (2002), then president of the Chamber, voiced concern that adding PFL to the SDI system would threaten to bankrupt an already overwhelmed SDI Trust Fund. Should the legislation proposed by then State Senator Sheila Kuehl (Democrat of Santa Monica) become law, argued Martyn Hopper (2002), then state director of the National Federation of Independent Businesses, "it will unleash on California specters far worse than anything Dickens threw at Scrooge."

Even after a coalition of opponents succeeded in removing the proposed payroll tax on employers and in reducing the duration of the paid time off, business groups continued to oppose the program. In particular, Julianne Broyles (2003), a leading California Chamber of Commerce lobbyist, voiced concern that the legislation would wreak havoc on small businesses, "which will experience severe disruptions due to increased unscheduled and unplanned absences of workers." Furthermore, Broyles predicted that the program "will force all businesses … to shoulder more costs, including more overtime when other workers need to pick up the slack caused by absent workers, costs for replacement workers, additional training costs and lost productivity and service due to a worker's prolonged or unscheduled absence."

More than 6 years after the law's implementation, however, Appelbaum and Milkman (2011) found that the law has not been onerous for employers. In their phone survey of 253 private for-profit and nonprofit business establishments, nearly 89% of respondents said the law had no or a positive effect on productivity, 91% said it had no or a positive effect on profitability, 93% said it had no or a positive effect on employee turnover, and nearly 99% reported that it had no or a positive effect on employee morale.

Nearly 87% of employers surveyed indicated that the paid leave law had not increased their costs; about 9% said the law had generated cost savings by decreasing turnover. To the extent that employers reported problems with the paid leave policy such as increased costs for temporary hiring or training, most of the complaints came from large rather than small businesses. Most employers covered the tasks performed during the paid leave period by shifting the work temporarily to other existing employees.

In background interviews conducted for this book, a small business owner, Michelle Horneff-

Cohen (personal communication, August 7, 2009), pointed out that PFL actually helped her company's bottom line. The owner of a residential property management company with 13 employees in San Francisco, she had had two babies born in the prior 3½ years, and she used both the Pregnancy Disability and PFL to take time off for the recovery from caesarian deliveries and to get to know her new babies. "It was great to be able to take the part-paid leave paid by the program," she said, "and not be a burden to my company's small payroll."

■ How much does the California paid leave program cost?

The biggest concerns voiced by employers prior to the passage of the California PFL program related to the high anticipated program costs. The specific complaints of businesses were mitigated when legislation shifted the entire burden for funding the program to payroll taxes paid by workers (rather than employers).[22] Still, there remained questions about how much the program would increase worker payroll taxes and whether funding it would jeopardize the solvency of the temporary disability program to which PFL financing was tied. Data on the first few years of the law's implementation indicate that costs are modest and the entire SDI program is on solid ground.

The PFL program paid about $469 million in benefits in 2009–10 for about 181,000 claims (out of 190,743 claims filed, according to EDD program data). As shown in Table 6.4, total benefits rose nearly 10% each year in real terms in the first 3 years, but the increase slowed to around 6% in 2008–09. The increase in total benefits roughly tracks the increase in the number of claims paid each year. Just as actual claims have been below the "likely" bound of estimates by Dube and Kaplan (2002) prior to passage of PFL legislation, so have the expenditures. Dube and Kaplan projected that expenditures would be $786 million and $844 million in 2004 and 2005, respectively, more than twice what they were in 2004–05 and 2005–06.

There are also administrative costs associated with the program. From nonpublic data tables obtained from the EDD, we calculated that total personnel and operating expenses for SFY 2004–05 were $17 million, or 5.7% of total benefits paid. Assuming that administrative costs were also 5.7% of total benefits for later years, we estimate that the total costs (benefits plus administration) were $40.79 per worker in SFY 2009–10.[23]

---

[22] *It is worth noting that economists tend to view it as less important whether employers or employees make the payroll tax payments, because it is generally possible for businesses to shift the incidences of the taxes onto workers by lowering wage rates or other types of compensation. This ability to shift the tax burden may be limited, however, for minimum wage workers or when there are other institutional constraints.*

[23] *SFY 2009–10 total benefits paid were $468,785,192 (California EDD, n.d.-c), implying total costs of $495,505,948, assuming that administrative costs were 5.7% of benefit costs. Dividing by the 12,146,313 nonpublic employees in the state during the third quarter of 2009 (California EDD, n.d.-c) gives the per capita amount.*

Table 6.4: Paid Family Leave (PFL) Benefits and Number of Claims Paid, by State Fiscal Year (SFY)

Benefits and Claims	SFY 2004–05	SFY 2005–06	SFY 2006–07	SFY 2007–08	SFY 2008–09	SFY 2009–10
Total benefits paid	$300,416,959	$349,325,387	$387,876,893	$439,487,315	$472,105,361	$468,785,192
Number of claims paid	139,593	153,446	165,967	182,834	187,889	180,675
% increase from previous year		9.9%	8.2%	10.2%	2.8%	–3.8%
Total benefits paid in 2008 dollars	$337,419,583	$377,958,687	$409,090,581	$446,961,498	$473,523,385	$465,686,599
% increase from previous year		12.0%	8.2%	9.3%	5.9%	–1.7%
Avg. taxable wage ceiling in 2008 dollars	$83,253	$85,928	$85,856	$86,490	$88,950	$91,993
% increase from previous year		3.2%	–0.1%	0.7%	2.8%	2.7%

Note. EDD PFL program data (California EDD, n.d.-c).

Another way of looking at the impact on employees is to consider how much they actually pay into the system. Although the payroll tax for family leave is combined with that for TDI, some rough calculations can be made. In 2003, prior to the implementation of the PFL program, the tax on wages funding the SDI system, otherwise known as the worker contribution rate, was 0.90%. To fund PFL, the worker contribution rate was initially increased to 1.18% for 2004, a difference of 0.28 percentage points. Since enactment of PFL, the rate has fluctuated and currently is at 1.20% for 2011, or 0.30 percentage points above the rate prior to enactment. Using this 0.30-percentage-point difference as an estimate of the portion of the payroll tax attributable to the PFL program, a full-time worker earning $45,000 a year pays an extra $135 per year in taxes to fund this benefit, while one at the 2011 taxable wage ceiling ($93,316) contributes $280 to fund the program.[24]

Finally, prior to its passage, some were concerned that PFL would bankrupt the SDI system in California. However, enactment of the program actually caused the SDI trust fund balance to grow rapidly at first, most likely because usage was low at first. The SDI trust fund consists of the money collected from workers for the disability and family leave programs and is maintained separately from other funds in the state budget. As the balance grew in the first few years, the payroll tax rate financing the entire SDI system was reduced, dropping to a low of 0.60% in

[24] *California median earnings were $44,313 in 2009: $48,389 for men and $40,019 for women (Getz, 2010).*

2007, but it has since been brought back up to 1.20% for 2011. If claims continue to grow, it is possible that the contribution rate may need to be increased. However, at least in these first years of the program, fears that PFL would bankrupt the SDI system appear unfounded.

Summary

California has pieced together a parental leave system that approaches the benefits offered to families in Canada, Australia, and some (less generous) European nations and is similar to what we propose to be established nationally. The state's PFL program, in combination with SDI, is an important part of a patchwork of laws that together can add up to 16 weeks of paid leave for new mothers, an additional 12 weeks of job-protected but unpaid leave for women who qualify, and 6 weeks of paid leave for new fathers. The California experience offers tentative but useful lessons for both state and national policymakers:

- Paid parental leave, especially for purposes of getting to know their newborn or newly adopted children, is popular with working parents.

- Offering paid leave to augment job-protected leave particularly helps low- and middle-income employees take time off to be with a new baby, reversing the pattern where FMLA job-protected leave disproportionately benefits higher paid workers.

- Partial wage replacement appears to increase the duration of leaves taken and to promote a longer period of breastfeeding.

- Access to partially paid leave makes it easier for fathers to take time off after the birth or adoption of a baby.

- Paid parental leave, at least that financed by employees, does not appear to adversely affect employers or pose a major burden for small business.

- PFL in California costs less than initially anticipated.

At the same time, the experience with paid family leave in California—and from what we know to date in New Jersey and Washington—illustrates the challenges in replicating such a policy at the state level and suggests the benefits of a more unified federal approach:

- Implementing a paid family leave program requires an infrastructure to administer leave payments. Both California and New Jersey have been able to build on existing TDI programs, but only three other states have such an infrastructure. Conversely, the state of Washington has postponed implementation of its law, in part because lack of such an administrative infrastructure has raised the administrative costs of implementing it.

- Establishing 50 different paid family leave policies could be confusing to both families and employers.

- Patching together intersecting laws is complicated; the best policy would offer both job protection and wage replacement in one package easily understood by employees, employers, and the public at large.

References

Appelbaum, E., & Milkman, R. (2004). Paid family leave in California: New research findings. *The State of California Labor, 4,* 45–67).

Appelbaum, E., & Milkman, R. (2011). *Leaves that pay: Employer and worker experiences with paid family leave in California.* Retrieved December 22, 2011, from www.cepr.net/documents/ publications/paid-family-leave-1-2011.pdf

Broyles, J. (2002). Paid leave bill threatens employers and workers with billions in new taxes. *Cal-Tax Digest.* Retrieved February 12, 2009, from www.caltax.org/documents/2002/8.2002. Broyles-PaidLeaveBillThreatensEmployers.04.htm

Broyles, J. (2003). *Chamber fights flaws in paid family leave rules.* Retrieved February 10, 2009, from www.calchamber.com/Headlines/HumanResourcesHealthSafety/Pages/ ChamberFightsFlawsinPaidFamilyLeaveRules.aspx

California Department of General Services. (2000). *Family and Medical Leave Act and California Family Rights Act VMLA/CFRA policy and procedures.* Retrieved July 25, 2011, from www.documents.dgs.ca.gov/ohr/supervisor/DGSFMLAPolicyProcedures.pdf

California Employment Development Department. (n.d.-a). *FAQs for disability insurance.* Retrieved August 20, 2009, from www.edd.ca.gov/Disability/FAQs_for_Disability_ Insurance.htm#Pregnancy

California Employment Development Department. (n.d.-b). *FAQs for paid family leave.* Retrieved July 25, 2011, from www.edd.ca.gov/Disability/FAQs_for_Paid_Family_Leave.htm

California Employment Development Department. (n.d.-c). *Quick statistics.* Retrieved July 25, 2011, from www.edd.ca.gov/About_EDD/Quick_Statistics.htm

California Office of the Attorney General. (1998). *Women's rights handbook.* Retrieved July 25, 2011, from http://ag.ca.gov/publications/womansrights/wrh.pdf

Cantor, D., Waldfogel, J., Kerwin, J., McKinley Wright, M., Levin, K., Rauch, J., et al. (2001). *Balancing the needs of families and employers. Family and medical leave surveys, 2000 update.* Rockville, MD: Westat.

Dube, A., & Kaplan, E. (2002). *Paid family leave in California: An analysis of costs and benefits.* Retrieved May 2, 2011, from www.irle.berkeley.edu/cwed/policy_briefs.html

Economic Opportunity Institute. (2008). *Family Leave Insurance: Security for our families, stimulus for our economy.* Retrieved July 25, 2011, from www.eoionline.org/work_and_family/fact_sheets/FamilyLeaveBrief_Dec08.pdf

Economic Opportunity Institute. (2009). *Keeping your job while you care for your family.* Retrieved February 9, 2010, from www.eoionline.org/work_and_family/Family_Leave_Insurance.htm

Getz, D. M. (2010). *Men's and women's earnings for states and metropolitan statistical areas: 2009* (American Community Survey Briefs ACSBR/09-3). Retrieved July 25, 2011, from www.census.gov/prod/2010pubs/acsbr09-3.pdf

Hamilton, B. E., Martin J. A., & Ventura, S. J. (2010). Births: Preliminary data for 2009. *National Vital Statistics Reports, 59*(3). Hyattsville, MD: National Center for Health Statistics.

Han, W., Ruhm, C. J., & Waldfogel, J. (2009). Parental leave policies and parents' employment and leave-taking. *Journal of Policy Analysis and Management, 28*(1), 29–54.

Hopper, M. (2002, August 11). Paid family leave bill isn't as great as it sounds. *Silicon Valley/San Jose Business Journal.* Retrieved December 29, 2011, from www.bizjournals.com/sanjose/stories/2002/08/12/editorial3.html?

Klerman, J., & Leibowitz, A. (1994). The work-employment distinction among new mothers. *The Journal of Human Resources, 29*, 277–303.

Labor Project for Working Families. (2003). *Putting families first: How California won the fight for paid family leave.* Retrieved July 25, 2011, from www.working-families.org/learnmore/pdf/paidleavewon.pdf

Martin, J. A., Hamilton, B. E., Sutton, P. D., Ventura, S. J., Matthews, T. J., Kirmeyer, S., & Osterman, M. J. K. (2010). Births: Final data for 2007. *National Vital Statistics Reports, 58*(24). Hyattsville, MD: National Center for Health Statistics.

Martin, J. A., Hamilton, B. E., Sutton, P. D., Ventura, S. J., Matthews, T. J., & Osterman, M. J. K. (2010). Births: Final data for 2008. *National Vital Statistics Reports, 59*(1). Hyattsville, MD: National Center for Health Statistics.

Martin, J. A., Hamilton, B. E., Sutton, P. D., Ventura, S. J., Menacker, F., & Kirmeyer, S., (2006). Births: Final data for 2004. *National Vital Statistics Reports, 55*(1). Hyattsville, MD: National Center for Health Statistics.

Martin, J. A., Hamilton, B. E., Sutton, P. D., Ventura, S. J., Menacker, F., Kirmeyer, S., & Matthews, T. J. (2009). Births: Final data for 2006. *National Vital Statistics Reports, 57*(7). Hyattsville, MD: National Center for Health Statistics.

Martin, J. A., Hamilton, B. E., Sutton, P. D., Ventura, S. J., Menacker, F., Kirmeyer, S., & Munson, M. L. (2007). Births: Final data for 2005. *National Vital Statistics Reports, 56*(6). Hyattsville, MD: National Center for Health Statistics.

Milkman, R. (2008). *New data on paid family leave.* Retrieved July 25, 2011, from www.familyleave.ucla.edu/pdf/NewData08.pdf

New Jersey Department of Labor and Workforce Development. (n.d.). *Family leave insurance benefits—general information.* Retrieved July 25, 2011, from http://lwd.dol.state.nj.us/labor/fli/content/program_info_menu.html

New Jersey Department of Labor and Workforce Development. (n.d.) Family leave insurance – Program statistics; 2011 monthly statistics. Retrieved December 29, 2011, from http://lwd.dol.state.nj.us/labor/fli/content/2011_monthly_report_fli.html

Schuster, M. A., Chung, P. J., Elliott, M. N, Garfield, C. F, Vestal, K. D., & Klein, D. J. (2008). Awareness and use of California's paid family leave insurance among parents of chronically ill children. *The Journal of the American Medical Association, 300,* 1047–1055.

U.S. Census Bureau. (n.d.). *American Community Survey.* Retrieved November 12, 2009, from www.census.gov/acs/www/

U.S. Department of Labor. (2010). *Fact sheet #28: The Family and Medical Leave Act of 1993.* Retrieved July 25, 2011, from www.dol.gov/whd/regs/compliance/whdfs28.pdf

Walsh, J. (2011). *Failing its families: Lack of paid leave and work-family supports in the U.S.* New York: Human Rights Watch. Retrieved March 28, 2012, from www.hrw.org/sites/default/files/reports/us0211webwcover.pdf

Washington State Employment Security Department. (2008). *Family Leave Insurance.* Retrieved July, 25, 2011, from www.esd.wa.gov/newsandinformation/legresources/factsheets/archives/fli-factsheet.doc

Wisensale, S. (2006). California's paid leave law: A model for other states? *Marriage and Family Review, 39*(3–4), 177–195.

Zaramberg, A. (2002, August 5). Paid family leave bill would hurt small business. *San Diego Business Journal, 23,* 39.

CHAPTER

Recommendations for a Paid Care Leave Policy

I n the preceding chapters, we have assessed what is known about the timing of return to work after childbirth and, specifically, its impact on child development, maternal and child health, and the economy. Here we draw on that cross-disciplinary evidence base and our own years of experience to inform our policy recommendations. The challenge is to craft a policy that will allow working parents to spend a significant portion of the first few months of life with their new or newly adopted babies without jeopardizing the nation's overall productivity, women's long-term career prospects, or family income.

To reiterate, here is a summary of our findings:

■ **A large body of social and medical science underscores the special importance of parent–infant interaction in the first half-year of life.** It takes several months of focused attention to become a responsive caregiver, establishing a pattern that will influence the baby's long-term cognitive, social, and emotional development. Profound changes are still occurring during the early postnatal period in the circuitry and neurochemistry of the baby's brain, underscoring the wisdom of families having adequate time to get to know and nurture the infant. There is also evidence that families need adequate time to recover from the delivery and sleep disruption, to adjust to the addition of a new family member, and to make sure the baby gets off to a healthy start. Mothers who stay home for a time find it easier to breastfeed and protect the baby from infection. Parental time off also facilitates taking the baby for checkups and detecting potential developmental delays early when problems can most effectively be addressed. Fathers who spend some time at home with their newborn babies tend to continue to play a more active role in child rearing as their children grow. The presence of a mother—or father—at home during the early months after childbirth also reduces the need for out-of-home care during the stage of the baby's life when good-quality care is most expensive and difficult to find.

■ **Although surveys of employed mothers in the United States indicate that most would prefer to take off 6 months from work to focus on their new babies, they typically take considerably less.** Whether because they do not qualify for job-protected leave or cannot afford to take time off without pay, one in four first-time mothers in the United States is back at work within 2 months after giving birth, and two out of five within 3 months after delivery, as compared with only 7% of their counterparts in the United Kingdom. Moreover, in the United States, it is the mothers with relatively fewer resources, and hence potentially more vulnerable infants, who are most likely to return to work in the 2nd month after giving birth. Although less is known about paternal preferences regarding leave duration following the birth or adoption of a new child, a small but growing number of fathers with access to paid leave through their employers or state policies in the United States are electing to spend up to a couple of weeks at home with their new babies, but this pattern tends to be limited to fathers in higher paid occupations.

■ **There is evidence that Americans would support a paid family leave program.** While Americans are typically skeptical of public efforts to solve social problems, there is evidence of public support for a paid care leave policy (Ruhm, 2011). A poll conducted by the Rockefeller Foundation and *Time* in 2009 showed "broad and deep support" for government and business policies to better address the needs of modern families (Halpin & Teixera with Pinkus & Daley, 2009, p. 411). Of the adults surveyed, 76% thought that "businesses should be required to provide paid family and medical leave for every family that needs it" (Halpin et al., p. 412). It is interesting that the support for paid care leave was bipartisan, with 61% of Republicans supporting such a policy. Although the poll did not inquire about how the paid care leave should be financed, the findings indicated general support for a publicly required paid leave policy.

■ **On the basis of experiences in Europe, Canada, and California, it appears possible to craft a paid parental leave policy that does not place undue constraints on employers or undermine the economy, women's career opportunities, or the family's long-term economic security.** In Europe, most evidence suggests that leave entitlements of 6 months to a year do not adversely affect women's career prospects or lifetime earnings, although rights to extremely extended leaves may have some detrimental consequences. Despite long durations and relatively high wage replacement rates in many European countries, total costs of the parental leave are relatively modest. Costs represent 0.1% to 0.2% of gross domestic product (GDP) in seven Western European nations (Austria, Germany, Ireland, the Netherlands, Portugal, Switzerland, and the United Kingdom)[1]—a very small fraction when compared, for example, to the cost of education, which represents between 5% and 6% of GDP in these nations (and 7.1% of GDP in the United States), or health care, which ranges from 8% to 11% of GDP in these countries (and 16% in the United States).

U.S. employers indicate that the expenses of providing 12 weeks of job-protected but unpaid leave under the Family and Medical Leave Act (FMLA) are minimal. In California, the cost of a partially paid leave policy for 6 weeks has proved to be considerably less than originally predicted, and organizations representing California employers no longer seem to have a focused agenda opposing the law. In the most recent year for which data are available, total claims for California's Paid Family Leave were $469 million. Considering that California has about 10% of the nation's population, expanding this leave nationwide at current usage rates might very roughly translate to $4.7 billion for a 6-week leave or about $9.4 billion for a 12-week leave.[2]

■ **A paid care leave policy would also help generate both public and private savings by reducing expenditures for treatment of infectious disease in children, maternal depression, compensatory education, and employee recruitment or re-training.** As discussed in chapter 2, providing paid time off for new mothers, by facilitating breastfeeding, alone could save up to $13 billion in reduced expenditures for treatment of children's infectious disease, such as respiratory and gastrointestinal illnesses and even meningitis. Additional savings for medical care would be expected from reducing maternal depression and the many costly social–emotional problems to which it contributes in young children. Providing a paid care leave available to both mothers and fathers would also facilitate well-baby visits for immunizations and provide an opportunity to identify and treat special needs and health problems early when they are easiest to correct or

---

[1] *The paid care leave policy we recommend here is more modest than that in any of these western European nations. However, if we use the low range of the expenditures for paid leave in these nations, 0.1% of GDP in the U.S. would be about $14.5 billion (0.1% x the U.S. GDP of $14.5 trillion in 2010). By comparison, the U.S. spends 3 times that much, or on average, about $45.8 billion annually for each grade from kindergarten through 12th grade (National Center for Education Statistics, n.d.)*

[2] *For sake of comparison, the annual cost of implementing a preschool-for-all policy in California was once estimated at $1.7 billion (Karoly & Bigelow, 2005), more than 3 times the current state worker payroll expenditures for PFL.*

ameliorate. By promoting a strong foundation for healthy parent–child relationships and support for infant brain development, a paid care leave policy would help reduce expenditures for special and compensatory education.[3] As discussed in chapter 3, investing in several months of paid care leave would also save families money that might otherwise be spent on out-of-home care for infants, which is difficult to find at any price. Finally, as discussed in chapter 4, a publicly financed paid care leave policy would benefit both employees and employers. By helping mothers to take a few months off and then return to work, the policy would reduce the wage penalty that typically affects women who exit the workforce after giving birth. In addition, a paid care leave policy could save employer expenditures for hiring and training a new employee, which have been estimated at 1.5 times a departing worker's annual salary, at least among employees with professional training.

Thus, from the standpoint of both child development and the economy, offering a paid parental leave policy during a portion of the 1st year of life does seem feasible in the United States. In this chapter, we offer the general framework for such a policy. At the onset, we should emphasize that our recommended leave provisions, although considerably less generous than those in most other industrialized nations, are consistent with the areas of strongest international consensus on what is needed to protect child development and enhance labor market outcomes. Moreover, our recommendations are designed to minimize the financial and administrative burden on employers, to be gender-neutral where feasible, and, where possible without detracting from desirable objectives, to build on existing structures and policy.

Below we make recommendations in sequence on each of the following components of parental leave:

- Duration of leave package

- Wage replacement rate

- Worker eligibility

- Prior work history

- Business size

- Finance mechanism

- Administration

---

[3] *The U.S. spends at least $50 billion annually on special education, nearly $14 billion for compensatory education under Title 1, and $25 billion on No Child Left Behind (Chambers, Parrish & Hall, 2004; National Center for Education Statistics, n.d.)*

- Scope of leave legislation (i.e., whether paid parental leave should be considered stand-alone or as part of more comprehensive family and medical leave legislation)

Following each recommendation, we present and discuss one or more "hard" questions.

Duration of Leave Package

■ Recommendation

We propose a 6-month package composed of 3 months of job-protected, paid leave, supplemented by 3 months of job-protected, unpaid leave, to care for a newborn or adopted baby. Specifically, the policy would allow a single parent to take, or both parents to share, 14 weeks of paid leave. The total period of paid leave would extend to 16 weeks in cases where both parents claim at least 2 weeks of leave. The purpose of such a provision, as is already in place in some nations, would be to offer an incentive to encourage fathers (or domestic partners) to take some time to spend with their new babies

Essentially, we propose adding 14–16 weeks of job-protected, paid parental leave to the existing 12 weeks of job-protected, unpaid leave already available to each eligible parent working for employers covered by the FMLA. (For brevity of exposition, we refer to the 14–16 weeks as 3 months of paid leave.)

As described in Table 7.1, at least one parent would qualify for an additional 12 weeks of job-protected leave beyond the initial 14 weeks of partially paid, job-protected leave. The minimum total leave package available to a single parent would thus be 26 weeks, or 6 months,

Table 7.1: Recommended Parental Leave Package

Eligible Worker	Paid, Job-Protected Leave	Unpaid, Job-Protected Leave	Total Paid and Unpaid, Job-Protected Leave
Parent A (typically mother)	Maximum of 14 weeks	12 weeks	26 weeks (14 weeks paid plus 12 weeks unpaid)
Parent B (typically father or domestic partner)	Portion of above or 2 additional "bonus" weeks if Parent B claims at least 2 weeks	12 weeks	14 weeks (2 paid bonus weeks plus additional 12 unpaid)
Family total	14–16 weeks	12–24 weeks, depending on extent to which both parents claim unpaid leave	40 weeks, depending on extent to which both parents claim unpaid leave

Note. Table refers to leave durations for two-parent families. Total amounts of leave are calculated assuming that the mother takes the maximum amount available.

of which 14 weeks would be partially paid and the remaining 12 unpaid. The maximum total leave package, if both parents claimed all benefits for which they were eligible, would be a total of up to 16 weeks of paid leave and 24 weeks of additional job-protected, unpaid leave, or 40 weeks, about the same duration of parental leave currently available in the United Kingdom, though still considerably less than the 50 weeks of parental leave available in Canada. Furthermore, unlike in the United Kingdom and in Canada, after the initial 14–16 weeks of paid leave, the remainder of the time off in our recommended package would be job-protected but unpaid.

Hard Question: Is the proposed period of paid leave long enough to protect maternal health, child health, and child development?

Strictly from the standpoint of maternal recovery from childbirth, 3 months of partially paid leave would more than cover the 6 to 8 weeks that physicians say mothers typically need to recover from childbirth. In addition, that period of leave would help many families handle the most acute period of sleep disruption. Three months of paid leave, supplemented by a similar period of unpaid leave, would also facilitate breastfeeding. As mentioned in chapter 2, the American Academy of Pediatrics recommends "human milk" (as opposed to formula) exclusively through the first year of life, but only 12% of mothers are still breastfeeding even 6 months after giving birth, and early return to work is often a factor in women's decisions to stop breastfeeding. Providing breast milk exclusively even for 4 months and partially thereafter has been found to significantly reduce respiratory and gastrointestinal illness in infants. Of course, even when mothers return to work from leave, they still need access to employer provisions to help them continue breastfeeding through the remainder of the 1st year of their baby's life.

From the perspective of establishing a reciprocal relationship between parent and child, our paid leave recommendation represents a substantial improvement over current U.S. policy, but it clearly falls short of the ideal. Fourteen weeks of paid leave taken by a single parent, or 16 weeks shared by the parents, would at least allow the family to get a start on the attunement process and the carefully choreographed "dance" described in chapter 2. The parent(s) on leave would have time to learn to recognize the baby's special signals, to get a sense of how to soothe the child, to witness the baby's first social smiles, and perhaps to prompt the infant's first giggles. However, pediatricians and developmental psychologists counsel that a longer period of focused attention is typically needed to establish a solid pattern of reciprocal interaction between parent and child. Perhaps most important, parents themselves typically stress the importance of the 6th-month marker. That is, at about the age of 6 months, babies usually learn to sit up and seem less vulnerable; parents may then start to feel more comfortable leaving the infant for a portion of the day in someone else's care. Concern about all of the above developmental issues underlies our recommendation to supplement the 3 months of paid leave with 3 months of job-protected, albeit unpaid leave.

With respect to concerns expressed in chapter 3 about early use of out-of-home care for infants, our recommended leave package would reduce but clearly not eliminate the need for access to quality, nonparental child care before the end of the 1st year of the baby's life. We recognize that many parents would still have to return to work by the 4th month after the baby's birth when the paid leave expired. The proposed leave package would, however, help parents avoid nonparental care during the period when babies are least able to protect themselves and most vulnerable to sudden infant death syndrome. Equally important, the leave package would buy some time for the family to search for an appropriate child care arrangement, an effort that in and of itself often amounts to a significant piece of work for many new parents.

Hard Question: **Why don't we recommend 6 months of paid leave?**

Although we would prefer that all families have access to 6 months of paid leave following the birth or adoption of a baby, we think it is important not to let the perfect become the enemy of the good: Three months of paid leave, supplemented by 3 months of job-protected, unpaid leave, seems to us to be the maximum possible federally supported leave policy goal currently achievable in light of existing American precedents.

Our recommended duration of paid leave is similar to the benefits already in place in two U.S. states—California and New Jersey. As discussed in chapter 6, California and New Jersey are among the five states that offer partially paid temporary disability insurance (TDI), with a period prior to the birth and following delivery included as conditions eligible for partial wage replacement. In California, doctors determine the length of the leave, but the typical period for a normal birth is 6 weeks, with 2 weeks more granted following a birth by cesarean section. In addition, as a part of paid family leave programs, both states offer up to 6 weeks of partial wage replacement per 12-month period for "bonding" with a newborn or adopted baby. Thus, if the mother claims the typical 6 weeks of disability insurance following delivery and then subsequently paid family leave, she can obtain a total of 12–14 weeks of partially paid time off for purposes of recovery from childbirth as well as bonding and attunement. Moreover, if the father or other parent claims a full 6 weeks of paid family leave, the family together can obtain 18–20 weeks of partial wage replacement following the birth of a baby, or 12 weeks following the adoption of a baby.

Our proposal of entitlements to up to 3 months of paid leave (taken by either parent or in combination) also matches the current minimum European Union standard of 3 months of paid parental leave, with the right to return to the same job or, if that is not possible, to an equivalent or similar job. In addition, our recommendation that an additional 2 weeks of paid leave be available when both parents claim at least 2 weeks is consistent with the paid paternity leave policy in several European nations, such as France, Spain, and the United Kingdom.

For all of the reasons cited in chapter 1, we acknowledge that families with fewer financial resources would be the least likely to be able to claim the second 3 months of unpaid leave. It is important to remember a primary rationale for paid leave, namely that the use of purely job-protected leave under the FMLA has been lopsided: A majority of those claiming the leave have been the better educated, better paid employees, and three quarters of the eligible workers not claiming the leave said they could not afford to take unpaid leave. Partly because they tend to be young, without having had many years to accumulate savings, and partly because they suddenly face new and sometimes even unpredictable expenses, families with new babies frequently find it especially difficult to deal with a total loss of one parent's earnings (and, obviously, this is even more true in single-parent households).

However, less advantaged families would almost certainly benefit from the 3 months of paid leave that we advocate, and it is our hope that many of these households might be able to take at least some of the additional job-protected though unpaid leave already provided under the FMLA. Doing so would no doubt require some of the same measures that families currently use to obtain a month or two of paid time off from work after the birth or adoption of a baby, such as piecing together vacation or sick leave to help finance the unpaid portion of the parental leave. The partial wage replacement in the first 3 months after the birth or adoption would at least help reduce financial stress and make it more likely that one or both of the parents would be able to take a longer period of time off to focus on the baby than would otherwise have been possible.

Also, we think it is possible that, over time, employers would become accustomed to the idea of 3 months of paid parental leave and more open to the idea of their employees claiming additional job-protected, albeit unpaid leave. This change in institutional culture would in and of itself represent a dramatic improvement over current practice, in which, as described in chapter 1, low-wage workers are often discouraged from taking any leave, and even many well-paid employees get the message that taking leave will undermine their careers.

In summary, we advocate a 3-month partially paid leave supplemented by 3 months of job-protected, unpaid leave with health and other benefits. This recommendation builds on the existing precedents in two states, California and New Jersey. These state policies appear to be helping new parents balance family and work responsibilities without posing an undue burden on either employers or employees. At the same, our recommended paid leave policy would match the minimum standard of the European Union, where generous leave policies have been in place for some time, without risking the negative effects on women's employment associated with leaves of a year or more in duration. As recommended by the Yale Bush Center Advisory Committee on Infant Care Leave (Zigler & Frank, 1988), we support supplementing the 3 months of partially paid leave with 3 months of job-protected, unpaid leave with continuing health and other benefits.

An alternative policy with considerable appeal would be to have the FMLA unpaid leave and the first 12 weeks of paid leave run concurrently. Consistent with this direction, in the 112th Congress, U.S. Representative Lynn Woolsey (D-CA), joined by 57 co-sponsors, proposed "The Balancing Act of 2011" (H.R. 2346, 2011), which would amend the FMLA to provide 3 months of paid, as opposed to just job-protected, leave. If both parents claimed this leave in succession, it would be possible for a family to carve out 6 months of job-protected, paid leave. This approach might have the advantage of encouraging more fathers to take significant time off to care for their babies, though it would most likely be less effective in facilitating breastfeeding. In addition, for a single-parent household, the total package of paid and unpaid leave available would be substantially less than what we recommend.

Wage Replacement Rate

■ Recommendation

Consistent with the policy in California, and with Canada's paid leave policy, we recommend that the wage replacement rate for the paid portion of the parental leave package be 55% of weekly earnings up to the cap on earnings subject to Social Security tax ($106,800 in 2011). In addition, the leave payment should be treated as income and should therefore be subject to taxation.

Hard Question: **Is the recommended wage replacement rate high enough to help low-income workers take parental leave?**

Our recommended wage replacement rate for parental leave is substantially less generous than that in most nations in Western Europe. For example, France, Germany, and the Netherlands all offer 100% wage replacement for the first 14–16 weeks, and the United Kingdom provides 90% for the first 6 weeks, followed by a flat rate for the remaining 33 weeks of paid leave. The Yale Bush Center Advisory Committee on Infant Care Leave, led by the first author some years ago, recommended income replacement at 75% of salary for 3 months, up to a realistic maximum benefit (Zigler & Frank, 1988). A high rate of wage replacement can be seen as critical to making parental leave policy gender-neutral. In their book *Families That Work*, Gornick and Meyers (2003) hypothesize that only with 100% wage replacement up to a high ceiling would couples be "economically agnostic" regarding who takes the leave. Citing a study by the U.S. Department of Labor that workers who take leave under the unpaid FMLA are 50% more likely to be women, Gornick and Meyers argue that because women on average earn less than men, they are substantially more apt to be the parent who claims the leave.

However, we think that the 55% wage replacement rate up to a ceiling of the current Social Security earnings cap is appropriate for several reasons. First, as a basic principle of personal responsibility, we believe that it is important for families to share in financing time off for parental leave. Second, some expenses related to working, such as transportation, are actually lower when a parent is away from the job, although the birth of a baby creates some new expenses as well. As discussed in chapter 5, regarding paid family leave in other countries, the 55% rate of wage replacement, albeit now available for 50 weeks, has been sufficient to result in a majority of mothers taking the full available leave in Canada. Since Canada introduced a "use it or lose it" policy, a majority of fathers take some of the partially paid leave.

Finally, in California, the 55% replacement rate up to a ceiling ($93,316 in 2011) has been sufficient to reverse the pattern of FMLA usage which has disproportionately benefitted higher-educated and higher-paid employees: As we pointed out in chapter 6, most California paid leave claims (for care of newborn or newly adopted children) are among the lower end of the income spectrum, at least for women, exactly opposite to the pattern observed with the FMLA. At the same time, upper-middle-income families do claim the California leave and praise its benefits.

Some leading advocates of paid family leave, including Representative Woolsey (D-CA) and former U.S. Senator Christopher Dodd (D-CT), the chief Senate champion of the FMLA, have proposed a family leave insurance program with leave benefits graduated on the basis of income. The scale for leave benefits would range from 40% to 100% of wages up to a ceiling of the cap on earnings subject to Social Security premiums, with tiers indexed to inflation. For example, FMLA-eligible employees earning up to $20,000 would receive 100% of their daily wages, those earning up to $60,000 would receive 55% of their earnings, and those earning more than $97,000 would receive 40% of the daily earnings.

Although such an approach may be more politically viable than our proposal, we are concerned that introducing a graduated scale would tend to make paid parental leave seem like a welfare or income redistribution program. Thus, we prefer providing a flat percentage of 55% of weekly earnings up to the income ceiling, with that ceiling typically rising with inflation. In this way, all families with newborn or newly adopted children would have the right to claim some benefits from the paid parental leave program, but no one would get a windfall. Under our recommendation, the highest leave payment an individual would receive would be 55% of the weekly wage related to an annual income of $106,800 in 2011, and the leave payment would be subject to income tax. We view making leave benefits taxable to be desirable because we see no rationale for treating them differently, in this regard, from any other source of income.

Eligibility—Worker Characteristics

■ Recommendation

Consistent with the FMLA and with efforts to make parental leave gender-neutral to the extent feasible, we recommend that both men and women, whether married or single parents, be eligible for the paid and unpaid portions of the job-protected parental leave. As in New Jersey's and California's paid family leave laws, domestic partners, stepparents, and foster parents would also be eligible for paid family leave benefits to care for a new or newly adopted child.

Hard Question: **Is it not likely that mothers will claim the overwhelming majority of the 3 months of paid leave? If so, why not just call it paid maternity leave?**

In our discussion of recommendations on leave duration, we began by citing the minimum standard of 3 months of parental leave in the European Union. Given that physicians recommend 6 to 8 weeks for recovery from childbirth, and the fact that mothers are the only gender that can breastfeed, we acknowledge that mothers will most likely claim the bulk of the 14 weeks of paid leave in the proposed paid parental leave policy. Moreover, this is the experience in virtually all European nations, where women have traditionally taken almost all of the available leave, except in cases where a portion of it is explicitly reserved for fathers.

However, in cases where each parent claims at least 2 weeks of paid leave, we propose that the total duration be extended to 16 weeks. This is a transparent effort to provide an incentive for fathers to take at least 2 weeks of leave to spend with their new babies. Furthermore, our recommendation provides flexibility in cases where the mother wants or needs to return to work sooner than 14 weeks after giving birth, so that the father or other domestic partner can stay at home with partial wage replacement for the remainder of the paid leave period. In cases of adoption, where neither recovery from childbirth nor breastfeeding is an issue, the ability to split the paid leave may be particularly helpful. Our goal in designing the policy this way is to supply families with the maximum ability to make the choices that suit their situation, while providing a mild incentive to promote recognition that balancing the competing demands of work and family is a joint responsibility—shared by both parents—rather than resting exclusively with mothers.

Eligibility—Prior Work History

■ Recommendation

We propose that to be eligible for job-protected parental leave an employee must have worked at least 1,000 hours over the preceding 12 months. This provision would allow many part-time workers to be eligible for leave. However, for a worker to be eligible for paid leave, work history is less germane, and a percentage of earnings accompanied by contributions to the insurance fund may suffice to determine eligibility.

Hard Question: **Will any prior work requirement disqualify the most vulnerable workers?**

As discussed in chapter 1, only 19% of all new mothers and 31% of those employed for 1 year prior to giving birth are estimated to be eligible for job protection under the FMLA. Many women are ineligible because they work in small businesses, a topic we discuss separately later. However, another factor contributing to ineligibility of women is that they are generally more apt than men to work part-time, and, in an economic downturn, many have no option but to work part-time. Similarly, women in their prime child-bearing years, perhaps especially those who have pursued years of advanced training, are likely to be starting families at the same time that they are launching careers.

Nevertheless, as we saw in chapter 5, virtually all nations providing paid parental leave have some prior work requirement. As stated earlier, the purpose of our recommended paid parental leave policy is not to be a welfare program replacing income regardless of the reason for its loss but rather to provide a period of respite from work to employed parents to focus on infant care. In fact, as we have discussed in several chapters of this book, one important motivation behind the FMLA and the paid leave legislation at the state level has been actually to encourage continued ties to the workforce and to prevent employee turnover. By offering a worker a limited period of extended time off, the intention is to eliminate the need for the employee to sever ties to the particular place of work, much less to the overall workforce. As such, the job protection component of the leave makes sense only if the parent has been employed during the previous year.

And the paid leave component is logically tied to a percentage of earnings in the previous year. The previous employment requirement also provides incentives for some individuals to work or increase their hours, prior to childbirth, so as to qualify for paid leave. Such effects may be particularly pronounced for low-paid workers (whose net wage replacement rate will be relatively high because their tax rate tends to be low) and those with intermittent employment histories. These incentives seem consistent with current public policies (e.g., welfare reform), which stress the importance of work for such individuals.

Those points made, we recommend reducing the current FMLA requirement of 1,250 hours to 1,000 hours to enable more part-time workers (e.g., those averaging about 20 hours of work per week) to qualify for job-protected leave. This 1,000-hour threshold for job protection benefits is provided in the New Jersey Family Leave Act enacted in 2008. An alternative that deserves consideration is the 6-month work history requirement of 650 hours proposed by Representative Woolsey in the 2011 bill described earlier. Many employers have a probationary period of 6 months before new employees are considered permanent or eligible for employee benefits. A 6-month tenure requirement might be sufficient to provide evidence that the new employee's performance had been satisfactory.

For paid leave benefits, the better approach may be to set a minimum amount of earnings for the prior year. For example, the California Paid Family Leave Act, which provides partial wage replacement though no job protection, does not require that a recipient have worked any specific number of hours in the previous year; the only work-related requirement is that the leave applicant have earned at least $300 (from which state disability insurance deductions have been withheld) during one of the four quarters in the year spanning roughly 5 to 17 months prior to the start of the leave. However, if an earnings requirement is considered, care must be taken not to set the minimum too high, or it will put low-income workers at a disadvantage.

Business Size Requirement

■ Recommendation

As recommended by the Obama presidential campaign in 2008, we recommend reducing the business size requirement for providing job-protected, unpaid parental leave from the current FMLA requirement of 50 or more employees to 25 or more. For the paid leave provision, we recommend following the precedent set by the paid family leave statutes in both California and New Jersey, where there is no minimum business size for an employee to qualify for paid leave.

Hard Questions: **Can job protection be expanded to more employees without hurting small business? Should there be a business size requirement for paid leave?**

From the perspective of employees, size of the firm does not affect the need for parental leave following the birth or adoption of a baby (except that small companies might offer greater flexibility in working conditions or be more willing to make informal arrangement to address work–family issues). Thus, it would be desirable for all eligible workers to be covered, regardless of employer size. However, small firms might find it more burdensome to manage their companies with absent employees or to provide job protection. Reflecting these competing demands, recommendations to reduce the business size requirements for job-protected leave are among the most contentious in the debates on family and medical leave.

As discussed in chapter 1, associations representing small business remain adamant in their opposition to such proposals. However, it is interesting to note that several states, such as Minnesota and Oregon, have already reduced the employee threshold to 25 or lower for eligibility for job-protected family and medical leave (National Partnership for Women and Families, n.d.).

Whether business size requirements become an issue in paid family leave legislation depends, in part, on how the leave is financed and whether employers are required to contribute to the premiums to support the program. Because the paid leave programs in both California and New Jersey are financed entirely by employee payroll deductions (and do not include job protection provisions), business size requirements ultimately were not included in these statutes. However, both former Senator Dodd and Representative Woolsey proposed requiring both employers and employees to pay premiums to finance the leave. The Dodd bill (S. 1681, 2007) made participation mandatory for all businesses with more than 50 employees; businesses with fewer than 50 employees could opt in, with a 50% discount on premiums. Similarly, the self-employed could also opt in, paying both the employer and employee shares at the 50% discounted rate for small business. The 2011 Woolsey bill made participation in the paid leave program mandatory for employers with 20 or more employees but allowed small employers and the self-employed to opt in.

On the basis of our review of the impact of paid family leave legislation in California since its implementation in 2004, some reduction in the business size requirement for the job-protected leave provisions in the FMLA is clearly needed. The California paid leave law, like that in New Jersey, does not provide job protection; hence, job protection is limited to those employees whose employers meet the business size requirements in the FMLA. As a result, as discussed in chapter 6, although some employees of small businesses ineligible for FMLA protection have claimed the paid leave in California (90 claims per every 100,000 workers in businesses with fewer than 50 employees), proportionally more claims are from workers in large companies (235 claims per every 100,000 workers in businesses with 50 or more employees).

Finance Mechanism

■ Recommendation

Consistent with the practice in most nations in Western Europe, we propose financing paid parental leave at the federal level through a combination of general revenue and payroll taxes for both employers and employees.

Hard Question: **Given the budget deficit, how likely is it that Congress would consider any new tax to pay for this program? (Or: Are you kidding?)**

Clearly, proposing an increase in taxation is always a risky enterprise, and it may seem foolhardy in the current budget climate. However, our premise, supported by the Nobel-winning economist James Heckman among many others, is that investing in the early years of child development helps prevent far greater expenditures for compensatory education and social welfare programs later on. Making it easier for working parents to spend at least a portion of the first half year of life focusing on their newborn or newly adopted baby seems like a wise investment. In addition, making it possible for parents, without permanently giving up their chance for a meaningful career or income security, to spend time at home with infants is likely to preserve and enhance the human capital of the parents, with direct benefits not only to them but also to the broader economy. More fundamentally, we believe that providing parents with the ability to balance the needs of work and home life is a basic family value, that it speaks to who we are and who we wish to be as a nation. We know of no more important investment, and we are not alone in this view. The parental leave policies we have proposed would considerably enhance the policies currently in place in the United States, but they remain modest relative to those in most other industrialized countries. Although there is an expense associated with our proposed parental leave benefits, as discussed earlier, a modest paid leave policy would cost less than a third of the cost of a year of public education, and, given all the brain development going on during the first months of life, would be at least as important an investment in the child's future..

Former Senator Dodd's proposed paid Family Leave Insurance Act and Representative Woolsey's proposed Balancing Act of 2011 offer an interesting twist on the payroll tax approach for financing paid family leave. Under these bills, both employees and employers would pay an insurance premium equivalent to 0.2% of each employee's earnings. Under the Dodd bill, employers with fewer than 50 employees could opt into the fund at a 50% discount, as could the self-employed. For an employer's workers to claim the leave payment, the employer would have to pay at least 12 months of that amount to insurance premiums. Alternatively, as indicated above, the employers could choose to self-insure so long as they were able to offer equivalent or better benefits. The federal government would then use general revenues to pay administrative costs not covered by the employer and employee contributions. Under the Woolsey bill, both employers and employees of businesses with 20 or more employees would pay a premium of 0.2% of each employee's earnings, but those with fewer employees would pay only 0.1%.

The Dodd and Woolsey bill finance mechanisms are similar to one of the options recommended many years ago by the Yale Bush Center Advisory Committee on Infant Care Leave, led by the senior author of this book. That committee recommended establishing a federally managed insurance fund modeled on short-term disability insurance with contributions from both employers and employees.

The Congressional and the Yale Bush Center Advisory Committee recommendations notwithstanding, we now think that paid leave for infant care would ideally be financed entirely through general revenues. As indicated in chapter 4, this option has the merit of spreading the cost across all taxpayers and of including investments as well as wages in the sources of revenues; imposing a payroll tax, especially one limited to employees, tends to be regressive. However, as we have noted, the vast majority of the Western European nations finance paid parental leave through a combination of payroll taxes and general revenue or through payroll taxes alone. Given that payroll taxes (or premiums, as they are called in Canada and in the Dodd and Woolsey bills), are the most likely route to financing paid parental leave, we recommend that there be no income ceiling threshold on the tax or premium, as is currently the case with Medicare but not Social Security.

Having stated our preferred approach to federally financing the paid portion of parental leave with general revenue, or in combination with payroll taxes, we recognize that there are alternative routes, such as proceeding state-by-state. The two states that have implemented paid family leave legislation, California and New Jersey, have both chosen to finance the leave solely through employee payroll taxes. The tax is estimated to cost $40 per employee per year in California and $33 per employee per year in New Jersey. Earlier versions of the paid family leave bill in California imposed a payroll tax on both employers and employees, but the former was ultimately eliminated as a condition to secure passage of the program.

Even if states dictate the finance mechanism for paid parental leave, the program should be national in scope in the sense that there should be a federal requirement that all states have such a policy. We think this state-by-state approach, however, would be more complicated and administratively expensive than our proposed federal approach to financing paid leave. In addition, having 50 different approaches to financing paid leave would potentially be confusing to both employers and employees.

Administration

■ Recommendation

In line with the principle of building on existing law and structures to the extent feasible, and given our preference that the paid parental leave program be financed at the federal level, we recommend that the program be administered by the Social Security Administration.

Hard Question: **Isn't the Social Security system already overburdened? (Or: Would any perceived linkage to Social Security prompt fears that the paid parental leave benefits would reduce pensions for the elderly?)**

We recommend administration through the Social Security Administration strictly because the infrastructure already exists, and there would be no need to set up a new administering agency. Administrative costs are low in the current Social Security system, and these efficiencies would be likely to extend to the administration of the parental leave. If, as we have recommended earlier, the leave program were financed through general revenue in combination with payroll taxes, the general revenue funds collected to administer the benefits could be transferred to the Social Security Administration. If funded by payroll taxes alone, the system for collecting these (from employers and employees) could easily be extended to financing parental leave, and applicants could apply for paid parental leave at local Social Security Administration offices. The parental leave payroll taxes would be paid into a paid leave trust fund that would be entirely separate from the Old-Age, Survivors, and Disability Insurance trust fund and the Medicare Hospital Insurance trust funds. Indeed, the long history of separation between retirement and Medicare trust funds should allay concerns that the parental leave benefits would affect retirement or health care security.

Alternative administrative structures, although possible, seem less desirable. Both California and New Jersey have built their paid family leave programs on the foundation of their state TDI program: Applications are sent to—and benefits are paid by—the TDI administrators, and revenues are collected through an increase in the preexisting TDI payroll tax. However, only three other states (Hawaii, Illinois, and Rhode Island) and Puerto Rico have TDI programs, so the administrative and financing structure for the California and New Jersey programs is likely to be quite difficult to replicate in the 45 states without TDI programs.

We also see difficulties with administering paid family leave through state unemployment insurance systems. All states and jurisdictions have unemployment programs, but there are a number of reasons why California and New Jersey have found that paid family leave is more suited to a TDI structure than an unemployment insurance structure. First, unemployment insurance is funded through a payroll tax paid by employers, and that tax rate for employers varies depending on the quantity of claims made by former employees. Under TDI, the tax rate to employers does not vary with the number of claims made. Second, in each state, the same unemployment insurance program covers all workers regardless of employer. For TDI, states have provisions that allow businesses to offer greater coverage through private insurers and that allow self-employed persons to elect to opt in or not.

With support from advocacy groups such as the National Partnership for Women and Families and MomsRising, much of the momentum for paid family leave has been at the state level over the last decade (Walsh, 2011). Many families have already obtained paid leave under the leave policies enacted in California and New Jersey, and studies of the impact of these laws can help inform policy development in other states as well as at the federal level. The Obama 2008 presidential campaign proposal to provide $1.5 billion to assist states and employers with start-up costs for paid leave programs would have been an important step to explore other finance and administrative mechanisms at the state level. Start-up support would certainly help Washington State, which enacted a paid family leave statute but, for lack of an administrative and financing structure, has of this writing not implemented the law. However, while policies such as paid parental leave may well begin at the state level, we think a federally administered program would ultimately be simpler and less expensive.

Representative Woolsey's 2011 bill contains an interesting proposal on the administration of a paid care leave program. That bill recommends establishing a Family and Medical Insurance Program in the Department of the Treasury. The Secretary of Labor would lead the administration of the federal program, and a Board of Trustees composed of the Secretary of the Treasury, the Secretary of Labor, the Commissioner of Social Security, the Secretary of Health and Human Services, and two members of the public appointed by the president would oversee the program. States would have the option to establish or expand their own paid leave program, funded by the federal insurance fund; or to request that the Commissioner of Social Security set up a State Family and Medical Insurance Program for the state.

Scope of Leave Legislation—Stand-Alone Parental Leave or Comprehensive Family and Medical Leave

▌ Recommendation

Although we are agnostic regarding the legislative vehicle in which paid parental leave might ultimately be enacted, we recommend that the provisions of paid and job-protected parental leave for the care of newborn and newly adopted children be fully developed separately from other types of family and medical leave before attempting to incorporate them with provisions with any other conditions eligible for such leave.

Hard Question: **Won't any separate discussion of parental leave endanger the carefully crafted alliance that supported the FMLA?**

Although the policy recommendations in this chapter focus on parental leave for the care of newborn or newly adopted infants, we recognize that in the political process the issue of paid leave for infant care might ultimately be combined with that of family and medical leave. Paid leave for a personal health condition or to address a serious health issue of a child or aging parent is certainly an important component of a comprehensive work–family policy; these issues arguably affect at least as large a portion of the workforce as does paid parental leave.

As was discussed in the chapter on the FMLA, early versions of that legislation focused more on maternity leave. The Yale Bush Center Advisory Committee's use of the term "infant care leave" in 1985 was deliberate and was intended to expand the concept of maternity leave to promote a gender-neutral policy whereby either parent would be eligible to take time off to care for a newborn or newly adopted infant. The purpose of infant care leave was not only to allow the mother time off for recovery from childbirth but also to allow either parent to begin to establish a reciprocal relationship with the baby.

During the nearly decade-long congressional deliberations on leave policy that followed, the concept of infant care leave was ultimately combined with that of the broader issues of family and medical leave. In a fascinating history of that legislation, Ronald Elving (1995) explained that among the key supporters of the legislation, female lawyers, unions, and the American Association for the Advancement of Retired Persons favored a more comprehensive approach. Some of these groups felt that medical and family leave would have a better chance of passage if combined with what might be construed as the "motherhood and apple pie issue" of parental leave for the care of newborn babies. But on a more fundamental level, women lawyers favored the broader framework for the leave legislation because they thought any leave package limited to infant care would undermine the basic principle of "equal treatment" for which many had fought so hard in civil rights legislation. Even if theoretically available to both genders, they argued, a leave policy focused on the care of newborn infants would ultimately be used primarily by women and would hence lead to discrimination against them in hiring. As summarized by Elving, from the point of view of the Women's Legal Defense Fund, "a leave bill had to be justified on the basis of something more common than motherhood, or even parenthood. It had to be something anyone might face, such as a temporary disability or medical necessity within the family" (Elving, p. 23).

Continuing in the same vein, in more recent policy discussions of paid leave, Workplace Flexibility 2010 at Georgetown University Law Center coined the term "Extended Time Off (EXTO)" to cover time off for a broad range of conditions, including a need for time off from work for a single reason that extends for more than 5 days but less than 1 year (e.g., caring for a newborn or newly adopted child, having a serious health condition, caring for a family member with a serious health condition, or serving in the military; Workplace Flexibility 2010, n.d.).

However, it is interesting to note that there is a recent legislative precedent for considering the special components of paid parental leave separately. In 2009, the U.S. House of Representatives passed a bill by Congresswoman Carolyn Maloney (D-NY) to provide paid parental leave to federal employees (H.R. 626, 2009). The bill essentially would add 4 weeks of paid leave for parents following the birth or adoption of an infant within the scope of the 12 weeks of FMLA job-protected leave already available to federal employees for a broader range of conditions.

Whether or not paid parental leave for infant care is ultimately combined with paid family and medical leave, we have limited our recommendations in this book to those related to parental leave for the care of infants for two reasons. First, our primary expertise is in the area of child development and the economic analyses of the impact of parental leave policies rather than on issues related to the eligibility, duration, or payment level for care of one's own illness or that of an elderly parent. Second, in our view, the policies needed to address leave following the arrival of a new baby are potentially quite different from those related to time off work for other reasons. For instance, it seems quite plausible that the optimal duration of leave and conditions under which it can be taken will diverge substantially across the various types of leave. One important source of differences is that the circumstances related to welcoming a new baby into the world are somewhat more predictable than those related to other types of family and medical leave, and hence it is both possible and important to address them separately and give them their due before launching into the negotiations and compromises involved in the development of broader legislation. Part of this predictability occurs because birth and adoption are clearly defined events that occur with limited frequency and with fairly clear delineation of caregiving responsibilities.

Many of the other potential types of leave are less clear-cut. Consider the example of caring for a sick relative. In this case, there are questions regarding the frequency, duration, and severity of the relative's illness; perhaps a different range of choices of caregivers; and the general lack of predictability in the occurrence of the illness. Thus, there may be increased concern about issues such as how the leaves should be structured to provide appropriate incentives to employees while minimizing disruptions to employers.

Conclusion

In this chapter, we have provided recommendations on the primary components of a parental leave policy, including at least 3 months of partially paid leave and an additional 3 months of job-protected, unpaid leave available to either parent. Although our recommended leave duration and wage replacement rates are less generous than those in Canada and most of Europe, our policy proposals would meet the minimum requirements of the European Union, build on existing federal and state law in the United States, and go a long way toward promoting child development without jeopardizing families' career chances or the nation's economy.

Research across the fields of maternal and child health, child development, and economics all converge to support our thesis: Paid family leave for infant care is a wise investment. The cost of a modest leave policy is low, and the projected benefits are substantial. By increasing the rates of breastfeeding and childhood immunizations, a paid leave policy would reduce expenditures for treatment of infectious disease. By supporting a period for families to attune with their new babies, the policy would have long-term benefits in children's cognitive and social and emotional development. By allowing mothers to take time off with a new baby without exiting the labor force, a modest paid leave policy could help reduce the lifetime wage penalty that most women currently pay for becoming mothers. A publicly supported paid leave policy might also benefit employers by reducing employee turnover and expenditures for retraining. In short, we see little downside to offering a modest paid leave policy for infant care and great cost in having the United States continue to be the only advanced industrialized nation without such a policy.

References

Chambers, J., Parrish, T., & Hall, J. (2004). *What are we spending on special education services in the United States, 1999-2000?* Special Education Expenditures Project, Center for Special Education Finance. Retrieved January 12, 2012, from http://csef.air.org/publications/seep/national/AdvRpt1.pdf

Elving, R. (1995). *Conflict and compromise: How Congress makes the law.* New York: Simon & Schuster.

Gornick, J. C., & Meyers, M. K. (2003). *Families that work: Policies for reconciling parenthood and employment.* New York: Russell Sage Foundation.

Halpin, J., & Teixeira, R., with Pinkus, S., & Daley, K. (2009). Battle of the sexes gives way to negotiation. In H. Boushey. & A. O'Leary (Eds.), *The Shriver report: A woman's nation changes everything* (pp. 395–417). Washington, DC: Center for American Progress.

H.R. 626, 111th Cong. (2009).

H.R. 2346, 112th Cong. (2011).

Karoly, L., & Bigelow, J. (2005). *The economics of investing in universal preschool education in California.* RAND Labor and Population. Retrieved January 4, 2012, from www.rand.org/pubs/monographs/MG349.html

National Center for Education Statistics (n.d.) Common core of data, surveys, and unpublished data. Retrieved January 12, 2012, from www2.ed.gov/about/overview/fed/10facts/edlite-chart.html

National Partnership for Women and Families. (n.d.). *State family and medical leave laws that are more expansive than the federal FMLA.* Retrieved September 25, 2011, from www.nationalpartnership.org/site/DocServer/StateunpaidFMLLaws.pdf?docID=968>

S. 1681, 110th Cong. (2007).

Ruhm, C. J. (2011). Policies to assist parents with young children. *The future of children, 21*(2), 37–68.

Walsh, J. (2011). *Failing its families: Lack of paid leave and work-family supports in the U.S.* New York: Human Rights Watch. Retrieved March 28, 2012, from http://hrw.org/sites/default/files/reports/us0211webwcover.pdf

Workplace Flexibility 2010. (n.d.) *Extended time off.* Retrieved July 10, 2011, from http://workplaceflexibility2010.org/index.php/policy_components/time_off/extended_time_off/

Zigler, E., & Frank, M. (Eds.). (1988). *The parental leave crisis: Toward a national policy.* New Haven, CT: Yale University Press.

About the Authors and Contributor

Authors

Edward Zigler, PhD, founded and is director emeritus of Yale's Edward Zigler Center in Child Development and Social Policy, one of the first centers in the nation to combine training in developmental science and social policy construction. Currently Sterling Professor of Psychology, Emeritus, he helped design several national programs, including Head Start, Early Head Start, the School of the 21st Century, and the Child Development Associate training credential. In the early 1970s, he served as the founding director of the Office of Child Development (now Administration on Children, Youth and Families) and chief of the U.S. Children's Bureau. He chaired an advisory commission that produced recommendations for what became the Family and Medical Leave Act. The author of nearly 40 books, he earned his doctorate in developmental psychology from the University of Texas, is a member of the Institute of Medicine and the American Academy of Arts and Sciences and has received many honorary degrees.

Susan Muenchow, MS, a principal research analyst at the American Institutes for Research, is a policy specialist and writer in the area of child development and social policy. She recently coauthored a report to California's governor and legislature on the design of a quality rating system for early learning and care. Prior to joining AIR, she administered subsidized early care and education programs and served as the director of the Children's Forum and the Florida Partnership for School Readiness. For her work in promoting the expansion and improvement of child care, she has received multiple awards and has testified before Congressional and state legislative committees on early learning and care policy. A graduate of Stanford University who has a master's degree from Columbia University School of Journalism, she has written on child development and social policy for the *Christian Science Monitor*, *Parents* Magazine, and the *New York Times*. With Dr. Zigler, she coauthored *Head Start: The Inside Story of America's Most Successful Educational Experiment*.

Christopher J. Ruhm, PhD, professor of public policy and economics at the University of Virginia, received his doctorate in economics from the University of California, Berkeley, and a bachelor's degree from the University of California, Davis. He previously held faculty positions at the University of North Carolina at Greensboro and Boston University. During the 1996–97 academic year he served as senior economist on President Clinton's Council of Economic Advisers. He is a research associate at the National Bureau of Economic Research and a research fellow at the Institute for the Study of Labor (IZA) in Germany. His recent research focuses on the role of government policies in helping parents with young children balance the competing needs of work and family life and on examining the relationship between macroeconomic conditions and the status of health. Dr. Ruhm has published extensively on the economic impact of parental leave policies and the timing of maternal employment after childbirth for both academic and policy audiences.

Additional Contributor

Sami Kitmitto, PhD, a senior research analyst at the American Institutes for Research, was the lead author along with Ruhm and Muenchow on chapter 6 on California's paid leave program. An economist specializing in education finance and policy, he currently serves as deputy project director on the National Assessment of Educational Progress-State Analysis project with the U.S. Department of Education where he leads tasks measuring the change in inclusion rates of students with disabilities on NAEP and analyzing achievement gaps using NAEP data. Dr. Kitmitto has previously served as project director on an evaluation of the federal Impact Aid program and analyst for the California Comprehensive Center investigating school and district effectiveness. Dr. Kitmitto earned his doctorate in economics with a multidisciplinary emphasis in Economy, Justice, and Society from the University of California, Davis.

Index

A

Abecedarian Project, 60, 64

Accounting firms: views on paid leave and employee retention/reduced turnover, 27

Administration of parental leave: recommendations, 166–168

Administration for Children and Families, 75

Adoptive parents, leave for: under Family and Medical Leave Act; in state policies, 20, 25; special reasons for leave needed, 39; California Family Rights Act, and, 128; Paid Family Leave (PFL) and, 129, 131–132, 133–135; recommendations, 157

Ainsworth, Mary, 47, 60

American Academy of Pediatrics: recommendations for breastfeeding, 35, 40, 67, 156; recommendations for child care standards, 72

American Association of Retired Persons, 17, 20, 169

American Public Health Association, 72

Americans with Disabilities Act, 18

Appelbaum, Eileen, 125, 137, 140, 142, 143

Association of Junior Leagues, 17

Attachment: definition of, 43; role of attunement and, 44, 46; stages of and time needed to develop, 47; impact on brain development, 47; implications for parental leave policy, 49; impact of nonparental care on, 62. See also Child development.

Attunement: definition of, 43; role of compared to attachment, 44; time needed to establish reciprocal pattern of interaction, 45; early intervention programs to promote, 45–46; impact on attachment and brain development, 46–48; implications for parental leave policy, 49, 156. See also Child development.

Australia: newcomer to parental leave, 102, 111; parental leave provisions, 111

Austria: Parental leave provisions, 106

B

"Back to Sleep" Campaign, 69

Barker hypothesis, 84

Barnard, Kathryn, 61

Becker, Gary, 84

Belsky, Jay, 60

Belgium: parental leave provisions, 106

Berman, Howard, 17, 19

Birth rates: impact of paid leave policies on birth rates/fertility in Europe, 116–117. See also Pronatalism.

Bond, Kit, 19

Bonding: definition of, 43; role of hormones in, 44; role of compared to attunement, 44. *See also* Child development

Brain development: wiring/development of neural pathways, 43, 47–49; Still Face study; effect of stress on, 48–49, 63; impact of attunement, attachment and parent–child interaction, 151. *See also* Child development.

Brazelton, T. Berry, 15, 20, 44, 45, 60

Breastfeeding: Link to reduction in postneonatal mortality and other benefits for child health, 33, 40, 86; difficulties with, 35 (infections, soreness, inadequate milk supply), 35; rate of, 40, 86; impact on maternal health, 37; American Academy of Pediatrics recommended duration, 40; pumping, 41; positive impact of California Paid Family Leave on, 142; relation to recommendations for paid care leave policy, 151, 156; projected savings in reduced expenditures for treatment of infectious disease, 153, 156, 170

Britain: See United Kingdom.

Bronfenbrenner, Urie, vii, x, 42

Bunning, Jim, 18

Burggraf, Shirley, 87

Bush, President George H. W., 17

Business: opposition to leave laws at federal level in U.S., 3, 17, 18–19; estimates of costs of FMLA to employers, 18; opposition to mandated benefits, 17–18; challenges associated with implementing leave private leave policies, 19; support for public leave policy, 19; small business exemption, 22; findings on cost of administering FMLA, 24; opposition to California Paid Family Leave Law, 143–144

Business size: FMLA requirements, 22; state policies, 25; recommendation for U.S. leave policy, 163–164. *See also* Small business.

C

Caldwell, Bettye, 60

California Chamber of Commerce, 143

California Employment Development Department (EDD): 126, 130, 133, 144

California Family Rights Act: 128, 129

California Manufacturers and Technology Association, 143

California Paid Family Leave: 123–149; planning grant for, 125; Labor Project for Working Families, 125; historical background, 126–128; added value of, 129; provisions of (with examples), 130–132; use for "bonding" with a new baby or newly adopted child, 133–135; impact on duration of leave, 135–137; impact on proportion of fathers taking parental leave, 137–138; impact on low–income employees' access to leave, 138–139; combining pregnancy disability leave and PFL, 139–140; public awareness of PFL, 140–141; impact of lack of job protection (focus on small–business employees), 141–142; impact on breastfeeding and child care, 142–143; effect on employers, 143–144, 153; benefits and claims, 144–145; cost of PFL, 144–146

California Senate Research Office: 133

California State Disability Insurance (formerly Temporary Disability Insurance): 25, 124, 126–127, 128, 129

California State Fair Employment Practices Act: 127

California State Fair Employment and Housing Act: 127

Canada: timing of return to employment following childbirth, 1, 12; female employment rate, 13; "use it or lose it" leave provisions for fathers, 14, 60; parental leave provisions, 16, 106, 110–111; duration of parental leave, and impact on breastfeeding, 86, 112; administration at provincial level, 112; wage replacement rate, 112; more generous benefits in Quebec, 112; impact of leaves on job continuity, 113; impact of leaves on child health and development, 115

Cesarean deliveries: increase in, 35; risks of and recovery from, 36

Chatterji, Pinka, 37

Childbirth: delay in age of childbearing, 12–13; safety of, 34; time needed for recovery, 34–38; complications of (incl. episiotomy, cesarean delivery, depression/"baby blues"), 35–36; increase in multiple births and low birthweight, 41

Child care: Types of nonparental care, 58; rate of use of early child care, 58, 59; research on effects of early nonparental care, 59–61, 62–66; quality of care, 62, 65, 86; safety of care, 67–70; safety of care in relation to types of care, 69–70; quality and availability of care, 70–72; affordability and cost of care, 72–73 . *See also* Infant care and Nonparental care.

Child Care and Development Block Grant, 76

Child and Dependent Care (tax) Credit, 73

Child development: bonding, 43; attunement, 43, 45; attachment, 43,47, 62; cognitive development, 45, 46, 64, 65, 84–85; social and emotional development, 63–64; stages in and brain development, 43, 47–49, 84–85

Child Welfare League of America, 2, 59

Children's Center at Syracuse Family Development Research Program, 60

Children's Defense Fund, 17

Clarke–Stewart, Alison, 60

Clay, William, 19

Clinton, Hillary Rodham, 17

Clinton, President William, 17

Coats, Dan, 19

Cohen, Wilbur, 15

Commission on Family and Medical Leave, 24

Communicable disease: In child care settings, 67–68

Connecticut, and family and medical leave legislation, 17

Contraception: Impact on maternal participation in workforce, 12–13

Cost savings: estimated for paid parental leave policy from expenditures for treatment of infectious disease, 40, 115, 153, 156, 170; 115; reduction in employee turnover and training costs, 23, 27, 89; potential reduction in early use of nonparental care, 74, 76; as an early investment, x, 84–86; in protecting good job matches, 87–88; in reduction of

health care costs, public assistance, 90–91; positive effects on job continuity and employment in Europe, 112–113; and in California, 142–143; other anticipated cost savings, such as in maternal depression and compensatory education, 153; summary of benefits, 170–171. *See also* Heckman's curve.

D

D'Amato, Alfonse, 19

DeLay, Tom, 18

Denmark: parental leave provisions, 106

Depression, maternal: See postpartum depression.

Disability insurance: state temporary disability insurance programs in 5 states, 25; use of for pregnancy leave before and after childbirth, 124; as foundation for Paid Family Leave (PFL) in California, 126–128; provision of infrastructure for administering paid family leave, 146; difficulty in replicating TDI infrastructure in other states, 167

Discrimination, against women: concerns about unintended consequences of paid leave, 3; rise in claims of by pregnant women, 28

District of Columbia, Temporary Disability Insurance policy, 25

Dodd, Christopher, 19, 20, 159, 160, 164, 165

Domestic partners: eligibility for paid leave, 129; recommendations, 161

Duration of leave: International Labor Organization (ILO) minimum for maternity leave, 16; of package of paid maternity and parental leave in advanced industrialized nations, 16; in Canada, 16; of FMLA, 21; of TDI in 5 states, 25; in Washington statute, 26; economic feasibility of length of leave, 95; in Europe and Canada, 106–107; of paternity leave, 108; comparative generosity of, 108–109; in Canada, 110–111; in Australia, 111; consequences of short or intermediate vs. long duration, 112–114, 116; of leave package in California, 129; impact of PFL in California, 135–137, 139; recommended parental leave package, 155–159, 170

E

Early Childhood Longitudinal Study, Birth Cohort (ECLS–B), 12, 37, 58

Early Head Start, 64, 65, 75

Early intervention programs: Benefits for low–birth–weight and other at–risk children, 45–46, 57, 60, 64–65; importance of parental involvement in, 66; recommendations for, 75

Economic impact of paid parental leave: on children, 83–86, 115–116; on mothers, 86–89, 112, 171; on employers, x, 3, 4, 89, 113, 143–144, 146, 152–153; on families, as an alternative to early use of nonparental care, 74; on taxpayers, x, 3, 5, 40, 153–154; on gender–wage gap, 3; negative impact of lengthy leaves, 113–114, 117; on employers in California, 143–144; on low–income and middle–income employees in California, 139; on payroll taxpayers in California, 144–146; in Europe, 152–153; costs to taxpayers in Europe, 109–110, 153; estimated cost savings in U.S. 153–154

Educare, 65, 73, 75

Eligibility: for FMLA, 20, 21–23; more generous eligibility requirements in some states, 25; business views on, 3; for private sector leave policies, 26–27; 28; less access for lesser educated, 28; for self–employed in Europe; variations in Europe and Canada, 106–107, 108; transferability in Australia, 111; for Paid Family Leave in California, 124; for Temporary Disability Leave/Pregnancy Disability Leave in California, 127, 128; for Paid Family Leave (PFL) in California, 129; proportion of eligible workers who apply for PFL, 134–135; recommended worker requirements, 161–163; for stand–alone paid parental leave vs. comprehensive paid family and medical leave, 168–170

Elving, Ronald, 17, 169

Employee retention/turnover: cost of turnover, hiring and retraining, 27; reduction in employee turnover and training costs, 23, 89; positive effects on job continuity and employment in Europe, 112–113; and in California, 142–143

"Employer–employee match quality," 87, 88

Employment, of mothers: dramatic changes in rate of in U.S, vii, 2, 9, 58; in U.S. compared to United Kingdom and Canada, 1, 13; of first–time mothers, 10–11; by level of education, 11–13; impact of early return to on maternal health, 34–38; on family well–being, 38–39; on child health, 39–41; on child development, 41–50; increase in prior to giving birth, 11; job segregation and glass ceiling, 114; managerial and professional, 28; service and part–time workers, and FMLA, 21; and private sector leave, 27; recommendations for work history requirements, 162–163; timing of return post–birth, in U.S. compared to Canada and United Kingdom, 2. *See also* Timing of return to employment postbirth in U.S.

Employment, of fathers: impact of extra hours of on child development, 50

Episiotomy, 35

Equal Employment Opportunity Commission, 28

Erikson, Erik, 45

Externalities and impact on privately negotiated leave arrangements, 90

F

Family child care homes: safety of, 68; quality of, 71

Family and Medical Leave Act: history and provisions of, 16–22; vetoes of, bipartisan support for, 19; eligibility for, 21; gender neutrality, 20; lack of access among part–time workers and small–business employees, 21, 22, 88; impact on leave use by better educated employees, 23; spillover effect on businesses not covered by FMLA, 22; costs to employers, 24; impact on timing of mothers' return to employment, 23; impact on father's taking time off, 23; child outcomes, "yuppie" bill, 23; impact on strengthened ties to workforce, 23

Family Day Care Rating Scale (FDCRS), 71

Family leave: definition of, 16; statutes in California, New Jersey, Washington, and other states, 123–124; stand–alone parental leave vs. comprehensive family and medical leave. *See also* Family and

Medical Leave Act, Maternity leave, Paternity leave, Parental leave, and State leave policies.

Fathers: effects of time spent with new or adopted babies, 44; focus on role of fathers, 33; impact of FMLA on, 23–24; leave utilization by, 14; impact of paternity leave on reduction in maternal depression, 39; paternity leave policies and, 96, 103–105; "use it or lose it" leave provisions and, 14. *See also* Paternal employment, Paternity leave.

Federal Interagency Day Care Requirements, 74

Feminist movement: attitudes toward and influence on leave policy, 20, 104, 169

Fertility: impact of paid leave on, 116

Finance mechanism for leave: obstacles to self–financing by families, 96; payroll deduction, 94–95; unemployment insurance, attachment to temporary disability insurance, general revenue tax, 95; recommended finance mechanism, 164–166

Finland: parental leave provisions, 106

Firestein, Netsy, 141

Fraiberg, Selma, 60

France: parental leave provisions, 106; length of job–protected leave, 108; length of paid leave, 109; cost of leave policy, 110

G

Gasper, Jo Ann, 15

Gender gap: in wages, 86–89; concerns about parental leave policy exacerbating gap, 3, 114; in parental leave utilization, 14; policies to encourage fathers to take leave, 14, 16, 96, 104–105; role in formation of FMLA, 20; impact of California PFL on share of leave taken by men, 137–138; recommendation for incentives for fathers to take leave, 161

Germany: first maternity leave policy, 102; gender gap in leave utilization, 104; parental leave provisions, 106, 108; paternity leave provisions, 14, 108; comparative generosity of leave provisions, 109; cost of leave policy, 110; provisions for flexibility, 110; impact of leave policy, 113–114, 116

Google, 73

Greece: parental leave provisions, 107

Greenspan, Stanley, 45, 60

H

Han, Wen–Jui, 49

Hatch, Orrin, 18, 23

Hawaii: Temporary Disability Insurance, 25; proposed paid leave, 124

Healthy Families America, 75

Heckman, James, x, 3, 85

"Heckman's curve": 85

Hess, Earl, 18

Hormones: role of in bonding process, 43–44, 47; impact of elevated stress hormones on child development, 63–64

Hyde, Henry, 19

I

Iceland: parental leave provisions, 106

Income, impact of: on leave access and utilization, 11–12, 96; on access and utilization of FMLA, 21–23, 88–89; on access to private sector leave policies, 26–27, 92–93; on type of nonparental care used, 59; on benefits of early nonparental care, 64–65; on access to quality child care, 75; on access and utilization of PFL in California, 138–139

Infant care (nonparental): age of entry and rate of use of early nonparental care, 2, 58; benefits of quality nonparental care for at–risk infants and toddlers, 60; cost of, 72–73, 74; debate on effects of, 2, 4, 57, 59–66; types of (center–based, family child care, informal or relative care), 58–59; health of children in, 67–68; impact on attachment, 60, 62; on cognitive development, 64–66; on social and emotional development, 63–64, 66; implications for parental leave policy, 66, 73–74; paucity of quality settings, 70–72; recommendations for improvements, 74–76; safety of, 68–70. *See also* Child care; Child development, Early Head Start, Educare, Child development, and Nonparental care.

Infant Health and Development Project, 64

Infant mortality: See Postneonatal mortality.

Infant/Toddler Environment Rating Scale, 70, 71

Insurance, health: continuation during FMLA–related leave, 21; small business exemption and health care reform legislation, 18; parallel between reductions in private sector leave policies and in contributions to health care premiums, 26

Insurance, temporary disability: states with TDI policies, 25; and wage replacement for pregnancy leave, 124; TDI infrastructure for administering paid family leave in California and New Jersey, 124–125; 127–129; example of, 131; pregnancy disability leave combined with PFL in California, 139; confusion about eligibility for typical pregnancies, 140; as potential administrative structure for national policy on paid leave, 167

Institute for Women's Policy Research, 27

Institute of Medicine (National Academy of Sciences), 61

International Labor Organization, 16, 102

Ireland: parental leave provisions, 107

Italy: parental leave provisions, 107

J

Job–protected leave: business opposition to, 18–19; duration of in Europe and Canada, 105–106, and Australia, 111; impact of FMLA, 21–23; impact of lack of job protection in PFL in California, 141; state policies on, 25; spillover effect on non–FMLA–covered employers, 22; in private sector, 26–28; recommendations for, 155–159

Junior League: See Association of Junior Leagues

K

Kagan, Jerome, 60

Kamerman, Sheila, 15, 20, 102–103

L

Labor Project for Working Families (California): 125, 141

Labor unions: involvement in leave legislation, 17, 125; impact on private sector leave policies, 26

Lally, J. Ronald, 46, 49, 76

Larson, John B., 17

Leave policies: types relevant to recovery from childbirth and care for new or adopted baby, 15–16. *See also* Family leave, Maternity leave, Parental leave, Paternity leave, and State leave policies.

Low birth weight: increase in, 41; role of early intervention programs in minimizing developmental delay, 45–46

M

Maloney, Carolyn, 169

Mandatory leave policies: pros and cons of, 94, 97; history of compulsory leave in western Europe, 102–103, 104

"Market failure" as barrier to private sector provision of leave policy, 89–90; role of "externalities", 90–91, and "asymmetric information", 91–94

Markowitz, Sara, 37

Maternal age: delay in age of childbearing, 12–13; role of access to contraception and education, 13

Maternal depression: see postpartum depression.

Maternal employment: cross–national comparisons in rate of, 13, 113; disparities of timing of return to employment, 11–13, 28; during first year after giving birth, vii, 1, 10; educational levels, 13; impact on child outcomes, including cognitive development, social and emotional development, 86; increase in, 2; job segregation, 114; part–time employment, 21, 27, 162–163; prebirth as predictor of postbirth, 11; wage penalty ("mommy tax"), 87, 114

Maternity leave: definition, 15; ILO minimum duration, 16; economic benefits for mothers, 86–89; history of in relation to FMLA, 17–20; and in western Europe, 102–103; and in California, 126–129; impact on maternal and child health, 37–41; package of paid maternity and parental leave in advanced industrialized nations, 16; generosity of, compared across nations, 108–109; impact of current policies in western Europe and Canada, 104–107; state TDI policies, 25. *See also* Parental leave policies and legislation.

Maternity Protection Convention, 103

McCain, John, 19

Milkman, Ruth, 125, 137, 140, 142, 143

Miller, George, 19

"Mommy tax", 86–89. *See also* Wages.

Mothers' views (on time off following childbirth, on timing of return to employment), 39, 41–43, 152

Murkowski, Frank, 19

N

National Association of Child Care Resource and Referral Agencies, 72

National Association of Manufacturers, 17

National Association of Wholesaler–Distributors, 17

National Center for Clinical Infant Programs (ZERO TO THREE), 61

National Child Care Information and Technical Assistance Center, 75

National Compensation Survey, 92

National Federation of Independent Business, 17

National Institute of Child Health and Development (NICHD) Study of Early Childcare (SECC), 49, 61, 62, 63, 65, 66, 67, 72

National Longitudinal Study of Youth—Child Supplement, 49, 50

National Organization for Women, 17

National Partnership for Women and Families, 28

National Retail Federation, 19

National Study of Employers, 26

National Survey of America's Families, 22, 59

Ness, Debra, 28

Netherlands: Parental leave provisions, 107

Newborns' and Mothers' Health Protection Act, 34

New Jersey, Temporary Disability Insurance and Paid Family Leave Insurance, 25, 124, 133, 146, 162

New York: Temporary Disability Insurance, 25; proposed paid family leave, 124

Nonparental care: debate on effects of, 62–66; impact on children's health and safety, 67–70; recommendations concerning, 74–76. *See also* Child care and Infant care.

Norway: parental leave provisions, 107

Nurses' Health Study, 37

O

Obama 2008 presidential campaign: proposed incentives for states to develop approaches to paid family leave, 126, 163

P

Packard (David and Lucile) Foundation: Planning grant for Labor Project for Working Families, 125

Paid Family Leave: In California, 123–149; in New Jersey, 124, 146; in Washington State, 124, 146; *See also* California Paid Family Leave Act, New Jersey Paid Family Leave Insurance, and Washington Family Leave Insurance Law.

Parental leave policies: history of parental leave policies (public) outside the U.S., 102–104 (Western Europe); overview of existing policies, 104–105 (Western Europe), 110–111 (Canada), 111 (Australia); summary table, 106–107 (Western Europe and Canada); cross–national variations, 108–109; worker eligibility requirements, 103, 108; wage replacement rate, prior work history, business size, administration , flexibility of, 110; cross–national comparison of overall generosity of benefits, 15, 16, 108–109; state policies, economic benefits of paid leave to mothers, economic benefits of paid leave to employers, costs of leave policies in Western Europe, 109–110; consequences of parental leave entitlements, 113 (of brief duration), 114 (of longer duration); 114 (on women's wages and prospects for advancement); association with child health and developmental benefits, 115–116 (Western Europe, Canada); impact on fertility, 116–117. *See also* Private sector leave policies and State policies.

Parent–child interaction: bidirectional and reciprocal, 44–47; impact on wiring of brain, 33, 47–49; stages of, time needed for pattern to establish, 45, 47; special role of fathers, 50; early intervention programs to promote, 45–46, 75; 151; recommended leave to promote, 156. *See also* Reciprocal pattern of interaction.

Parental time investments: impact on child development, 84–85; Heckman's curve, 85; return to investment during infancy, 86

Paternal employment: impact of increased hours on children's math and reading performance, 50

Paternity leave: in U.S., 14; concerns about gender gap in leave usage in western Europe and Canada, 14; definition of, 15; paternity leave packaged with maternity and parental leave, 16; comparison of Family and Medical Leave benefits with those in Europe and Canada, 21; impact of FMLA on duration of paternity leave, 23–24; impact of California's PFL on duration of paternity leave, 137–138; role of paternity leave in reducing maternal depression, 39; provisions and utilization of, 103–108, 111, 112 (in Europe and Canada); incentives for fathers to take leave, 96, 108; attitudes toward, 14; wage replacement rate and, 159; recommendations for incentives, 155

Parttime employees: and eligibility for FMLA, 21–22; benefits of part–time work in 1st year of life, 50; paid family leave in California, 124; recommendations, 161–163

Payroll tax: pros and cons of use to finance parental leave, 94–95; use to finance leave in Canada and western Europe, 106–107; employee payroll tax as leave finance mechanism in California and New Jersey, 124; provisions of in California, 130–132; employer views, 143–144; impact on employees, 145; recommendations for paid leave finance mechanism, 164–166

Phillips, Deborah, 47, 63

Portugal: parental leave provisions, 107

Postneonatal mortality: (in relation to timing of mother's return to employment), 39–40; (rates across types of child care settings), 68; (in Western Europe and Canada), 115

Postpartum depression: postpartum "Baby blues", 36; clinical depression, reduction in associated with access to time off, 37–38; 42; role of paternity leave in reducing maternal depression, 39

Pregnancy Discrimination Act, 25, 28, 127

Premature infants: 41; and early intervention to minimize developmental delay associated with low birth weight, 45–46; benefits of high quality early care for, 60

Private sector leave policies and practices: Types of employers with generous policies, 26, 27; accounting firms and rationale for generous leave policies, 27; decline in full pay policies, 26, 28; impact of externalities on likelihood of privately negotiated leave policies, 90–91; impact of asymmetric information, 91–94; percentage of private sector workers in establishments with paid and unpaid family leave, 93; mandating employers to provide, 94

Pronatalism, 103

Protectionist impetus for leave policy, 102–103

Provence, Sally, 15

"Public provision" of parental leave, 94

Public sector employees: access to leave, Carolyn Maloney bill, 169

Public awareness of leave policy in California, 140

Public support, for leave policies: internationally, 102; coalition supporting in California, 135; Rockefeller Foundation and Time magazine poll, 152

R

Reciprocal pattern of parent–child interaction, 44–46. *See also* Parent–child interaction.

Recommendations for child care policy, 74–76

Recommendations for paid care leave policy: duration of leave, 155–159; wage replacement rate, 159–160; eligibility (worker characteristics), 161; (prior work history), 161–163; business size requirement, 163–164; finance mechanism, 164–166; administration, 166–168; scope of leave legislation, 168–170; summary, 170–171

Rhode Island: Temporary Disability Insurance, 25, 126

Ricciuti, Henry, 60, 61

Rockefeller Foundation poll, 152

Roukema, Marge, 18, 19

S

Savings, estimated cost: See Cost savings.

Schroeder, Patricia, 17, 19

Self–employed: access to Paid Family Leave in California, 124; proposal for access to paid Family Leave Insurance Act, 165

Sen, Gita, 87

Shellenbarger, Sue, 28

Shonkoff, Jack, 47

Sick leave: use by parents for time off with new babies and unequal access to, 27–28; use by fathers for time off with new babies, 14, 24; ongoing anticipated role of, 158

Single parents: impact of welfare reform on timing of return to employment, 2; greater access of married parents to unpaid leave, 40; and recommendations for eligibility for cash assistance, 75; benefits of high quality care for children of low–income (single) parents, 60, 64–66; benefits of work for children, 49; impact of recommendations on duration of leave for, 159

Sleep deprivation, 38–39, 151

Small business: opposition to Family and Medical Leave Act, 17–18; opposition to California's Paid Family Leave (PFL) law, 143; legal exemptions, 18, 22; percentage of small businesses offering unpaid and paid leave, 93; spillover effect of FMLA on exempt employers, 22; state leave laws and small business, 25; coverage under California's State Fair Employment and Housing Act, 127; no size limitation in eligibility for paid leave under California's Pregnancy Disability Leave or PFL, 129, 131; employees of file fewer claims for PFL, 141–142; positive impact of PFL on small business, 143–144; recommendation for business size requirement, 163; options for small business to participate in federally proposed family leave insurance program, 165

Small Business Administration: study on cost to employers of leave policy vs. terminating and replacing employees, 19

Social Security Administration: as potential administrative structure for paid parental leave, 166–168

"Specific human capital," 87–88

Spain: parental leave provisions, 108

State government: temporary disability leave insurance, 25; payroll taxes to support leave; laws more generous than FMLA, movement to support paid leave, 124, 146–147, 166, 167

State leave policies: States with more generous leave policies than FMLA, 25–26; states with proposed family leave bills, 124; feasibility of state–by–state adoption, 166–168. *See also* California, New Jersey, and Washington State.

Stevens, Ted, 19

"Still Face" study, viii

Stress: on marriage following childbirth, 38; impact of "toxic stress" on young children, 63–64

Sudden Infant Death Syndrome (SIDS): 69, 70, 157

Sweden: parental leave provisions, 107; leave duration, 108; leave generosity, 109; leave policy costs, 110; job segregation, 114; wage replacement rate, 104

Switzerland: parental leave provisions, 107

Syracuse Family Development Research Program, 60

T

Tanaka, Sakiko, 39, 115

Thompson, Ross, 43, 44, 47, 48

Time magazine poll, 152

Timing of return to employment postbirth: 1, 10, 12; effect on mother's health, 36–37; effect on family well–being, 38–39; effect on child's health and development, 39–41, 49–50; 156–158

Tronick, Ed, viii

U

Unemployment insurance: as financing and/or administrative structure for paid leave, 167

United Kingdom: timing of return to employment post–birth compared to U.S., 1, 10, 13; education of women, 13; employment of women, 13; conservative government and leave expansion, 16; link between timing of return to employment and breastfeeding, 40; parental leave provisions, 107;

comparative generosity of leave policy,
109; cost of leave policy, 110; impact of
leave policy on job continuity, 113

U. S. Catholic Conference, 17

U. S. Census Bureau, 27, 28, 87, 133

U. S. Centers for Disease Control and
Prevention, 133

U. S. Chamber of Commerce, 17, 18, 24

U. S. Department of Labor, 24, 27, 159

"Use It or Lose It" policy: in Canada, 14, 60;
"father's quota" in Iceland, and "bonus"
in Finland, 108; recommendations for
U.S., 155, 157

V

Vacation leave: use by parents for time off
with new babies and unequal access to,
27–28; use by fathers for time off with
new babies, 14, 24; ongoing anticipated
role of, 158

Vandell, Deborah, 61, 66

W

Wages: of workers claiming FMLA benefits,
23, 88; of working women, wage penalty
or "Mommy Tax", 86–89; wage penalty
for paternity leave, 14; impact of lengthy
leaves on, 113–114

Wage replacement rate: comparison of rates in
Europe and Canada, 106–107; 108–109;
less generous rate in Canada, 111; at
minimum wage level in Australia, 111;
in California and New Jersey, 124, 129–
132 impact on low–income employees,
138; for TDI in California, 127;
Recommendation, 159–161

Waldfogel, Jane, 49

Washington State, Family Leave Insurance
program, 26, 124

Weil, David, 19

Welfare reform, 2, 75

WestEd Center for Child and Family Studies,
46

Williams, Wendy, 15, 20

Woolsey, Lynn: 126, 159, 160, 164, 165, 168.
See also Dedication.

Women's Legal Defense Fund, 17

Work history requirements: for FMLA
benefits, 21–22; state policies on, 25;
in Europe, 108; no prior work
requirements for TDI or PFL in

California, 127, 130; as proposed in
The Balancing Act of 2011, 162;
recommendations, 161–163

World Health Association, 40

Workplace Flexibility, Georgetown University
Law Center, 169

Y

Yale Bush Center Advisory Committee on
Infant Care Leave, 15, 17, 20, 21, 158,
159

Yale Bush Center in Child Development and
Social Policy, 41

Z

ZERO TO THREE (formerly the National
Center for Clinical Infant Programs), 61